BRICS: Architects of a New Global Order

Exploring the Growth, Challenges, and Potential of Emerging Giants in Shaping the Future of Global Governance

Claudio Pacardi

1. **Introduction to the BRICS**: history, formation of the bloc and common objectives.

2. **Comparative Economic Analysis**: comparison of the BRICS economies with those of the G7 nations.

3. **Economic Development Policies**: description of the economic development strategies adopted by each BRICS country.

4. **Role in Global Governance**: BRICS impact on international financial and political institutions.

5. **International Trade and Investment**: analysis of trade and investment relations between the BRICS and with the rest of the world.

6. **Innovation and Technology**: focus on how the BRICS are driving innovation in key sectors such as technology, renewable energy and space.

7. **Environmental Challenges and Sustainability**: exploration of environmental policies and initiatives for sustainable development in BRICS countries.

8. **Population and Social Dynamics**: Demography, Urbanization, and Social Issues in the BRICS.

9. **Culture and Soft Power**: BRICS cultural influence at a global level.

10. **Defense and Security**: analysis of defense policies and initiatives for regional and global security.

11. **Education and Research**: state of higher education and scientific research.

12. **Infrastructure and Urban Development**: significant infrastructure and urban development projects.

13. **Energy and Natural Resources**: management of natural resources and energy policies.

14. **Agriculture and Food Security**: strategies for sustainable agriculture and food security.

15. **Domestic Policy and Challenges**: discussion on domestic political challenges and reforms in each country.

16. **Health and Wellbeing**: state of health systems and welfare initiatives in the BRICS.

17. **Future of the BRICS**: future prospects and potential scenarios for the development of the bloc.

18. **Bilateral and Multilateral Relations**: examination of key relationships between BRICS members and with other nations.

19. **Criticism and Controversies**: analysis of the main criticisms and controversies concerning the BRICS.

20. **Conclusions and Final Reflections**: summary of key points and reflections on the future role of the BRICS in the world.

1. Introduction to the BRICS: history, formation of the bloc and common objectives.

The introduction to the BRICS should lay the foundation for understanding this block of emerging nations, highlighting their rise and their role in the world economy. Here's how you could develop this chapter:

Introduction to BRICS: History, Bloc Formation, and Common Objectives

History and Formation

- **Origin of the Term**: The term "BRIC" was first coined in 2001 by Jim O'Neill, an economist at Goldman Sachs, to identify the emerging economies of Brazil, Russia, India and China, seen as engines of future economic growth. South Africa joined the group in 2010, transforming the BRIC into BRICS.

- **First Meetings and Official Formation**: BRIC leaders held their first official summit in 2009 in Russia, marking the formal birth of the bloc. South Africa was officially admitted in 2010, reinforcing the group's diversity and geopolitical influence.

Common Objectives

- **Economic Cooperation**: Promote economic cooperation, trade and investment among members, with the objective of supporting the growth, economic development and diversification of their economies.

- **Unified Political Voice**: Strengthen the political weight of BRICS countries on the international stage, working for fairer representation in global financial institutions such as the International Monetary Fund (IMF) and the World Bank.

- **Sustainable Development**: Jointly address the challenges of sustainable development, including climate change, food security, and access to energy.

- **Cooperation in Key Sectors**: Increase collaboration in strategic areas such as science and technology, energy, security and education.

- **New Financial Architecture**: The establishment of the New Development Bank (NBD) in 2014 and the Contingent Reserve Arrangement (CRA) aims to provide an alternative to Western financial institutions and to support infrastructure and sustainable development projects in emerging and developing countries.

Importance of Blocking

- **Economic Growth**: Collectively, the BRICS represent a significant portion of world economic growth, global population, and foreign exchange reserves, playing a crucial role in the global economy.

- **Diversity and Potential**: Despite differences in terms of economy, politics and culture, the BRICS union reflects the potential for collaboration between emerging countries to redefine the balance of global economic and political power.

To explore in more detail and in depth the introduction to the BRICS, expanding our understanding beyond the history, the formation of the block and the common objectives, we can delve into additional aspects that characterize this economic and political alliance. This more detailed approach will allow us to appreciate the complexity and nuances of the BRICS as a global entity.

Geopolitical Depth and Economic Implications

The BRICS are not just a group of countries with rapidly growing economies; they also represent a geopolitical force that seeks to redefine the norms and practices of international relations and the global economy. Their rise coincides with a period of global transition, characterized by a shift of economic power from the West to the East and the South of the world. This dynamic has created new opportunities for the BRICS to propose alternatives to the traditional economic and political dominance of the United States and Europe.

Internal and Dynamic Challenges

Despite the unity presented on international stages, the BRICS face several internal challenges, including economic disparities, political tensions, and social issues. Managing these challenges is crucial for the cohesion of the group and for its effectiveness as a block:

- **Economic Disparities**: Although united under the acronym BRICS, member countries have significant differences in terms of economic dimensions, levels of development and growth models. These disparities represent both a challenge and an opportunity for the group to work toward common goals while respecting the individual needs of member countries.

- **Political Tensions**: Political differences and regional tensions between some BRICS members can complicate cooperation. Diplomacy and continuous dialogue are essential to mitigate these tensions and promote a common agenda.

- **Social Issues**: Problems such as inequality, poverty, and limited access to basic services such as education and health, remain significant challenges within BRICS countries. Working on these issues can not only improve internal stability, but also strengthen the block's legitimacy as an alternative model of development and cooperation.

Innovation and Sustainable Development

The BRICS are also trying to position themselves as a leader in sustainable development and technological innovation. Investments in research and development, green technologies, and initiatives to combat climate change are an integral part of their national agendas. Cooperation in these areas not only helps the BRICS achieve their sustainable development goals, but it also contributes to their global soft power, showing a commitment to pressing global issues.

The New Global Financial Architecture

The establishment of the New Development Bank (NBD) and the Contingent Reserve Arrangement (CRA) represents a significant step towards creating a more inclusive and equitable global financial architecture. These institutions not only offer alternatives to the IMF and the World Bank, but they also reflect the BRICS' ambition to play a more central role in the global financial system, while providing financial support to developing countries.

Confluence of Cultures and Societies

Beyond economic and political aspects, the BRICS represent a rich variety of cultures, languages and traditions. This cultural diversity is a force that, if well exploited, can further enrich cooperation between members through cultural, educational and tourist exchanges

By continuing to delve into the internal and external dynamics of the BRICS, we can explore how these interactions affect not only the members themselves but also the wider global order. This approach allows us to understand the scope and depth of their collective commitment to a new paradigm of international cooperation.

Multilateralism and Diplomacy

The BRICS bloc is actively committed to promoting a more multilateral world order. This view is particularly evident in their critiques of existing global governance structures, which they perceive as biased in favor of Western advanced economies. Through forums such as the G20 and the United Nations, the BRICS seek to reform these institutions to reflect more equally the distribution of economic and political power in today's world.

Challenges to Global Governance

The unique position of the BRICS as emerging but still developing economic powers places them in a complicated situation. On the one hand, they aspire to greater rights and representation in global institutions; on the other, they must face challenges within the block, such as economic disparities and geopolitical tensions. The BRICS' ability to navigate these internal dynamics will significantly influence their effectiveness in promoting a global reform agenda.

Building Regional Partnerships

In addition to domestic cooperation, the BRICS are expanding their relations with other developing nations and regional groups. These efforts, often manifested through initiatives such as BRICS Plus, aim to build a larger network of countries that share similar views on global governance and economic development. Such partnerships could not only strengthen the position of the BRICS at the global level, but also promote more inclusive and sustainable development models.

Impact on Global and Economic Policy

The BRICS commitment to a fairer and more representative world order brings with it significant implications for global politics and the economy. Their search for alternatives to Western financial institutions and their support for more inclusive global governance could redistribute power in ways that alter existing balances, challenging dominant narratives and promoting new forms of international cooperation.

Technology and Innovation as Vehicles of Change

The BRICS recognize the crucial role of technology and innovation as engines of economic growth and tools to address global challenges such as climate change and inequality. By investing in research and development, BRICS not only seek to improve their national economies, but also to contribute to global solutions. In addition, the emphasis placed on innovation opens up new avenues for cooperation both within the bloc and with other countries and regions.

Culture and Identity

Finally, it is essential to recognize the cultural and identity impact of the BRICS on the world stage. Celebrating cultural diversity and promoting intercultural dialogue are key aspects of the BRICS agenda. These efforts not only enrich bilateral and multilateral relations, but they also contribute to building bridges of understanding between peoples of different backgrounds, challenging stereotypes and prejudices.

This holistic approach to the role and aspirations of the BRICS in the global context highlights their complexity as an alliance and their potential impact on multiple aspects of geopolitics and the world economy. By exploring these dimensions, we can gain a deeper understanding.

The Evolution of Global Socio-Economic Dialogue

The BRICS play a crucial role in the evolution of global socio-economic dialogue, supporting not only the need for greater equity in international economic relations but also the importance of addressing transnational issues such as poverty, inequality and climate change. Their emphasis on inclusive and sustainable development offers a different perspective than dominant narratives, often focused on a market-driven development model that prioritizes economic growth over other factors.

Reorientation of the Dynamics of Economic Power

Through initiatives such as the creation of the New Development Bank and the Contingent Reserve Arrangement, the BRICS are actively working to reorient economic power dynamics at the global level. These institutions not only offer alternatives to traditional financial bodies, but they also represent an attempt to establish a more balanced economic order that respects the principles of national sovereignty and equitable cooperation. The aspiration for greater control over global financial resources and a greater voice in international economic decisions reflects the BRICS ambition to transform existing power structures.

Challenging the Western Paradigm

The BRICS, through their commitment to South-South cooperation and their support for a multipolar world order, challenge the dominant Western paradigm in many sectors, from foreign policy and security to economic governance and sustainable development. This does not necessarily mean a direct opposition to the West, but rather the search for a more balanced dialogue and an international system that reflects the diversity and plurality of global voices. The BRICS' ability to present alternative models of cooperation and development could encourage greater flexibility in existing global institutions.

Implications for the International System

The emergence of the BRICS as a significant block has profound implications for the international system, urging adaptations both in the foreign policies of established powers and in the structures of global governance. Their call for reforms in international financial institutions, for example, calls into question the current distribution of decision-making power and requires greater inclusivity. Similarly, their commitment to collective security and regional cooperation offers alternatives to traditional balances of power and military alliances.

Future Perspectives

Looking to the future, the prospects and potentials of the BRICS in shaping the new world order will depend on their ability to overcome internal challenges, maintain a common strategic vision and manage complex dynamics both within the block and in their external relations. Their success in promoting a more inclusive and equitable model of cooperation could not only strengthen their position at the global level but also offer valuable lessons on how to collectively address transnational challenges in an era of uncertainty and change.

Through these efforts and initiatives, the BRICS continue to play a central role in redefining the rules and norms of the global order, seeking to promote a fairer and more sustainable future. Their evolution as an economic and political block remains a dynamic field of study and interest, reflecting the tensions and potential of a rapidly changing world.

The Influence of BRICS on Global and Regional Governance

As the BRICS continue to exert their influence, there is an increasing impact on global and regional governance. This impact is manifested through various channels, such as the strengthening of existing multilateral institutions, the creation of new platforms for South-South cooperation, and the initiative of reforms that aim to make global governance more representative of emerging and developing economies.

A New Pole of Attraction for Emerging Economies

The BRICS are positioned as an alternative pole of attraction for other emerging and developing economies, offering a model of cooperation based on principles of mutual respect and mutual benefit. This aspect is particularly relevant in a global context in which many nations feel marginalized by financial and commercial institutions dominated by advanced economies. Through forums such as BRICS Plus and the New Development Bank, BRICS are committed to building a more inclusive and equitable world order.

Reorienting International Norms

The BRICS actively seek to reorient international norms in areas such as trade, investment, and environmental protection, promoting standards that reflect their priorities and those of other emerging economies. This effort includes negotiating trade agreements that emphasize sustainable development and the protection of workers' rights, as well as promoting responsible investment practices that take into account social and environmental impacts.

Dialogue and Diplomacy

Through an ongoing commitment to dialogue and diplomacy, the BRICS are also strengthening their capacity to act as mediators in regional and global conflicts. This mediation capacity reflects the growing importance of the BRICS in promoting peace and global stability, based on their principle of non-interference in countries' internal affairs and on respect for national sovereignty.

Challenges and Criticisms

Despite their successes, the BRICS face a series of challenges and critiques, including the coherence of their foreign policies, internal differences in terms of economic and political models, and concerns related to respect for human rights and fundamental freedoms. The BRICS' ability to face these critiques and to maintain a united position in the face of external challenges will be crucial for their future impact on global and regional governance.

Projections on the Future Global Impact

Looking to the future, the role of the BRICS in shaping the world economy and politics will depend on their ability to navigate a rapidly changing global landscape, characterized by new challenges such as digitalization, climate change, and geopolitical tensions. Their emphasis on more inclusive global governance and sustainable development models could offer important lessons on how to collectively address these global challenges.

Innovation and Digital Collaboration

The adoption of advanced technologies and the promotion of digital innovation will be fundamental aspects for BRICS in strengthening their economies and responding to the needs of their societies. Collaboration in areas such as artificial intelligence, blockchain, and the digital economy will not only stimulate economic growth, but also improve governance and civic participation.

Towards a Renewed Global Order

In conclusion, even without concluding the discourse permanently, the BRICS are progressively outlining the contours of a renewed global order, in which emerging and developing economies play a more central and active role. Their aspiration for a more balanced and representative world is at the heart of efforts to reform existing international institutions and to create new cooperation mechanisms that better reflect the geopolitical and economic reality of the 21st century. This process is not without challenges, but the path taken by the BRICS underlines their growing importance in shaping the future of global governance.

Economic Integration and Flexible Cooperation

The BRICS strategy is based on economic integration and flexible cooperation, allowing members to coordinate on issues of common interest while respecting their national diversity and priorities. This pragmatic approach facilitates collaboration in key areas such as energy security, infrastructure, sustainable finance and the fight against climate change. Through these joint initiatives, the BRICS not only strengthen their economies, but also help to shape global norms and policies in these areas.

Strengthening South-South Ties

An essential component of the BRICS vision is the strengthening of South-South ties, promoting closer cooperation between developing nations beyond their membership in the bloc. This commitment translates into support for the poorest countries through development initiatives, financial assistance and technology transfer. The potential of this South-South cooperation lies in promoting a more inclusive development agenda that addresses global disparities and supports the national development efforts of the most vulnerable countries.

Demographic and Social Challenges

The BRICS also face significant demographic and social challenges, ranging from an aging population in some countries to the need to create economic opportunities for young growing populations in others. Addressing these issues requires innovative policies in education, employment, health and social protection. The BRICS' successes and challenges in these areas not only influence the well-being of their citizens, but they also offer valuable lessons for other emerging and developing economies.

Environmental Governance and Climate Action

In the context of the global climate crisis, the BRICS play a crucial role in environmental action, given their significant ecological footprint and their ability to influence global environmental policies. The BRICS commitment to clean energy, the conservation of natural resources and the reduction of greenhouse gas emissions is essential to achieve global sustainable development goals and to mitigate the impacts of climate change. Their strategies and policies in this area have the potential to drive a global transition to more sustainable development models.

Cultural Influence and Soft Power

In addition to their economic and political influence, the BRICS wield significant soft power through the promotion of their culture, values and worldviews. Through cultural exchanges, education and public diplomacy, the BRICS are building bridges of understanding and cooperation with the rest of the world. This cultural dimension enriches global dialogue and underlines the importance of diversity and intercultural dialogue in promoting peace and global understanding.

Towards a New Paradigm of International Cooperation

In conclusion, the BRICS journey illustrates their crucial and increasingly influential role in redefining the global geopolitical and economic landscape. As they seek to overcome domestic challenges and navigate a complex international environment, BRICS represent a catalyst for change, promoting a new paradigm of international cooperation that emphasizes equity, sustainability and multilateralism. This commitment reflects a shared vision that goes beyond simply achieving economic growth to include promoting global development that is inclusive and respectful of cultural and environmental diversity.

Contribution to Global Peace and Security

The BRICS also have a role to play in promoting peace and global security. Through their commitment to dialogue and diplomacy, they strive to address regional tensions and conflicts through peaceful means, promoting solutions that respect national sovereignty and territorial integrity. Their unique position as a bridge between the global North and the global South makes them key players in facilitating understanding and mediating in international disputes, thus contributing to a more stable and peaceful world order.

Technology as an Engine of Change

In the field of technology, the BRICS are pushing the boundaries of innovation to address social and economic challenges, from the digitalization of the economy to the creation of smart and sustainable cities. Their emphasis on innovation opens up new avenues for growth and development, allowing BRICS countries to skip traditional industrialization trajectories and adopt cleaner and more efficient development models. Cooperation in the field of research and development, in particular in the field of renewable energy, information technologies and biotechnology, underlines their commitment to using science and technology as tools for sustainable progress.

Challenging Global Inequalities

The BRICS are also pursuing an agenda to address global inequalities, both within their borders and internationally. Through shared development initiatives and aid programs, they seek to reduce the gap between rich and poor countries, promoting a fairer approach to global development. This includes efforts to improve access to education, healthcare and decent employment, stressing the importance of inclusive growth that benefits all segments of society.

Cultural and Humanitarian Cooperation

In addition to their economic and political initiatives, the BRICS value cultural and humanitarian cooperation as a means of building understanding and solidarity between the peoples of different countries. Through cultural, educational and scientific exchange programs, they promote intercultural dialogue and mutual respect, enriching international relations with a sense of shared humanity and curiosity about different traditions and ways of life.

The Way to the Future

As the BRICS move into the future, their trajectory will continue to be closely watched from around the world. Their ability to maintain internal cohesion, to face global challenges with innovative solutions and to promote a more just and sustainable world order will determine their long-term success and their lasting impact on future generations. With their growing economic, political and cultural influence, the BRICS have a unique opportunity to shape the future in ways that reflect the principles of diversity, equity and collaboration, offering new perspectives and solutions to the global challenges that lie ahead.

As the BRICS continue to shape the global landscape, their strategy and initiatives span various dimensions, highlighting the complexity and ambition of their collective commitment. This section explores additional facets of the BRICS influence and potential in the international context.

Reform of Global Financial Institutions

One of the key objectives of the BRICS is the reform of international financial institutions to make them more representative and sensitive to the needs of emerging and developing economies. Through negotiations and concrete proposals, the BRICS seek to change the voting quotas and lending practices of organizations such as the International Monetary Fund (IMF) and the World Bank, to ensure that the decisions taken reflect a wide spectrum of interests and not only those of the richest and most industrialized nations. This push for greater equity in global financial institutions underscores the BRICS' desire to promote a more balanced world economic system.

Economic Resilience in an Uncertain World

In an era characterized by global economic uncertainty, the BRICS are focusing on building resilient economies that can withstand external shocks. This involves not only strengthening internal economic ties through trade and investment but also diversifying their economies to reduce dependence on individual sectors or markets. Economic resilience is also seen in their ability to implement prudent macroeconomic policies and in the construction of substantial currency reserves that can act as shock absorbers against fluctuations in global financial markets.

Food Security and Sustainable Agriculture

The BRICS are addressing issues of food security and sustainable agriculture through joint research and the development of agricultural technologies that can increase productivity while reducing environmental impact. These efforts are crucial to ensure that rapidly growing BRICS populations have access to sufficient, nutritious, and sustainable food. Collaboration in this sector also aims to share best practices and innovations with other developing countries, thus contributing to the global fight against hunger and poverty.

The Commitment to Universal Access to Healthcare

The BRICS are working together to improve access to health services for their populations, with a particular focus on communicable diseases, maternal and child health, and the response to global health emergencies. Cooperation in this area includes the exchange of knowledge and resources, as well as supporting the development of stronger and more responsive health systems. In addition, the BRICS are promoting research and development of affordable drugs and vaccines, stressing the importance of equity in global health.

The Promotion of Smart and Sustainable Cities

Recognizing urbanization as one of the major challenges and opportunities of the 21st century, BRICS are investing in the development of smart and sustainable cities. These initiatives aim to improve the quality of urban life through the adoption of innovative technologies for efficient resource management, sustainable mobility, and intelligent public services. BRICS cooperation in this sector aims to share experiences and solutions that can be adapted and implemented in different geographical and socio-economic realities.

Comparing and Learning from Diversity

One of the most significant aspects of BRICS cooperation is their ability to compare, learn and derive value from their diversity. Despite differences in political systems, economies, and societies, the BRICS have found common ground on issues of global importance, demonstrating that diversity can be a force rather than an obstacle to international cooperation. This approach allows not only to enrich the dialogue between members but also to explore innovative development models that can be adapted and applied in various contexts.

The Challenge of Climate Change

Climate change represents an urgent challenge and the BRICS play a key role in finding sustainable solutions. As among the largest emitters of greenhouse gases, BRICS countries are aware of their responsibility and are taking ambitious actions to reduce emissions and promote clean energy. Cooperation in this field extends to joint research on green technologies, the exchange of effective policies for adaptation to climate change, and mutual support in international climate negotiations. The BRICS commitment to climate action is crucial to achieving the global goals set out in the Paris Agreement.

Digitalization and Cybersecurity

In the digital age, the BRICS are jointly tackling the challenges and opportunities presented by digitalization. This includes developing strategies to promote the digital economy, improve access to technology, and protect data and cybersecurity. Collaboration in this area aims to develop a shared approach to Internet governance and cybersecurity, while strengthening national capacities in information and communication technologies (ICT). Digitalization offers BRICS the opportunity to accelerate economic growth, improve public services and promote social inclusion.

The Educational Agenda

Education is another priority for the BRICS, who recognize its crucial role in sustainable development and the reduction of inequalities. Joint efforts in this field focus on improving access to quality education, exchanging good practices in the field of higher education, and strengthening research and innovation. Initiatives such as BRICS universities and shared scholarship programs aim to promote academic mobility and build knowledge networks that transcend national boundaries.

Contribution to Global Health Governance

The COVID-19 pandemic has underlined the importance of international cooperation in managing health emergencies. The

BRICS have responded by exchanging information, cooperating in the research and development of vaccines and treatments, and supporting the equitable distribution of health resources. Their collaboration in this area demonstrates their commitment to strengthening global health governance and to better preparing for future health emergencies.

Towards a Shared Future

Overall, the BRICS journey reflects a deep commitment to building a shared future that is more equitable, sustainable and resilient. Through multilateral cooperation, they are tackling some of the most pressing challenges of our time, seeking to create a positive impact not only within their borders but around the world. Their ability to work together, while respecting differences and valuing diversity, offers valuable lessons on how nations can collaborate for the common good in an era of increasing global challenges.

In the context of the continuous evolution of the role of the BRICS on the global stage, these countries emerge as protagonists in the promotion of a new, more balanced and multipolar international order. Let's explore additional dimensions that highlight their growing influence and the challenges they face.

The Strategy Towards Economic Diversification

The BRICS are intensifying efforts to diversify their economies in order to reduce dependence on commodity exports and stimulate growth in high value-added sectors such as advanced manufacturing, financial services and information technologies. This diversification strategy is critical to improving economic resilience and promoting long-term sustainable development. The collaboration between the BRICS in this context includes the development of common platforms for innovation and the exchange of knowledge and expertise in key sectors.

Investments in Sustainable Infrastructure

Recognizing the critical role of sustainable infrastructure in stimulating economic growth and improving quality of life, BRICS are investing massively in infrastructure projects that take into account environmental, social and governance (ESG) considerations. These investments include initiatives in renewable energy, sustainable transportation, water resource management, and smart urban development. The BRICS New Development Bank plays a key role in financing these projects, highlighting the block's commitment to sustainable development.

The Role in International Peace and Security

The BRICS seek to take a more active role in promoting international peace and security, supporting diplomatic solutions to conflicts and contributing to peace operations under the aegis of the United Nations. Their collective position on global security issues reflects a preference for multilateralism and for a balanced approach that takes into account different international perspectives and interests. Collaboration in this area aims to contribute to global stability and to support an international order based on respect for international laws.

Cooperation in Space and Scientific Research

The shared interest in scientific research and space exploration opens new frontiers for cooperation between the BRICS. Joint efforts in these fields not only enhance their position as a leader in technological innovation but also provide an opportunity to address global challenges such as climate change, natural resource management and food security from a new perspective. Collaboration in space and scientific research symbolizes the BRICS aspiration to contribute significantly to human progress.

Addressing Global and International Inequalities

The BRICS are committed to developing strategies to address inequalities both within their borders and at the international level. This commitment translates into policies aimed at improving access to education, health, and economic opportunities for vulnerable groups. Globally, the BRICS promote a development agenda that emphasizes the need for fairer trade, equitable access to technologies, and financial support for less developed countries. These efforts are essential to building a more just world and reducing global inequalities.

The Challenges of Multilateralism and Global Governance

As the BRICS strive to promote a more multipolar world order, they are faced with the challenges of maintaining internal cohesion and navigating the complex dynamics of multilateralism. The diversity of political, economic and social systems within the BRICS group presents both opportunities and challenges for their cooperation. The BRICS' ability to act cohesively on global issues is crucial to their success in reforming global governance. This requires a delicate balance between promoting national interests and supporting a common agenda that reflects the shared objectives of sustainable development, equity and global justice.

The Commitment to Building Resilient Societies

BRICS are aware that the resilience of societies — their ability to resist, adapt and recover from shocks and stress — is crucial in an era characterized by rapid change and transnational challenges. Through joint initiatives in public health, education, and technological innovation, BRICS work to build more resilient communities that are better equipped to face future pandemics, natural disasters and other crises. Cooperation in these areas not only improves the quality of life of their citizens but also reinforces global security and stability.

The Balance Between Development and Environmental Conservation

The BRICS are faced with the challenge of pursuing economic development without compromising the environment and natural resources. Their growing emphasis on sustainable development reflects the awareness that environmental conservation and the fight against climate change are global imperatives that require immediate and coordinated action. Through the promotion of renewable energy, sustainable agricultural practices and green development policies, BRICS strive to find a balance between economic growth and environmental protection for future generations.

The Promotion of Culture and Intercultural Dialogue

The rich cultural diversity of the BRICS is a source of strength and innovation. The promotion of intercultural dialogue and mutual understanding between the BRICS and beyond is essential to address prejudices and stereotypes, build bridges between societies, and support global peace and harmony. Through cultural festivals, educational exchange programs and artistic collaborations, BRICS celebrate their shared cultural heritage and stress the importance of cultural diversity as a pillar of international dialogue and cooperation.

The BRICS Enlargement Prospects

As the BRICS continue to consolidate their influence worldwide, the opportunity to expand the bloc to include other emerging economies that share similar objectives of global governance reform and sustainable development is also being discussed. A possible expansion could further strengthen the voice of the BRICS in international arenas, but it would also require addressing the challenges related to the integration of new members with different priorities and national contexts. Managing this enlargement process in a way that reinforces the cohesion and effectiveness of the group will be critical to its future success.

Dynamic Conclusion

Ultimately, the BRICS represent an ongoing experiment in reforming the world order to reflect the geopolitical realities of the 21st century. As they seek to navigate the complexities of global governance and promote equitable and sustainable development, the successes and challenges they encounter offer valuable lessons on the importance of cooperation, dialogue and multilateralism in an interconnected world. Their ability to face these challenges and to take advantage of

The dynamics and evolution of the BRICS in the context of global geopolitics and economic governance represent one of the most significant transformations in recent decades. This group of countries, originally united by the prospect of accelerated economic growth and a shared desire to reform the existing world order, has gradually expanded its scope of cooperation, addressing a wide range of global challenges and promoting a multilateral approach to international issues.

The detailed conclusion of the role and impact of the BRICS requires considering several key aspects that have characterized their trajectory and outline future prospects:

Economic Integration and Challenging Inequalities

The BRICS have promoted internal economic integration through initiatives such as the New Development Bank and the Contingent Reserve Arrangement, aimed at providing alternatives to Western financial institutions. These efforts reflect not only the desire for economic self-determination but also the intent to propose a more inclusive and equitable development model that can serve as an example for other developing nations.

Environmental Leadership and Sustainability

By tackling the challenges of climate change and promoting sustainable development, the BRICS have positioned themselves as key players in the global environmental arena. Their emphasis on clean energy, sustainable infrastructure, and responsible agricultural practices underscores a commitment to environmental protection that is intertwined with economic growth objectives.

Promoting Peace and Security

In the field of international peace and security, the BRICS have sought to balance geopolitical relations through dialogue and diplomacy, stressing the importance of multilateralism and respect for international law. This approach reflects a shared vision that global stability is intrinsically linked to economic prosperity and sustainable development.

Advances in Science, Technology and Innovation

The joint investment in research and development, especially in fields such as information technology, biotechnology and renewable energy, demonstrates the BRICS ambition to drive global innovation. These efforts not only aim to improve members' economic competitiveness but also to contribute to global solutions for common challenges such as food security, public health and climate change.

The Role of Soft Power and Cultural Dialogue

Through soft power and cultural dialogue, the BRICS have worked to build bridges between civilizations, promoting mutual understanding and cultural cooperation. This dimension of their commitment reinforces ties not only between the members of the group but also with other nations, underlining the importance of cultural diversity and mutual respect in a globalized world.

Future Challenges and Perspectives

Looking to the future, BRICS face the challenge of maintaining internal cohesion in the face of political and economic differences between members. In addition, their ability to effectively promote a fairer and more sustainable world order will depend on their ability to negotiate with other global powers and to successfully implement the proposed reforms. The potential expansion of the group to new members could strengthen their position worldwide, but it will also require a delicate balance to maintain unity of vision and action.

In conclusion, the BRICS path is marked by significant ambitions and concrete achievements, as well as by complex challenges that require innovative solutions and cooperation. Their rise represents a dynamic change in international relations, placing a new emphasis on emerging economies and their role in global governance. Over time, the BRICS have demonstrated a remarkable capacity for adaptation and leadership in various sectors, from economic to environmental, from global security to technological innovation. However, to fully realize their potential as a positive force for global change, they must face internal and external challenges with a renewed commitment to the principles of multilateralism, equity and sustainable cooperation.

Maintaining Cohesion and Strengthening Multilateralism

Internal cohesion remains one of the most significant challenges for BRICS, given the diversity of political, economic and development priorities among its members. The group's ability to act together in international forums and to promote a common agenda will depend on their ability to overcome these differences and find common ground. Strengthening multilateralism, through a shared commitment to reform global institutions and to promote a more just world order, remains a central objective that can help mitigate these challenges.

Innovation and Technological Development as a Priority

Innovation and technological development continue to be priorities for BRICS, as they seek to position themselves as leaders in the 21st century global economy. Adopting advanced technologies and promoting research and development can help BRICS members overcome barriers to development and create new opportunities for economic and social progress. Targeted collaborations in areas such as artificial intelligence, biotechnology and renewable energy can not only stimulate economic growth but also contribute to sustainable solutions for global environmental challenges.

A Renewed Commitment to Sustainability and Climate Action

Climate change represents an existential threat that requires urgent and coordinated global action. BRICS have an opportunity to lead by example, promoting policies and practices that reduce greenhouse gas emissions and promote climate resilience. The commitment to sustainable development and to a green economy can serve as a model for other countries and demonstrate that it is possible to achieve economic growth without compromising the environment.

Building Global Partnerships and Intercultural Dialogue

Finally, BRICS can further strengthen their global impact by building partnerships with other nations, regions, and international organizations. Promoting intercultural dialogue and mutual understanding can help overcome geopolitical divisions and build a sense of global community based on respect and cooperation. The expansion of cultural, educational and scientific exchange networks between the BRICS and the rest of the world can enrich the fabric of international relations and promote peace and global stability.

In conclusion, the BRICS journey across the global landscape is marked by significant successes and persistent challenges. Their evolution from an economic concept to a multidimensional partnership reflects the growing importance of emerging economies in world governance. By jointly tackling global challenges and promoting a more sustainable and equitable future, BRICS have the opportunity to shape a new world order that better reflects diversity

2. Comparative Economic Analysis: comparison of the BRICS economies with those of the G7 nations.

The comparative analysis of the BRICS economies with those of the G7 reveals substantial differences, but also common traits and interesting trends that reflect the global dynamics of economic power. The comparison between these two groups of countries can be examined through various key factors, including GDP, economic growth, demography, international trade, technological innovation, and environmental policies.

Size and Growth of GDP

- **GDP size**: The G7 countries (Canada, France, Germany, Italy, Japan, the United Kingdom and the United States) represent some of the most developed and industrialized economies in the world, with a combined GDP that constitutes a significant portion of the global economy. The BRICS (Brazil, Russia, India, China and South

Africa), although more heterogeneous in terms of the level of economic development, have shown impressive growth rates in recent decades, especially China and India, bringing their collective contribution to the constantly increasing world GDP.

- **Growth Rates**: BRICS tend to show higher growth rates than G7 countries, reflecting their more dynamic economic development phase and their catch-up potential. However, this growth may be accompanied by greater volatility and vulnerability to external shocks.

Demography and Labor Market

- **Demography**: BRICS generally have a younger population and higher population growth rates than G7 countries, where the population is on average older and with low or negative population growth rates. This offers BRICS the potential benefit of a larger working-age workforce, but it also presents challenges related to education, training and employment.

- **Labor Market**: G7 countries often have lower unemployment rates and higher income levels than the BRICS, where unemployment, especially among young people, and income inequality can pose significant challenges.

International Trade and Investments

- **Exports and Imports**: The BRICS have become increasingly important players in global trade, with China emerging as one of the world's leading trading powers. The G7 countries, however, maintain a dominant presence in international trade and foreign direct investment, benefiting from consolidated business networks and privileged access to global financial markets.

- **Investments**: Both groups attract significant flows of foreign direct investment (FDI), but G7 countries tend to be more integrated into global value chains, while the BRICS are trying to increase their participation through industrialization and innovation policies.

Technological Innovation

- **Research and Development (R&D)**: G7 countries have historically invested heavily in R&D and enjoy a solid innovation ecosystem. Some BRICS countries, especially China, are rapidly closing the gap, increasing investment in R&D and improving their technological innovation and production capabilities.

Environmental Policies and Sustainability

- **Sustainability**: While G7 countries have adopted comprehensive policies to address climate change and promote environmental sustainability, the BRICS are facing the challenge of balancing economic growth with environmental protection. China and India, for example, are among the biggest emitters of greenhouse gases, but they are also taking significant steps toward renewable energy and other green technologies.

Conclusion

The comparative analysis between the BRICS and the G7 reveals a complex fabric of economic intersections, shared challenges and strategic differences that shape the global landscape. This extended comparison highlights additional relevant dimensions that deserve attention to understand the dynamics between these two important groups of nations.

Structural Challenges and Economic Reforms

- **Structural Challenges**: Both blocks face internal structural challenges, but their nature and context differ substantially. The G7 countries, with mature economies, are confronted with issues such as the aging of the population, the sustainability of public debt and the need for labor market and welfare reforms. BRICS, on the other hand, are often struggling with inadequate infrastructure, economic governance, corruption, and social disparities. Both groups recognize the need for structural economic reforms to support long-term growth, but strategies and priorities vary.

Global Impact and Political Influence

- **Political Influence**: The economic growth of the BRICS has led to an increase in their political and diplomatic influence worldwide, challenging the international order traditionally dominated by the G7 countries. The BRICS seek to reform international financial institutions and promote a more multipolar world order, while the G7 countries tend to defend the current global architecture, although with some openings to change. This dynamic affects negotiations on global issues such as trade, climate change and security.

Regional Partnerships and Alliances

- **Regional Collaboration**: BRICS and G7 countries engage in regional partnerships and alliances to amplify their influence. While the BRICS work to strengthen South-South ties and to expand their presence in Africa, Latin America and Asia, the G7 countries maintain traditional alliances with Europe, North America and key allies in Asia and the Pacific. These alliances are crucial for political, economic and military support, reflecting the geopolitical strategies of both blocs.

Technology and Global Competitiveness

- **Technological Dominance**: The race for technological supremacy is a key battleground for the BRICS and the G7. While the G7 has enjoyed a historic advantage in innovation and technology, with a robust patent system and significant investment in research and development, the BRICS are rapidly gaining ground. China, in particular, has made great strides in the technology sector, becoming a global leader in areas such as 5G technology, artificial intelligence and e-commerce. This competition for technological dominance is critical to future economic competitiveness and political influence.

Sustainability and Energy Transition

- **Energy Transition**: The transition to a low-carbon economy is an issue of increasing importance for the BRICS and the G7. While the G7 countries have set ambitious goals for carbon neutrality and are moving towards renewable energy, the BRICS are at different stages of the energy transition, balancing economic growth needs with environmental commitments. International collaboration and technology transfer are essential to accelerate this transition, addressing the common challenges of climate change and promoting sustainable development.

Ultimately, the comparison between the BRICS and the G7 reveals a global landscape in which two influential groups navigate through challenges and opportunities in a context of growing economic and political interdependence. This dynamic reflects the fluidity of the current world order and the need for a continuous and constructive dialogue between advanced and emerging economies.

Response to Global Crises

- **Crisis Management**: The ability to respond effectively to global crises is another crucial aspect of the confrontation between BRICS and G7. The COVID-19 pandemic has tested the health, economic and governance systems of all countries, highlighting both vulnerabilities and strengths. The G7 countries, with their most advanced economies, have been able to mobilize significant resources for the response to the crisis, although not without difficulty. The BRICS, for their part, have faced additional challenges due to limited resources and less developed infrastructure in some cases, but they have also demonstrated resilience and the ability to implement innovative response measures.

Financial Integration and Stability

- **Financial Stability**: Global financial integration and stability are essential for both groups. While the G7 countries have an established role in the international financial system, the BRICS are trying to increase their influence through initiatives such as the New Development Bank and the use of local currencies in bilateral trade. These moves not only aim to reduce dependence on the US dollar but also seek to create a more diversified and resilient financial system.

Social Policies and the Reduction of Inequalities

- **Inequalities**: Reducing inequalities both nationally and globally is a common topic of interest, although the methods and effectiveness of policies may differ between the BRICS and the G7. The challenge of ensuring that economic growth results in tangible improvements for all segments of society is a daunting task, with the BRICS especially facing the task of lifting large sectors of their population out of poverty. At the same time, even in the

G7 countries, the increase in inequalities and the feeling of being left behind by certain strata of the population require innovative political responses.

Towards a More Inclusive Collaboration

- **Global Collaboration**: Finally, the comparison between BRICS and G7 underlines the importance of a more inclusive global collaboration that takes into account the voices of emerging and developing economies. The need to collectively address global challenges such as climate change, the pandemic, food security and access to clean energy requires a shared commitment to working together in ways that respect diverse perspectives and contribute to a sustainable future for all.

In conclusion, the comparison between the BRICS and the G7 reveals a wide range of challenges and opportunities that reflect the complexity of today's world economy. As both groups adapt to a rapidly changing global environment, their interaction will continue to influence the path to global economic growth, stability, and sustainable development.

Digitalization and the Fourth Industrial Revolution

- **Technological Adoption**: Digitalization and the fourth industrial revolution represent a key area in which the BRICS and the G7 are navigating with different strategies. The G7 countries, with their advanced economies, had an initial advantage in the adoption of digital technologies and innovation, integrating artificial intelligence, big data and the Internet of Things (IoT) into their production and service systems. However, some BRICS countries, in particular China, have made great strides in becoming world leaders in specific technological sectors, challenging the traditional dominance of the G7 and outlining new paths for innovation and technological development.

Energy Security and Green Transition

- **Energy and Environment**: Energy security and the transition to cleaner energy sources have become priorities for both the BRICS and the G7, but with different approaches and challenges. While G7 countries focus on decarbonizing their economies and investing in renewable energy, BRICS face the dual challenge of ensuring energy security to support their rapid economic growth and, at the same time, contributing to global efforts to combat climate change. This involves a delicate balance between the exploitation of the abundant natural resources available to some BRICS countries and the adoption of sustainable environmental policies.

Cultural Influence and Shared Values

- **Soft Power**: In addition to economy and technology, soft power plays a significant role in shaping the global influence of the BRICS and the G7. By promoting their culture, values and ideals, both groups seek to extend their influence far beyond economic boundaries. While the G7 has long benefited from a strong cultural and media presence worldwide, BRICS countries are gradually expanding their soft power through cinema, literature, art and education, seeking to present alternatives to Western values and to promote greater cultural diversity in global narratives.

Global Governance and Multilateralism

- **Reform of International Institutions**: The issue of global governance and multilateralism remains a field of tension and cooperation between the BRICS and the G7.

The BRICS push for a reform of international financial institutions and multilateral organizations to reflect more fairly the current distribution of global economic power. At the same time, the G7 countries are open to certain reforms but are trying to maintain a system that protects the interests of advanced economies. This debate on the future of global governance underlines the need for an inclusive dialogue that can harmonize the interests of developed and developing countries.

Demographic and Socioeconomic Challenges

- **Population and Work**: Demographic challenges represent another critical point of confrontation between the BRICS and the G7. While the G7 countries face problems related to population aging and the sustainability of social security systems, the BRICS are faced with the need to integrate large young populations into the labor market, while ensuring social equity and reducing poverty. The management of demographic dynamics and the implementation of inclusive labor policies are fundamental for the social stability and sustainable economic growth of both groups.

In conclusion, the continuous confrontation and interaction between the BRICS and the G7 highlight the complexity of international relations in the 21st century. While each block has its strategic objectives and priorities, the interconnected reality of today's world requires transnational cooperation on multiple fronts. This dynamic exchange between BRICS and G7 not only determines the trajectory of global economic and political development but also offers unique opportunities to collectively address some of the most pressing challenges facing the world.

Global Health Impacts and Pandemic Response

- **Health Cooperation**: The recent COVID-19 pandemic has highlighted the critical importance of international cooperation in the field of public health. BRICS and G7 both have essential roles to play in promoting global health security, from researching and developing vaccines to building more resilient health systems. The sharing of knowledge, resources and strategies can accelerate progress toward managing global health emergencies, demonstrating how collaboration can overcome geopolitical divisions for the common good.

Investments in Global Infrastructure

- **Infrastructure Development**: The BRICS and the G7 recognize the importance of investments in infrastructure for sustainable economic development. While the BRICS focus on infrastructure projects that can stimulate economic growth in developing countries, the G7 engages in initiatives that promote high standards in terms of sustainability, transparency and governance. Cooperation and dialogue between these blocks can facilitate the development of infrastructures that benefit global economies, while improving access to essential services such as water, energy and transport.

Food Security and Agricultural Development

- **Agricultural Sustainability**: Food security remains a global concern, with BRICS and G7 playing complementary roles in the development of sustainable and innovative agricultural practices. While BRICS countries can offer lessons from their experiences with agriculture in diverse environments and climatic conditions, G7 countries can contribute with advanced technologies and scientific research. Collaboration in this sector is crucial to address the challenges posed by climate change, the loss of biodiversity and the need to feed a growing world population.

Dialogue on Human Rights and Fundamental Freedoms

- **Promoting Human Rights**: Human rights and fundamental freedoms represent an area of dialogue and, at times, tension between the BRICS and the G7. While G7 countries tend to emphasize the promotion of human rights as part of their foreign policy, BRICS often stress the principle of non-interference in internal affairs and the right to development. Finding common ground that respects national sovereignty while promoting universal human rights is a challenge that requires a continuous commitment to dialogue and mutual understanding.

Future Prospects and Innovation

- **Frontiers of Innovation**: Finally, both the BRICS and the G7 are exploring the frontiers of innovation in sectors such as clean energy, biotechnology, nanotechnology and space exploration. Collaboration in these areas can lead to revolutionary discoveries that have the potential to transform economies and improve quality of life around the world. Encouraging a global innovation ecosystem that facilitates the sharing of ideas, resources and talents among the BRICS, the G7 and beyond can accelerate progress towards sustainable solutions for the environmental, health and technological challenges facing the world today.

Global Economic Integration and Fair Trade

- **Equity in Global Trade**: As global economic integration continues to progress, dialogue between the BRICS and the G7 can help promote fairer trade and trade rules that benefit both advanced and developing economies. Adjusting trade policies to ensure that global supply chains are more resilient, sustainable, and ethical can reduce economic inequalities and promote industrial development around the world.

Access to Education and Skills Development

- **Global Education**: Universal access to quality education is crucial for sustainable development. The BRICS and the G7, with their diverse experiences and resources, have the opportunity to collaborate on educational programs that promote literacy, digital skills and professional training. This can help prepare the global workforce for the economies of the future, while promoting innovation and social mobility.

Urban Challenges and Sustainable Development of Cities

- **Sustainable Urbanization**: With rapid urbanization, especially in BRICS countries, there is a need to develop cities that are sustainable, resilient and able to provide a high quality of life for their inhabitants. The sharing of best practices and innovative solutions for urban management, housing, public transport systems and waste management can help make cities engines of sustainable and inclusive growth.

Fight against Climate Change and Shared Actions

- **Shared Climate Action**: The fight against climate change requires coordinated global action. The collaboration between the BRICS and the G7 on climate policies, green finance and clean technologies can accelerate the transition to low-carbon economies. Working together to strengthen commitments under the Paris Agreement and to mobilize financial resources for climate adaptation and mitigation in the most vulnerable countries is crucial to address one of the greatest challenges of our time.

Medical Research and Public Health

- **Collaboration in Medical Research**: In an era characterized by global health challenges such as pandemics and antibiotic resistance, collaboration between the BRICS and the G7 in medical research and public health is more important than ever. Sharing data, resources and expertise can accelerate the development of more effective vaccines, treatments and health systems, improving global resilience to future health crises.

Partnerships for Development and Humanitarian Assistance

- **Development Support and Humanitarian Assistance**: Development assistance and humanitarian action are areas where BRICS and the G7 can collaborate to address the root causes of poverty, conflict and humanitarian crises. Working together to support sustainable development, promote peace and provide humanitarian aid where it is most needed can help build a safer and more prosperous world for all.

In short, dialogue and cooperation between the BRICS and the G7 are not only vital to address immediate challenges, but also to shape a global future that is sustainable, just and resilient. Through a shared commitment to transnational cooperation, these two influential blocs can contribute significantly to guiding the world towards a path of equitable development and shared prosperity. Their ability to collaborate, despite political and economic differences, serves as a powerful reminder of global interdependence and the need for collective action to solve problems that transcend national borders.

Innovation for Social Inclusion

- **Technologies for Inclusion**: In addition to innovation aimed at economic growth, there is a growing need to ensure that new technologies promote social inclusion. BRICS and the G7 can play a key role in ensuring that technological advances, from artificial intelligence to the digitalization of public services, are accessible to everyone and used to reduce inequalities rather than exacerbate existing divisions.

Strengthen Global Governance

- **Institutional Reform**: Effective global governance requires institutions that reflect the realities of the contemporary world. The collaboration between the BRICS and the G7 to reform international financial institutions, development agencies and climate governance mechanisms can help create a fairer and more flexible system, capable of dealing with global challenges more effectively.

Promoting International Peace and Security

- **Diplomacy and Conflict Prevention**: Peace and international security remain fundamental objectives, with BRICS and G7 that can play complementary roles in international diplomacy, conflict prevention and peacebuilding. By joining forces to mediate conflicts, support democratic transitions and strengthen the rule of law globally, they can contribute to a more stable and secure world.

Environmental Sustainability and Conservation

- **Environmental Protection**: In an era of ecological crisis, the protection of the environment and the conservation of natural resources are imperatives that require coordinated global actions. The collaboration between BRICS and G7 on initiatives for biodiversity, the fight against deforestation and the protection of the oceans can accelerate progress towards shared environmental objectives, while ensuring that economic development is sustainable and environmentally friendly.

Building a Culture of Cooperation

- **Intercultural Dialogue and Education**: Finally, the construction of a culture of global cooperation also involves intercultural dialogue and education. Promoting mutual understanding and respect between different cultures and societies is essential to overcome prejudices and stereotypes. BRICS and the G7 can support initiatives that encourage cultural exchange and global education, preparing future generations to navigate and thrive in an interconnected world.

Through their cooperation and continuous dialogue, the BRICS and the G7 have the opportunity to direct global priorities towards wider horizons of progress and the common good. Their interaction represents not only a practical necessity in the face of global challenges, but also an expression of hope in the ability of humanity to unite for a better future. The road ahead is complex and full of challenges, but also full of possibilities to create a fairer, more sustainable and peaceful world.

Intensifying the Fight Against Global Inequality

- Global **Equity: Global** inequality remains one of the greatest challenges faced by the international community. The BRICS and the G7, through concerted policies and multilateral initiatives, play a crucial role in promoting greater equity, both within countries and between nations. This includes the redistribution of resources, equitable access to global markets for developing countries, and supporting policies that promote an equitable distribution of the benefits of globalization.

Tackling the Climate Emergency with Innovative Solutions

- **United Climate Action**: As the world faces the urgent need to mitigate the impact of climate change, BRICS and the G7 can play a critical role in developing and implementing innovative solutions. This could include jointly financing clean technologies, promoting energy efficiency, and supporting agricultural practices that reduce carbon emissions. Collaboration in this field is essential to accelerate the transition to a low-carbon future.

Strengthening Food Security Through Technology

- **Agricultural Innovations for Food Security**: BRICS and the G7 can join forces to address global food security, exploiting advanced agricultural technologies to increase food production in a sustainable way. Adopting climate-smart farming practices, improving agricultural value chains and supporting small-scale agriculture can contribute significantly to the fight against hunger and malnutrition.

Promoting Global Health and Wellbeing

- **Global Response to Health Crises**: Global health is another area where cooperation between BRICS and G7 can make a difference. In addition to pandemic management, there is a growing need to address health issues such as non-communicable diseases, antibiotic resistance, and overburdened health systems. Investing in medical research, promoting the equitable production and distribution of drugs and vaccines, and supporting health systems in less developed countries are critical steps toward improving global health.

Expanding Access to Quality Education

- **Education for All**: Access to quality education is crucial for sustainable development. The BRICS and the G7 can work together to eliminate barriers to education, both in developed and in developing countries. This includes supporting primary and secondary education, promoting technical and vocational education, and investing in higher education and research. Education is the key to unlocking human potential and stimulating innovation and economic growth.

Building Resilient and Sustainable Infrastructure

- **Shared Infrastructure Development**: The need for resilient and sustainable infrastructure is another area of potential cooperation between BRICS and G7. Joint investment in green infrastructure, such as renewable energy, sustainable transport systems and smart cities, can drive economic development while reducing the ecological footprint. Collaboration on standards and funding can accelerate the implementation of infrastructure projects that benefit populations worldwide.

Joining Forces for International Peace and Stability

- **Supporting Global Peace**: Finally, the promotion of peace and international stability remains a fundamental objective, in which both the BRICS and the G7 can play complementary roles. Addressing the roots of conflicts, from poverty to inequality, from climate change to resource scarcity, requires a holistic and cooperative approach. Conflict mediation, support for peace missions and the prevention of radicalization through social and economic development are areas where collaboration between BRICS and G7 can contribute significantly to building a more peaceful world.

Strengthening Social Security Networks

- **Global Social Protection**: The expansion of social safety networks globally is another critical area of cooperation. Ensuring that people around the world have access to a decent standard of living, including food security, health care, and insurance against unemployment and poverty, is critical to reducing inequalities and promoting inclusive growth. The BRICS and the G7 can share best practices and collaborate on programs that promote social protection and economic well-being at the international level.

Accelerating Innovation for Sustainability

- **Green Technologies and Sustainability**: Accelerating the development and adoption of green technologies is essential to address contemporary environmental challenges. BRICS and G7, with their research and development capabilities, can drive innovation in areas such as renewable energy, energy efficiency, sustainable mobility and sustainable management of water resources. Collaboration in research and development, technology transfer and the funding of sustainable start-ups are crucial steps towards a greener future.

Supporting the Growth of Emerging Economies

- **Aid for Economic Development**: Supporting the growth of emerging and developing economies is in the best interest of both the BRICS and the G7. Through investment, fair trade, and development assistance, these groups can help raise living standards, promote sustainable industrialization, and stimulate global innovation. Building resilient and diversified economies around the world will contribute to global economic and political stability.

Cooperation in the Cybersecurity Sector

- **Cybersecurity**: In an era of increasing digitalization, cybersecurity is becoming a shared concern that requires coordinated action. BRICS and G7, benefiting from extensive expertise in the technological sector, can work together to develop security standards, promote cyber resilience and combat cybercrime at an international level. Protecting critical infrastructure, defending privacy rights, and promoting an open and secure Internet are common objectives that can strengthen confidence in the global digital economy.

Cultivating Cultural and Scientific Diplomacy

- **Cultural Exchange and Scientific Collaboration**: Finally, cultural diplomacy and scientific collaboration offer fertile ground for building bridges between the BRICS and the G7. Cultural exchanges, international education, scientific collaborations, and joint research can help overcome ideological barriers and promote a sense of global community. These joint efforts not only enrich international dialogue but also fuel innovation and mutual understanding, setting the stage for deeper global cooperation.

In a world characterized by complex transnational challenges, the BRICS and G7's ability to collaborate and build effective partnerships is more important than ever. As they navigate through political and economic differences, the potential for a joint positive impact on global issues offers a promising vision for the future. Addressing these challenges with a cooperative approach can not only lead to more sustainable and inclusive solutions, but it can also strengthen the international system, making it more resilient to future crises.

Joining Forces Against Poverty

- **Eradication of Poverty**: The fight against poverty requires a global commitment. The BRICS and the G7, through shared initiatives, can implement effective strategies to reduce extreme poverty, improve access to education and health care, and create economic opportunities. Investing in the world's most vulnerable communities not only improves the lives of individuals but also contributes to global stability and prosperity.

Promoting Gender Equity

- **Gender Equality: Gender** equity is fundamental to sustainable development. BRICS and G7 can amplify their efforts to promote gender equality, eliminate discrimination, and open economic and social opportunities for women and girls around the world. Policies that support women's education, employment and women's political participation are not only right but also stimulate economic growth and community development.

Facilitating Dialogue for Conflict Resolution

- **Peace and Mediation**: The ability to facilitate dialogue and mediate in conflicts is an area where BRICS and G7 can collaborate effectively. Supporting peace efforts, providing platforms for negotiation, and contributing to post-conflict construction are ways to promote global stability. Cooperation in this area can help prevent future conflicts and build more peaceful societies.

Economic Integration for a More Connected World

- **Trade and Investment**: Promoting an open and regulated global trade environment can benefit both the BRICS and the G7. Working together to address trade barriers, support trade multilateralism, and encourage responsible investment can stimulate global economic growth. Strengthened cooperation in this area can contribute to greater equity in the international trading system, offering shared benefits.

Cooperation for the Management of Natural Resources

- **Resource Sustainability**: The sustainable management of natural resources is another critical area for collaboration. The BRICS and the G7 can share knowledge and best practices for the conservation of water resources, the sustainable management of forests and the protection of biodiversity. These efforts not only protect the environment but also ensure that resources are available for future generations.

Strengthening Resilience to Climate Change

- **Climate Adaptation**: Working together to strengthen resilience to climate change is critical. BRICS and the G7 can collaborate to develop and implement adaptation strategies that protect vulnerable communities, improve food security, and manage natural risks. These shared initiatives can accelerate climate action and support resilient development.

Ultimately, cooperation between the BRICS and the G7 has the potential not only to effectively address global challenges but also to chart a path to a more promising future for everyone. As they continue to seek common ground and overcome differences, their joint commitment to international cooperation can serve as a catalyst for positive change on a global scale.

Supporting Innovation for Accessibility

- **Access to Technology**: Making technology accessible to everyone is crucial to reducing the digital divide between and within countries. The BRICS and the G7, through collaborations in the field of technological innovation, can facilitate access to the Internet, improve digital literacy and support the development of inclusive technologies. These joint efforts can transform access to information, education, and economic opportunities, promoting greater social equity.

Strengthening Cooperation for Emergency Management

- **Emergency Preparedness and Response**: In a world increasingly exposed to natural and man-made crises, the ability to respond effectively is essential. Collaboration between the BRICS and the G7 in emergency preparedness and response, including the sharing of information, resources and expertise, can save lives and reduce the impact of crises. Working together to improve early warning systems and build response capacity can strengthen global resilience.

Promoting Sustainable Development through Partnership

- **Sustainable Development Goals (SDGs)**: The BRICS and the G7 have a fundamental role to play in promoting and realizing the SDGs. By collaborating on projects that address poverty, health, education, gender equality, and environmental sustainability, they can accelerate progress toward these global goals. A shared commitment to sustainable development can help ensure that no one is left behind in the search for a fairer and more prosperous future.

Intensifying the Fight Against Corruption and Improving Governance

- **Global Governance and Anti-Corruption**: The fight against corruption and the improvement of global governance are essential to ensure that resources are used effectively and that the benefits of development reach everyone. BRICS and the G7 can join forces to promote transparency, strengthen the rule of law and combat corruption at all levels. This cooperation can help build stronger and more reliable governance systems worldwide.

Joining Forces for Environmental Conservation

- **Global Environmental Protection**: Cooperation for environmental conservation is more urgent than ever. By working together on initiatives aimed at protecting ecosystems, conserving biodiversity and sustainably managing natural resources, the BRICS and the G7 can help preserve the planet's natural heritage for future generations. Joint engagement in conservation projects can also promote global awareness and action for the environment.

Expanding Cultural Collaboration and Interfaith Dialogue

- **Cultural Exchange and Dialogue**: Promoting understanding and respect between different cultures and religions is fundamental in a globalized world. The BRICS and the G7 can support initiatives that facilitate cultural exchange and interreligious dialogue, helping to build bridges between communities and to prevent conflicts. These efforts can enrich mutual understanding and celebrate diversity as a force.

Through these and other areas of collaboration, the BRICS and the G7 can transform global challenges into shared opportunities, leading the world on a path of enhanced cooperation, sustainable progress and lasting peace. Their ability to work together, while respecting differences and valuing common objectives, will serve as the foundation for a more promising global future.

Improving Global Access to Clean Energy

- **Sustainable Energy for All**: Access to clean and sustainable energy is a prerequisite for sustainable development. The BRICS and the G7 can exploit their influence and resources to promote the global adoption of renewable energy, improve energy efficiency, and support the energy transition in developing countries. Joint initiatives to finance clean energy projects and share advanced technologies can significantly contribute to reducing dependence on fossil fuels and combating climate change.

Strengthening Cooperation for Water Security

- **Sustainable Water Management**: Water is a vital resource that is becoming increasingly scarce. The BRICS and the G7 can collaborate on strategies for sustainable management of water resources, including technologies for saving water, desalination, and efficient management of urban and agricultural water. These actions can help prevent future water crises and ensure that every person has access to clean and safe water.

Collaboration for Digitalization and Financial Inclusion

- **Inclusive Digital Finance**: The digitalization of the financial sector offers enormous opportunities to improve access to financial services. The BRICS and the G7 can work together to promote financial inclusion through technologies such as mobile payments, blockchain and cryptocurrencies, while ensuring that these systems are safe, equitable, and accessible to everyone. This type of collaboration can help reduce poverty, stimulate entrepreneurship, and support economic growth in developing countries.

Strengthening Innovation Support Networks

- Innovation **Ecosystems: The creation of innovation** ecosystems that support start-ups, research and development is essential to face the challenges of the future. The BRICS and the G7 can share experiences, policies and resources to build environments that promote creativity, entrepreneurship and scientific discovery. By facilitating exchanges between entrepreneurs, researchers and educators, they can help develop innovative solutions to global issues.

Promotion of Academic Mobility and Shared Research

- **International Academic Exchange**: Higher education and research benefit greatly from international cooperation. The BRICS and the G7 can intensify academic exchanges and research partnerships to address complex issues ranging from climate change to emerging diseases. Promoting joint scholarship programs, collaborations between universities and research centers can accelerate scientific progress and strengthen ties between different academic communities.

Development of Shared Strategies for Sustainable Mobility

- **Transportation and Urbanization**: With rapidly growing urbanization and the need to reduce greenhouse gas emissions, the development of sustainable transport systems is crucial. The BRICS and the G7 can collaborate in the development and implementation of sustainable mobility solutions, such as electric vehicles, efficient public transport systems, and infrastructure for cyclists and pedestrians. These efforts can help create more livable cities and reduce the ecological footprint of transportation.

By encouraging cooperation on these and other fundamental issues, BRICS and the G7 can play a decisive role in shaping a future that is both sustainable and inclusive. Their ability to join forces, transcending differences and focusing on common objectives, is essential to solving the problems we face globally.

Focus on Global Mental Health

- **Psychological Wellbeing**: In a world where mental health is becoming an increasingly pressing issue, BRICS and the G7 have the opportunity to promote awareness and improve access to psychological support services. By collaborating on awareness programs, research, and interventions, they can help reduce the stigma associated with mental illness and build stronger support systems for people with these conditions.

Strengthening Climate Resilience in Vulnerable Communities

- **Local Adaptation to Climate**: The communities most vulnerable to climate change require attention and support to build their resilience. The BRICS and the G7 can collaborate on projects that aim to strengthen the capacity of local communities to adapt to the impacts of climate change, through the construction of resilient infrastructure, the improvement of agricultural practices and the sustainable management of natural resources. These efforts can help prevent the loss of lives, livelihoods, and biodiversity.

Improving Data Security and Online Privacy

- **Protection of Digital Information**: In the context of increasing digitalization, data security and online privacy are becoming issues of global concern. By working together to establish international standards and best practices for data protection, the BRICS and the G7 can help ensure that digital technologies are secure and respect user privacy. This cooperation can also facilitate trust in electronic commerce and digital communications globally.

Supporting Green Growth and Bioeconomy

- **Nature-Based Economies**: The transition to nature-based economies or "bioeconomies" offers a path to sustainable development that values biodiversity and ecosystems. The BRICS and the G7 can collaborate in the research and development of bioenergy, biodegradable materials and other green innovations that promote the sustainable use of natural resources. These efforts can drive economic growth while reducing the ecological footprint.

Building Disaster Management Capacity

- **Disaster Preparedness**: Increasing global capacity to manage natural and anthropogenic disasters is critical to safeguarding communities and progress toward sustainable development. BRICS and the G7 can share knowledge, technology and resources to improve disaster preparedness, early warning systems and emergency responses. This collaboration can strengthen the resilience of societies to disasters, saving lives and preserving livelihoods.

Promoting Peace through Education

- **Peace Education**: Finally, education plays a crucial role in promoting intercultural understanding and peace. BRICS and the G7 can support educational programs that teach tolerance, respect for diversity, and conflict resolution. These programs can help form conscious global citizens capable of contributing to a more peaceful and collaborative world.

Through these broad areas of collaboration, the BRICS and the G7 can effectively respond to the needs of our time, tackling global challenges together and exploiting opportunities for shared progress. Mutual commitment to strengthened cooperation, based on respect, open dialogue and joint action, is vital to overcome the obstacles that stand in the way of a more prosperous and sustainable future for all.

Enhancing Youth Skills and Entrepreneurship

- **Youth Empowerment**: The empowerment of younger generations through education, access to economic opportunities and support for youth entrepreneurship is fundamental to sustainable development. The BRICS and the G7 can collaborate on programs and initiatives that equip young people with the skills necessary to thrive in the global economy and encourage them to become leaders and innovators in their field.

Consolidating Food Safety through Innovation

- **Agricultural Innovation for Food Security: Innovation in the** agricultural sector can play a key role in improving global food security. The BRICS and the G7, by harnessing their respective strengths in research and technology, can promote sustainable agricultural practices, develop climate-resistant crops and improve food supply chains. These joint efforts can help ensure that food is plentiful, accessible, and nutritious for growing populations.

Integration of Biodiversity Strategies

- **Conservation of Biodiversity**: Protecting biodiversity requires coordinated action at the global level. Collaboration between the BRICS and the G7 in developing and implementing conservation strategies can help protect vulnerable ecosystems, conserve endangered species and promote the sustainable use of natural resources. By joining forces, these groups can play a crucial role in counteracting the loss of biodiversity and supporting life on Earth.

Strengthening Climate Adaptation Policies

- **Climate Resilience**: As the world faces unprecedented climate challenges, strengthening adaptation policies is essential. BRICS and the G7 can work together to develop climate resilient solutions that protect communities, economies and ecosystems from the impacts of climate change. This cooperation may include the exchange of scientific knowledge, technical and financial support for resilient infrastructure, and the promotion of adaptable agricultural practices.

Development of Cultural Exchange Platforms

- **Cultural Dialogue**: Finally, strengthening dialogue and cultural exchange between the BRICS and the G7 can help build understanding and mutual trust. Joint initiatives such as international cultural festivals, artistic exchange programs and educational partnerships can enrich the fabric of international relations and promote values of peace, tolerance and friendship between peoples.

The cooperation between the BRICS and the G7, extended to these and other areas, represents a promising path towards resolving the most pressing global issues. As the world continues to evolve, the ability of these groups to adapt, innovate, and work together will largely determine the quality of the future we are building. A collective commitment to shared goals can not only lead to effective solutions for today's problems, but it can also pave the way for an era of progress, prosperity and peace for future generations.

In conclusion, the cooperation between the BRICS and the G7 underlines the importance of dialogue and joint action in an interconnected world, facing global challenges that go beyond the capabilities of any single country or group of nations. From improving access to clean and sustainable energy to promoting peace and international security, from innovation for social inclusion to the conservation of biodiversity, the areas of potential collaboration are vast and of fundamental importance.

The shared commitment to these initiatives can accelerate progress towards a more equitable, resilient and sustainable world, highlighting the need to overcome differences for the common good. Cooperation between the BRICS and the G7 not only has the power to effectively address immediate challenges, but it also offers a structure through which it is possible to build a better future for everyone, based on mutual understanding, respect and a common commitment to shared objectives.

In an era characterized by rapid change and increasing complexity, the ability of these groups to adapt, cooperate and innovate together will be crucial to shape the course of global progress. As we move forward, it is essential that BRICS and G7 continue to seek common ground and work together to address the challenges of our time, harnessing their unique capabilities, resources and visions for the benefit of all nations and future generations.

3. Economic Development Policies: description of the economic development strategies adopted by each BRICS country.

The BRICS countries, comprising Brazil, Russia, India, China and South Africa, have adopted different economic development strategies that reflect their unique socio-economic conditions, challenges and objectives. Below, we will explore the main policies and initiatives adopted by each country to stimulate economic growth and development.

Brazil

Brazil has traditionally focused on a development model focused on strengthening the domestic market, industrial diversification and the expansion of agriculture and exports. In recent years, the country has tried to address economic challenges through structural reforms, such as those of the pension system and the labor market, to increase competitiveness and attract foreign investment. The promotion of renewable energy and the development of infrastructure were other key areas of focus to stimulate sustainable economic growth.

Russia

Russia, with its vast natural resources, especially gas and oil, has based much of its economic growth on the export of these resources. However, recognizing the need to diversify its economy, Russia has undertaken efforts to develop sectors such as technology and innovation, manufacturing, and tourism.

Policies aimed at improving the business climate, attracting foreign investment and modernizing infrastructure have been an integral part of the country's economic development strategy.

India

India has followed an economic development path focused on liberalizing the economy, with reforms that have opened markets to foreign investment and promoted competition. With one of the youngest and fastest growing populations in the world, India is also focusing on education, skill development, and digitalization to take advantage of its demographic dividend. Initiatives such as 'Make in India' and 'Digital India' aim to transform the country into a global manufacturing hub and promote the use of digital technologies across various sectors of the economy.

China

China has experienced an unprecedented economic transformation, becoming the "factory of the world" through intense industrialization and urbanization. Its strategy has evolved towards promoting innovation, with significant investments in research and development to become leaders in advanced technologies such as artificial intelligence and telecommunications. China is also pursuing the 'Belt and Road Initiative' to expand its economic influence and improve trade connections globally.

South Africa

South Africa, the most industrialized economy in Africa, focuses on strengthening the manufacturing sector, attracting foreign investment and improving infrastructure to stimulate economic growth. The country faces significant challenges such as high unemployment and economic inequalities. Economic development policies include initiatives to promote entrepreneurship, skill development, and access to markets for small and medium-sized businesses, as well as efforts to improve access to energy and energy efficiency.

These economic development strategies reflect the wide range of approaches taken by BRICS countries to address their specific economic challenges and exploit growth opportunities. While each country pursues unique objectives based on its socioeconomic conditions, together, as a bloc, the BRICS represent a significant force in the world economy, supporting multilateralism and seeking to shape a new global economic order that reflects their growing weight and influence. Their joint commitment to multilateral and regional initiatives, as well as collaboration on issues of common interest such as trade, investment, sustainable development and climate change, underlines their aspiration to play a central role in global economic governance.

Despite internal challenges and geopolitical tensions that may emerge, collaboration between BRICS countries has the potential to contribute significantly to global economic stability, the reduction of poverty and the promotion of sustainable development. Their economic development policies, although different, share the common goal of improving the well-being of their citizens and increasing their impact on the world stage.

Looking to the future, it will be crucial for BRICS to balance growth aspirations with the need to address pressing issues such as social and economic inequalities, environmental protection and the transition to greener and more sustainable economies. In addition, the BRICS' ability to navigate changing global dynamics, to adapt to new technologies, and to respond effectively to global crises, such as pandemics, will largely determine their success in achieving their economic development goals and in contributing to a more balanced and resilient world order.

In the context of a world that is facing rapid technological, environmental and social changes, BRICS countries have a unique opportunity to shape economic development strategies so that they reflect not only immediate needs but also long-term prospects for sustainable and inclusive progress. Their collaboration and individual initiatives can serve as catalysts for a wide range of reforms and innovations.

Promotion of the Circular Economy

- **Circular Economy and Sustainability**: The transition to a circular economy represents a key strategy for BRICS in promoting sustainable economic development that minimizes waste and optimizes the use of resources. By investing in technologies that promote recycling, reuse and waste reduction, BRICS can reduce the environmental impact of their growing economies, while contributing to the creation of new jobs and the stimulation of industrial innovation.

Development of Green Infrastructure

- **Investments in Green Infrastructure**: The development of green infrastructure, such as sustainable public transport systems, efficient energy networks and smart cities, is critical to supporting urban growth and improving quality of life. BRICS, through strategic planning and investments, can guide the implementation of infrastructure projects that are not only economically advantageous but also ecologically sustainable.

Strengthening Food Security

- **Innovation in Agriculture for Food Security**: Addressing food security remains a priority for BRICS, who can apply innovative approaches to agriculture to increase production in a sustainable way. Biotechnology, precision agriculture, and climate-resilient agricultural practices are examples of how science and technology can be mobilized to ensure that rapidly growing populations have access to sufficient, safe and nutritious food.

Strengthening Access to Education and Skills

- **Education and Skills Development**: A renewed focus on education, in particular on STEM (science, technology, engineering and mathematics) training and digital skills, is crucial to prepare the BRICS workforce for the needs of the future labor market. Expanding access to quality education and investing in skill development can help unlock human potential and stimulate innovation.

Promoting Financial Inclusion

- **Financial Inclusion through Technology**: Using technology to promote financial inclusion is a key strategy for the BRICS. Digital finance platforms, such as mobile payments, cryptocurrencies, and blockchain technologies, offer new ways to expand access to financial services, especially for unbanked and underserved populations, while facilitating economic transactions and stimulating entrepreneurship.

Intensification of Regional and Global Cooperation

- **International Cooperation**: Intensifying regional and global cooperation is essential to address transnational challenges such as climate change, pandemics and international security. BRICS can play a leading role in promoting multilateralism, strengthening international institutions and working together with other countries and regional blocs to find shared solutions to global problems.

The continuous evolution of BRICS economic development strategies reflects not only their response to immediate challenges but also their long-term vision for a resilient and prosperous future. Their ability to innovate, adapt and collaborate will be critical to navigating the rapidly changing global economic landscape. As BRICS implement and refine their economic development policies, they can offer valuable lessons on how to deal with the complexities of development in an interconnected world.

Addressing the Digital Divide

- **Bridging the Digital Divide**: Reducing the digital divide remains a critical priority. BRICS, through targeted investments in information and communication technology (ICT) and digital infrastructure, can facilitate universal access to the internet and digital services. This is especially important for rural and remote areas, where digitalization can open up new economic opportunities and improve access to education and healthcare.

Supporting the Energy Transition

- **Just Energy Transition**: As the BRICS are on the road to low-carbon economies, a just energy transition that considers communities dependent on fossil fuels is essential. Implementing policies that support redevelopment, economic diversification and access to renewable energy can help ensure that the transition is fair and inclusive.

Consolidating Civic Participation and Community Development

- **Community Empowerment**: Stimulating civic participation and community development is crucial for sustainable development. BRICS can adopt participatory approaches that involve local communities in planning and implementing development projects, ensuring that policies respond to local needs and priorities. This can strengthen the social fabric and promote a sense of belonging and collective responsibility.

Promoting Diversity and Inclusion

- **Diversity and Inclusion**: Celebrating and promoting diversity within BRICS societies can enrich the development process. Implementing policies that ensure the inclusion of all social groups, including those who are marginalized, in economic and social opportunities, strengthens social cohesion and maximizes development potential.

In conclusion, the economic development strategies adopted by the BRICS reflect a wide range of approaches and initiatives, each adapted to the specificities of the national context but all oriented towards objectives of sustainable growth, equity and resilience. As these countries advance, their collective and individual experience in implementing these strategies offers important insights into how global development goals can be achieved through cooperation, innovation, and a shared commitment to the future.

As BRICS navigate through the changing global landscape, facing both emerging opportunities and persistent challenges, the drafting and implementation of economic development policies requires continuous adaptation and mutual learning.

This dynamic approach to economic progress underlines the importance of innovative and flexible strategies, able to respond to rapid technological, environmental and geopolitical changes.

Investing in Research and Development (R&D)

- **Focus on R&D**: Investment in research and development is essential to catalyze innovation and support long-term economic growth. BRICS can strengthen their commitment in this area, promoting collaborations between universities, research institutes and industries to develop new technologies and solutions. Such initiatives can range from clean and sustainable energy to biotechnology and advanced manufacturing, positioning the BRICS as leaders in fields critical to the global economic future.

Strengthen Social Security Networks

- **Social Protection Systems**: The development of robust and accessible social protection systems is essential to mitigate poverty, reduce inequalities and promote social inclusion. BRICS can explore innovative social security models that exploit technology to improve efficiency and accessibility, while ensuring that safety nets are resilient to economic and social crises.

Develop Green Economy Capacity

- **Green Economies**: The adoption of green economic models represents a strategic opportunity for BRICS to promote sustainable development. This requires policies that encourage sustainable production and consumption, support innovation in green technologies, and facilitate the transition to low-carbon sectors. Encouraging green entrepreneurship and investments in environmentally friendly projects can also stimulate job creation and open up new market opportunities.

Integration of Circular Economy Principles

- **Adoption of the Circular Economy**: The integration of circular economy principles into industrial and development policies can help BRICS to reduce the environmental impact of their economies. This involves promoting waste reduction, reuse and recycling throughout the entire life cycle of the products. Developing infrastructures and systems that support the circular economy not only improves sustainability but can also generate economic benefits through resource efficiency.

Strengthening International Cooperation

- **Global Dialogue and Cooperation**: International cooperation is crucial to address transnational challenges such as climate change, pandemics and global security. BRICS, through multilateral platforms and strategic partnerships, can play a leadership role in promoting global dialogue, facilitating the sharing of knowledge and good practices, and mobilizing resources for shared development initiatives. Building international coalitions for sustainable development and peace can amplify their influence and help shape a fairer and more collaborative world order.

Encouraging Financial Inclusion

- **Access to Financial Services**: Expanding access to financial services is critical to stimulating economic activity and promoting entrepreneurship. BRICS can implement policies aimed at improving financial inclusion, exploiting fintech technologies to reach unbanked populations and provide accessible and affordable financial services. Initiatives such as microfinance, digital payments, and peer-to-peer lending platforms can support small businesses, improve household economic security, and stimulate inclusive economic growth.

Supporting Professional Training and Continuing Education

- **Work Capacity and Future Skills**: To maintain competitiveness in a rapidly changing global economy, it is essential that BRICS invest in professional training and continuing education. Programs that focus on digital skill development, sustainable management, and emerging technologies can prepare the workforce to thrive in new industries. Collaborations between educational institutions, industries, and governments to create flexible and relevant learning paths can bridge the gap between formal education and labor market needs.

Valuing Biodiversity and Ecosystem Services

- **Environmental Conservation**: The BRICS, many of which are home to rich biodiversity, have the opportunity to lead global efforts in the conservation of ecosystems and in the enhancement of ecosystem services. Protecting natural areas, promoting the sustainable use of resources and implementing responsible agriculture and fishing practices can not only contribute to the conservation of biodiversity but also support the well-being of communities that depend on these ecosystems.

Expanding Access to Sustainable Energy

- **Affordable and Clean Energy**: Access to energy is a fundamental pillar of economic development. BRICS can play a key role in stimulating investment in renewable energy sources and clean technologies, while promoting energy efficiency. This not only contributes to the fight against climate change but also ensures that emerging and developing economies have the energy needed to support growth and improve the quality of life of populations.

Promotion of Public Health and Wellbeing

- **Resilient Health Systems**: Building strong and resilient health systems is vital for security and economic development. Facing both chronic and emerging health challenges, BRICS can benefit from enhanced cooperation in the field of public health. Initiatives to improve disease surveillance, expand access to basic health services, and promote medical research can strengthen the capacity to respond to health crises and improve the long-term health and well-being of their populations.

In summary, BRICS economic development policies, through a mix of innovation, sustainability, inclusion and cooperation, can provide a dynamic model for facing the challenges of the 21st century. As they continue to explore new strategies and adapt to changing global conditions, their approach to economic progress offers valuable insights for global development, highlighting the power of collaboration and innovation in building a prosperous and sustainable future.

As the BRICS continue on their path of economic development, facing the unique and shared challenges of our time, additional areas of strategic focus emerge that can help shape a resilient and prosperous future for these rapidly growing nations.

Integration of Emerging Technologies into the Economy

- **Adoption of Advanced Technologies**: The acceleration in the adoption of emerging technologies such as artificial intelligence (AI), robotics, blockchain and the Internet of Things (IoT) can transform key sectors of the BRICS economy, improving efficiency and stimulating innovation. Investing in digital infrastructure and promoting technological literacy within the workforce can facilitate this transition, ensuring that BRICS remain competitive in the global economic landscape.

Improving Urban Resilience and Sustainable Development

- **Sustainable and Resilient Cities**: With increasing urbanization, the development of sustainable and resilient cities becomes crucial. BRICS can implement policies to promote green urbanization, improve waste management, reduce pollution, and increase urban green spaces. Designing cities that are both livable and resilient to climate change and natural disasters can significantly improve the quality of life of citizens.

Promoting Gender Equity and Women's Empowerment

- **Women's Empowerment: Women's** economic empowerment is fundamental to sustainable development. BRICS can intensify efforts to eliminate barriers to female employment, promote female entrepreneurship, and ensure equal access to education and economic opportunities for women. Policies that support gender equality in workplaces and communities can accelerate economic and social progress.

Strengthening South-South and Triangular Cooperation

- **International Collaboration**: Expanding South-South cooperation and triangular cooperation can offer BRICS new opportunities to share knowledge, experience and resources for development. Through partnerships with other developing nations and developed countries, BRICS can explore innovative solutions to development problems, strengthen economic and political ties, and promote greater equity in the international system.

Deepening Food Safety Strategies

- **Innovative Food Security**: Given the critical importance of food security, BRICS can further explore innovative strategies to ensure that everyone has access to sufficient, safe and nutritious food. This may include supporting sustainable agriculture, using biotechnology to improve crop yields, and developing resilient food webs that can withstand economic and environmental shocks.

Implementation of Policies for Economic Diversification

- **Diversification and Competitiveness**: To reduce dependence on specific sectors, such as natural resources or low-cost manufacturing, BRICS can adopt policies aimed at economic diversification. This involves supporting high-tech sectors, promoting innovation in value-added services and investing in research and development. Diversification can help stabilize the BRICS economy, promote long-term sustainable growth, and increase resilience to global market fluctuations.

Through these strategic initiatives and the continuous evolution of their economic development policies, BRICS can not only effectively address domestic and global challenges but can also contribute significantly to building a more balanced and inclusive world economic order. Their capacity for adaptation and innovation, combined with growing economic and political influence, places them in a unique position to promote positive changes not only within their borders but also internationally.

Valorization of the Blue Economy

- **Sustainable Exploitation of Marine Resources**: Adopting an approach to the blue economy, which values the sustainable exploitation of marine and aquatic resources for economic growth, can offer BRICS new ways of development. This involves the responsible management of fish resources, the development of sustainable coastal tourism and investment in marine renewable energy, such as offshore wind energy, while contributing to the conservation of marine ecosystems.

Focus on Rural Development and Sustainable Agriculture

- **Revitalization of Rural Areas**: Strengthening rural development through sustainable agriculture and the economic diversification of rural areas can help reduce regional inequalities and improve food security. BRICS can encourage agricultural practices that are environmentally sustainable and resilient to climate change, while supporting agricultural innovation and facilitating access to markets for small farmers.

Support for the Social and Solidarity Economy

- **Promotion of Social Entrepreneurship: The social** and solidarity economy, which includes companies that have social, environmental and community objectives at the center of their mission, represents an important lever for development. BRICS can promote social entrepreneurship and cooperatives as a means to create jobs, combat poverty and respond to social and ecological challenges, while strengthening the social fabric.

Improving the Accessibility and Reliability of Public Services

- **Public Services for All**: Ensuring that all citizens have access to high-quality public services, such as healthcare, education, and transportation, is essential to promote equity and improve quality of life. BRICS can exploit digital technologies to make public services more accessible and reliable, improving efficiency and reducing disparities in access to essential services.

Encourage Youth Participation in Development Policy

- **Youth Empowerment**: Encouraging the active participation of young people in the definition and implementation of development policies can ensure that economic strategies are aligned with the aspirations and needs of future generations. Creating spaces for youth involvement, both politically and economically, can lead to innovative solutions and ensure that development is sustainable and inclusive in the long term.

The BRICS' holistic and multilateral approach to economic progress, which balances growth, sustainability and inclusion, demonstrates their growing role as engines of innovation and positive change in the global context. By continuing to explore and implement economic development policies that reflect contemporary realities and future prospects, BRICS can not only successfully navigate the challenges of the present but can also open new paths for a more prosperous and resilient world.

In conclusion, the economic development strategies adopted by the BRICS countries represent a complex mosaic of approaches and initiatives, each reflecting national specificities but all oriented towards objectives of sustainable growth, social equity and economic resilience. The diversity of the policies implemented — from the promotion of technological innovation and sustainable development, to the strengthening of financial inclusion and food security, to the enhancement of circular and blue economies — highlights the understanding by the BRICS of the importance of a multifaceted approach to economic development.

The BRICS economic development strategies emphasize not only the importance of adapting to the rapid transformations of the global context, but also the need to promote growth models that are inclusive and sustainable in the long term. By investing in education, research and development, sustainable infrastructure and green innovation, BRICS are seeking to position themselves as a leader in the transition to a more resilient and low-carbon global economic future.

At the same time, the emphasis placed on international cooperation, both within the BRICS group and with other nations and regional blocs, reflects the awareness that many of the challenges to contemporary economic development transcend national borders and require collective responses. Collaboration to address issues such as climate change, food security and the COVID-19 pandemic underlines the role that the BRICS intend to play not only as engines of economic growth but also as promoters of global solutions.

In addition, the recognition of the importance of gender equity, youth empowerment and civic participation in economic development policies signals a commitment by the BRICS to build more just and inclusive societies. This holistic approach, which considers economic development inseparable from social progress and environmental sustainability, is crucial for tackling the complex challenges of the 21st century.

Finally, as the BRICS continue to navigate a rapidly changing global landscape, their ability to adapt, innovate and collaborate will largely determine the success of their economic development strategies. The shared experience and mutual learning between these countries can offer valuable insights for other developing nations, helping to shape a global economic future that is not only more prosperous but also more resilient, equitable and sustainable.

The future trajectory of the BRICS, influenced by their economic development policies and their ability to collectively face global challenges, will be a key factor in determining the configuration of the world economic order of the future. Their strategy, intrinsically linked to the search for a balance between growth, sustainability and equity, offers a development model that could guide not only their national paths but also positively influence global development dynamics.

4. Role in Global Governance: BRICS impact on international financial and political institutions

The role of the BRICS in global governance, especially in international financial and political institutions, reflects the growing economic and political importance of these countries on the world stage. The BRICS, consisting of Brazil, Russia, India, China and South Africa, have sought to strengthen their influence and promote greater equity in global governance structures, often perceived as dominated by the advanced economies of the G7. The impact of BRICS on international financial and political institutions can be examined through various dimensions:

Reform of International Financial Institutions

The BRICS have lobbied for substantial reforms in international financial institutions such as the International Monetary Fund

(IMF) and the World Bank. The purpose of these reforms is to better reflect the growing economic weight of developing and emerging countries in the world economy. Efforts include calling for greater voice and representation in these institutions, as well as adapting lending policies to be more attentive to the development needs of these countries.

Creation of the New Development Bank (NBD)

Perhaps the most significant action taken by the BRICS to strengthen their impact on global economic governance was the creation of the New Development Bank (NBD), also known as the BRICS Bank, in 2014. This institution aims to mobilize resources for infrastructure and sustainable development projects in BRICS countries and other emerging and developing economies, acting as an alternative to traditional financial institutions dominated by the West.

The Contingent Reserve Arrangement (CRA) Agreement

In parallel with the NBD, the BRICS have established the Contingent Reserve Arrangement (CRA), a 100 billion dollar foreign exchange reserve fund intended to provide short-term financial support to members in case of balance of payments problems. This initiative aims to strengthen the global financial safety net and reduce dependence on the IMF.

Promoting Multilateralism

The BRICS have promoted multilateralism as the foundation of global governance, seeking to counter tendencies towards unilateralism and protectionism. Through their annual summits and other multilateral platforms, the BRICS have emphasized the importance of international cooperation to address global challenges such as climate change, terrorism, pandemics and poverty.

Influence in the United Nations

The BRICS seek to strengthen their influence in the United Nations and its agencies, promoting reforms that make the Security Council more representative of the 21st century international community. In addition, they have supported initiatives that promote sustainable development, human rights, and international peace and security.

Impact on Global Trade

BRICS play an active role in global trade discussions, supporting an open and rules-based multilateral trading system. They have lobbied for reforms in the World Trade Organization (WTO) and have promoted regional and bilateral trade agreements that reflect their interests and those of other emerging economies.

In summary, the BRICS are actively trying to shape global governance to reflect the emerging multipolar world, stressing the need for greater inclusivity, equity, and international cooperation. Although there are challenges, including internal differences among BRICS members, their joint commitment to promoting reforms of international financial and political institutions continues to offer a vital perspective for a more balanced global order. Their collective action underlines the importance of dialogue, mutual respect and cooperation between nations to effectively address global challenges and promote sustainable development.

The BRICS' continued commitment to greater representation and voice in global economic and political decisions not only reflects their growing economic power but also their desire for an international system that recognizes and respects the diversity of development trajectories and political aspirations. Through initiatives such as the New Development Bank and the Contingent Reserve Arrangement Agreement, BRICS have demonstrated their ability to offer constructive alternatives to existing structures, while promoting solidarity between emerging and developing economies.

The BRICS approach to global governance, which emphasizes multilateralism, cooperation and inclusive dialogue, offers an important contribution to the search for shared solutions to complex transnational issues. As they continue to navigate evolving global dynamics and face internal and external challenges, the BRICS' ability to work together and with other nations will be crucial to realizing their vision of a more just and equitable world order.

Ultimately, the impact of the BRICS on international financial and political institutions extends far beyond economic issues, touching on fundamental aspects of peace, security and global sustainable development. Their rise as a collective force on the international scene underlines the transition to a multipolar world in which global governance must be continuously adapted to reflect the reality of increasingly complex interconnection and interdependence.

The BRICS commitment to shaping global governance takes on an additional dimension when considering the emerging challenges of the 21st century, such as the digitalization of the economy, cybersecurity issues, and the implications of artificial intelligence on society and work. These challenges require innovative and collaborative responses that the BRICS are particularly positioned to help formulate, given their diversity and their experience in rapid technological evolution.

Digitalization and Global Governance

- **Economic Digitalization**: The BRICS are actively exploring how digitalization can be used to promote financial inclusion, improve the efficiency of public services, and stimulate economic growth. Their collective action can influence the formulation of global norms on the digital economy, promoting an approach that balances the opportunities offered by digital technologies with the need to address issues such as data privacy, cybersecurity and digital inequality.

Cybersecurity and Stability

- **Cybersecurity Cooperation**: With the increase in transnational cyber threats, BRICS have an opportunity to play a key role in strengthening global cyber stability. By collaborating on cybersecurity standards, threat information exchange and defense strategies, they can significantly contribute to creating a more secure and resilient digital environment.

Artificial Intelligence and Ethics

- **Artificial Intelligence (AI) Governance**: As AI continues to transform economies and societies, the need for ethical and inclusive governance of these technologies emerges. BRICS can bring important perspectives to the global debate on AI, promoting the development and responsible use of AI that respects human rights, promotes equity, and minimizes the risks of inequality and discrimination.

Environmental Sustainability and Climate Change

- **Action on Climate Change**: The BRICS commitment to promoting sustainable development extends to their active participation in discussions on climate change. As important global players and, in some cases, as major emitters of greenhouse gases, their cooperation in international climate initiatives, including efforts to reduce emissions and promote adaptation to climate change, is crucial to the success of global efforts to mitigate the impact of climate change.

Equity in Global Trade

- **International Trade Reforms**: BRICS play an active role in promoting a fairer and more open multilateral trading system. Through their commitment to global trade platforms such as the World Trade Organization, they seek to ensure that international trade rules are fair and promote sustainable development, reflecting the interests and concerns of emerging and developing economies.

In conclusion, as the BRICS continue to strengthen their presence in international financial and political institutions, their role as catalysts for positive and constructive change in global governance becomes increasingly evident. Through dialogue, cooperation and innovation, these countries are trying to address some of the most pressing issues of our time, proposing solutions that aspire to a more just, equitable and sustainable world order. Their collective action not only reflects the common aspirations and challenges of emerging countries, but also offers new perspectives and approaches to address the complexities of global governance in the 20th century.

First century. Their ability to navigate international dynamics, to propose alternative models of development and cooperation, and to influence the global agenda underlines the crucial role that the BRICS play in shaping the future of global governance.

Increase in Cultural Influence and Soft Power

- **Promotion of Soft Power**: The BRICS are increasing their cultural influence at the global level, recognizing that soft power is a fundamental aspect of international governance. Through the promotion of their languages, cultures, values and through educational and cultural exchanges, these countries can facilitate greater mutual understanding and build bridges of dialogue and cooperation with other nations. The increase in soft power can also strengthen their ability to influence global discussions and policies in a more subtle but significant way.

Strengthening South-South Partnerships

- **Deepening South-South Relations**: While the BRICS seek to reform existing financial and political institutions, they are also deepening South-South relations, offering an alternative to the traditional dependence on Western aid and influence. By strengthening economic, political and cultural networks between developing countries, BRICS can promote new models of cooperation and development that are more balanced and mutually beneficial.

Expansion of Multilateral Cooperation Initiatives

- **Renewed Multilateralism**: In promoting a multipolar world order, the BRICS are also seeking to expand multilateral cooperation initiatives that transcend their borders. By actively participating in international forums and promoting multilateral agreements on issues such as security, trade, technology and the environment, BRICS can support a more inclusive and cooperative international system.

Future Challenges and Opportunities

- **Navigating Global Challenges: BRICS face the challenge of maintaining cohesion and unity of action in** the face of internal differences and external pressures. However, their ability to overcome these challenges and to seize opportunities for enhanced cooperation will largely determine the effectiveness of their impact on global governance. By addressing issues such as global inequalities, climate change and pandemics with a unified and supportive approach,

BRICS can offer leadership and vision for a world that seeks shared solutions to common challenges.

Ultimately, the evolving role of the BRICS in global governance reflects an important shift towards a more pluralistic and diversified international order. As they continue to explore new avenues for cooperation and to exercise their influence constructively, BRICS have the opportunity to make a significant contribution to shaping a global future that values collaboration, mutual respect, and a commitment to shared progress. Their collective trajectory in the coming years will remain a key factor in determining the configuration of global governance in an increasingly interdependent world.

The rise of the BRICS on the global stage highlights a trend towards a more balanced world order, where emerging economies acquire a stronger voice in global governance issues. This shift in power offers a platform to address some of the inherent inequalities in the existing international system and opens up new avenues for international cooperation.

Promoting Sustainable Development

- **2030 Agenda for Sustainable Development**: BRICS can play a key role in promoting the United Nations 2030 Agenda for Sustainable Development, adopting and implementing policies that support the Sustainable Development Goals (SDGs). Through their economic and political influence, they can guide global efforts to address critical issues such as poverty, hunger, gender inequality and climate change, demonstrating their commitment to equitable and sustainable development.

Strengthening Crisis Response Capabilities

- **Global Crisis Management**: The ability to respond effectively to global crises, such as pandemics and climate emergencies, is a major challenge for global governance.

BRICS, through cooperation and coordination, can contribute to strengthening global response capacities, by sharing resources, knowledge and technologies. Their collaboration can be especially valuable in strengthening global health systems, promoting research and development of vaccines and treatments, and coordinating relief efforts in the event of natural disasters.

Innovation in Global Finance

- **International Financial Reforms**: BRICS can continue to push for reforms in international financial institutions to make the global financial system more representative, equitable and resilient. This includes promoting greater transparency, adopting fairer lending practices, and developing new financial instruments to support sustainable development and adaptation to climate change.

Strengthening South-South Trade and Investment

- **South-South Trade and Economy**: Expanding South-South trade and investment offers BRICS and other developing countries the opportunity to diversify their economies, reduce dependence on traditional markets and stimulate domestic economic growth. BRICS can play a leadership role in facilitating regional trade agreements, promoting economic integration, and supporting the creation of more inclusive regional and global value chains.

Addressing Global Security Issues

- **Security and Global Peace**: With their growing political influence, the BRICS can contribute significantly to international efforts to maintain global peace and security. This includes active participation in peacekeeping operations, mediation in international and regional conflicts, and support for disarmament initiatives. Their collaboration can help build a safer world, where security issues are addressed through dialogue and cooperation rather than through competition and conflict.

Integrating Youth into Governance Policies

- **Youth Empowerment**: BRICS recognize the importance of integrating young people's voices into global governance policies. Promoting youth empowerment through education, employment and political participation can ensure that future generations are better equipped to face global challenges, while at the same time helping to renew and strengthen international institutions with new ideas and perspectives. Investing in young people, not only as beneficiaries but also as active actors of change, can accelerate progress towards achieving sustainable development goals and promote more dynamic and inclusive global governance.

Supporting Innovation for Environmental Governance

- **Environmental Leadership**: Faced with the global climate crisis, BRICS have the opportunity to assume a leadership role in the development and implementation of innovative solutions for environmental governance. This includes promoting low-carbon economies, supporting research and development in clean and renewable technologies, and facilitating ambitious international climate agreements that take into account the needs and capacities of all nations. Their joint action can demonstrate that economic development and environmental protection can go hand in hand, offering sustainable models for the rest of the world.

Strengthening Global Health Networks

- **Global Health Cooperation**: The current COVID-19 pandemic has underscored the critical importance of effective international cooperation in the field of global health. BRICS can play a critical role in strengthening global health networks, promoting universal access to health services, supporting joint research and development of vaccines and treatments, and working to strengthen preparation for and response to future pandemics. Their collaboration can help ensure that resources and knowledge are shared fairly, helping to build a healthier and more resilient world.

Promotion of Cultural Diversity and Inter-cultural Dialogue

- **Dialogue and Cultural Diversity**: The BRICS, with their rich and diverse cultural heritages, are in a unique position to promote intercultural dialogue and mutual understanding at the global level. Through initiatives that enhance cultural diversity and facilitate exchanges between people from different countries and cultures, BRICS can help overcome prejudices and build bridges of friendship and cooperation between nations. These efforts are essential to address the deep roots of conflicts and to promote lasting peace based on mutual respect and global solidarity.

Expansion of Political Dialogue Platforms

- **Expanded Political Dialogue**: As the BRICS seek to expand their influence in international financial and political institutions, the creation and expansion of political dialogue platforms become crucial. These platforms can facilitate discussion on complex global issues, allowing BRICS and other countries to explore consensual solutions and promote a more inclusive world order. Through open and constructive political dialogue, BRICS can work with other nations to address global challenges, from international security to economic governance, from social justice to climate change.

In conclusion, while the BRICS continue to strengthen their role in global governance, their impact extends far beyond economic and financial issues, touching on fundamental aspects of international cooperation, peace and security, sustainable development and global health. Their ability to act as catalysts for positive change offers hope for a future in which global governance is more equitable, resilient and attentive to the needs of all nations and all peoples. The road ahead will require commitment, innovation and collaboration, but the BRICS are uniquely positioned to help drive the transformation toward this more inclusive future. Through the promotion of strengthened multilateralism, the enhancement of South-South partnerships, and the commitment to sustainable solutions to global problems, BRICS can not only shape global governance to better reflect the geopolitical landscape of the 21st century, but they can also offer new models of cooperation and development.

Priority on Human Development

- **Focus on Human Development**: A fundamental priority for BRICS in global governance is the recognition that economic development must go hand in hand with human development. This involves a commitment to the elimination of poverty, universal access to quality education, gender equality, and health and well-being for all. By working together to promote these goals, BRICS can play a key role in ensuring that global policies are designed to improve the lives of people around the world.

Fight against Climate Change

- **United Action against Climate Change**: Tackling climate change requires coordinated and ambitious global action. The BRICS, given their growing economic influence and their vulnerability to the impacts of climate change, have a special interest in leading and supporting international efforts to mitigate and adapt to climate change. Through joint initiatives and the promotion of clean and sustainable technologies, BRICS can make a significant contribution to the global fight against climate change, while promoting sustainable development in their countries and beyond.

Strengthening Global Food Security

- **Food Security and Sustainable Agriculture**: Food security remains a pressing global challenge, exacerbated by climate change and growing population pressures. The BRICS, many of whom are important agricultural producers, can play a crucial role in promoting sustainable agricultural practices, in agricultural research, and in the development of resilient food systems. By facilitating trade in agricultural products and promoting cooperation on food security, BRICS can contribute to the creation of a more stable and sustainable global food system.

Promoting Peace and Security

- **Contributions to International Peace and Security**: BRICS have the opportunity to promote international peace and security through multilateral diplomacy and support for peace missions and conflict resolution processes. Their active participation in security discussions and initiatives can help prevent conflicts, manage international crises and build lasting peace, exploiting their diversity of experiences and perspectives to find inclusive and sustainable solutions.

Supporting Cultural Diversity and Social Cohesion

- **Enhancing Diversity and Social Cohesion**: Finally, BRICS can promote cultural diversity and social cohesion not only within their borders, but also globally. By celebrating cultural diversity, facilitating cultural and educational exchanges and promoting respect for all cultures, BRICS can contribute to building more inclusive and tolerant societies and to strengthening dialogue and mutual understanding at the international level.

In conclusion, the BRICS' collective commitment to global governance represents a significant opportunity to address some of the most pressing challenges of our time. Through cooperation, innovation and a shared commitment to a fairer and more sustainable future, BRICS have the potential to profoundly influence the architecture of world governance. Their joint action can not only promote greater balance in the international system but also guide progress toward common global goals, such as sustainable development, peace, security, and prosperity for all.

The BRICS' ability to navigate the complexities of international relations, addressing both internal differences and external challenges, will be crucial to realizing their potential as a positive force in global governance. Successfully tackling these tasks will require not only a strategic vision and political commitment but also a capacity to adapt and respond to changing global dynamics.

Through collaborative initiatives, such as strengthening multilateral institutions, promoting South-South trade and investment, and leading efforts to combat climate change, BRICS can help shape a new paradigm of international cooperation. A paradigm that values diversity, promotes justice and equity, and recognizes the importance of shared solutions to shared challenges.

In addition, the active involvement of BRICS in global governance issues provides a platform for experimenting with new models of development and cooperation, which can serve as an example for other countries and regions. Their success in these areas could not only strengthen their position in the world but also provide valuable lessons on how to build a more inclusive and resilient future globally.

Ultimately, the role of the BRICS in global governance represents a unique opportunity to positively influence the course of international development. As they move into the future, their collective commitment to fairer, more responsible and inclusive governance could not only transform their own nations but also offer new hope and opportunities for the entire world. The road ahead is complex and full of challenges, but also full of possibilities for a significant and lasting change in the global governance landscape.

In conclusion, the growing role of the BRICS in global governance marks a crucial moment in the history of international relations, characterized by a shift towards a more multipolar world order. The collective influence of Brazil, Russia, India, China and South Africa on international financial and political institutions represents not only the recognition of their growing economic and political importance but also the desire for fairer representation and a more inclusive dialogue in the international community. This movement has the potential to rebalance global power, offering new perspectives and modes of cooperation that better reflect the diversity and complexity of the contemporary world.

The creation of the New Development Bank and Contingent Reserve Arrangement Agreement by the BRICS underlines their commitment to providing alternatives to traditional financial institutions and to promoting sustainable development through initiatives that respect the needs and priorities of emerging and developing countries. These institutions symbolize a significant step towards establishing a more inclusive and equitable global financial system.

In parallel, the BRICS' commitment to reform existing global governance structures, such as the International Monetary Fund and the World Bank, reflects their determination to ensure that these institutions are more representative of the current world economic order. Their collective actions aim to strengthen the voice of developing countries in global economic decisions, promoting principles of fairness, transparency and justice.

In addition, the emphasis placed by the BRICS on promoting multilateralism and international dialogue on key issues such as climate change, global security, and public health demonstrates their aspiration to contribute constructively to the solution of global challenges. Their approach to international cooperation, which emphasizes solidarity, mutual respect and joint action, offers a valuable model for tackling transnational issues in a collaborative and inclusive manner.

However, internal challenges, differences of interest, and geopolitical tensions represent significant obstacles to the cohesion and effectiveness of the BRICS as a bloc. The BRICS' ability to navigate these complexities, while maintaining a shared commitment to common objectives, will be crucial to their continued success in reforming global governance. Successfully tackling these challenges will require a delicate balance between promoting national interests and supporting multilateral ideals.

Ultimately, the evolving role of the BRICS in global governance offers a unique perspective on the transformation of international power dynamics. It represents an opportunity to promote a fairer and more inclusive dialogue on critical global issues, stressing the importance of a cooperative and multilateral approach to international development and security. As the BRICS continue to shape the global governance landscape, their collective commitment to reform, innovation, and cooperation remains essential to realizing the vision of a world order that is equitable, resilient and capable of meeting the challenges of the 21st century.

5. International Trade and Investment: analysis of trade and investment relations between the BRICS and with the rest of the world.

Trade relations and investments between the BRICS countries (Brazil, Russia, India, China and South Africa) and with the rest of the world have assumed increasing importance in the context of international trade and the global economy. These nations, with their rapidly expanding economies, have not only increased their global economic weight, but have also sought to diversify their economic partnerships and deepen mutual cooperation. Below is an analysis of the key dynamics that characterize BRICS trade and investment relations, both within the group and with the outside world.

Intra-BRICS trade

- **Trade Intensification**: In recent decades, there has been a significant increase in intra-BRICS trade, with a flow of goods and services that reflects the complementarity of their economies. China, in particular, has established itself as the main trading partner for many of the BRICS countries, exporting manufactured goods, while Brazil and Russia are important suppliers of raw materials.

- **Trade Barriers**: Despite growth, intra-BRICS trade is hampered by tariff and non-tariff barriers, regulatory complexities, and lack of efficient transport infrastructure. Reducing these barriers is essential to realizing the full potential of intra-BRICS trade.

Cross investments

- **Foreign Direct Investment (FDI) flows**: BRICS are both recipients and significant sources of foreign direct investment. China, in particular, has intensified its investments abroad, including those in the BRICS countries, mainly concentrated in key sectors such as energy, infrastructure and technology.

- **Infrastructure Development**: The New BRICS Development Bank plays a crucial role in financing infrastructure projects in member countries, thus facilitating intra-BRICS investments and promoting economic development.

Business Relations with the World

- **Exports and Imports**: The BRICS have established themselves as key players in world trade, with a significant share of global exports and imports. The diversification of exports beyond raw materials, in particular for Brazil and Russia, and the expansion into high-tech sectors, for India and China, remain important priorities.

- **Trade Agreements**: The BRICS have negotiated a series of bilateral and regional trade agreements to facilitate access to foreign markets and promote trade and investment. Participation in such agreements allows BRICS to better integrate into the global economy and to influence international trade rules.

Challenges and Opportunities

- **Protectionism and Trade Tensions**: The rise of protectionism and trade tensions, especially between China and the United States, present challenges for BRICS, as they seek to navigate a changing global trading environment. The promotion of multilateralism and the strengthening of global business institutions are seen as ways to mitigate these tensions.

- **Sustainability and Environmental Standards**: With the growing global focus on sustainable development, BRICS are called upon to integrate environmental and social considerations into their trade and investment policies. This includes adopting sustainable business practices and supporting green investments.

In conclusion, BRICS' trade and investment relations with the rest of the world and with each other represent a fundamental element of global economic dynamics. By addressing existing challenges and exploiting emerging opportunities, BRICS can further strengthen their role in the international trading system, promoting a more robust and resilient cooperation environment. The importance of adapting to a rapidly changing global landscape and of adopting inclusive and sustainable strategies is crucial to their continued success. Below, additional dimensions of this dynamic context are explored.

Digitalization of Commerce

- **E-commerce and Digital Trade**: Digitalization offers BRICS new opportunities to expand trade and investment. The adoption of cross-border e-commerce platforms can open up new markets for small and medium-sized enterprises (SMEs) and facilitate the trade of digital goods and services. The BRICS are trying to harmonize regulations on digital commerce and promote a safe and open online environment, recognizing the growth potential that electronic commerce represents for their economies.

Partnerships for the Global Value Chain

- **Integration into Global Value Chains (CVG)**: BRICS are working to integrate more deeply into global value chains, not only as suppliers of low-cost raw materials and manufactured goods, but also through high-value-added production and innovation. The development of logistics infrastructure, investment in research and development and the promotion of high production standards are essential to facilitate this transition and to improve the competitiveness of BRICS companies in the global market.

Green Finance and Sustainable Investments

- **Sustainability in Investments**: The promotion of sustainable investments and green finance has become a priority for BRICS, which seek to align investment flows with sustainable development goals. This includes encouraging responsible business practices, supporting projects that have a positive environmental and social impact, and adopting sustainability criteria in the allocation of financial resources. The BRICS New Development Bank plays an important role in this context, financing green projects and sustainable infrastructure.

Building Economic Resilience

- **Economic Diversification and Resilience**: Facing global market volatility and building resilient economies is a common goal of the BRICS. This involves diversifying economic bases to reduce dependence on individual sectors or markets, promote innovation and industrial competitiveness, and develop sound macroeconomic policies. Collaboration between BRICS to share knowledge, experience and best practices can support diversification efforts and help build economies that are more flexible and able to withstand external shocks.

Promotion of Commercial Multilateralism

- **Strengthening the Multilateral Trading System**: BRICS stress the importance of a strong, rules-based multilateral trading system, as embodied by the World Trade Organization (WTO). By working together to promote reform of the WTO and to ensure that the international trading system reflects the interests and concerns of developing countries, BRICS can contribute to fairer and more balanced global trade.

Engagement with Other Developing Countries

- **Extending Cooperation to Other Developing Countries**: In addition to cooperation within the BRICS bloc, there is also a growing commitment to extend collaboration to other developing countries. Through initiatives such as the BRICS Plus dialogue, BRICS seek to build broader alliances, promote the global South and address issues of common interest such as sustainable development, the fight against poverty and access to innovative technologies. This approach aims to further strengthen solidarity between developing countries, creating a united front to negotiate global issues and strengthening their voice in international platforms.

Addressing the Challenges of Protectionism

- **Countering Protectionism**: In an era characterized by growing protectionist sentiment and trade tensions, BRICS have the opportunity to promote free trade and multilateralism as fundamental pillars of the global economic order. By supporting an open and regulated business environment, BRICS can help mitigate the negative impacts of protectionism on international trade and investment, while promoting inclusive economic development.

Technological Innovation and Intellectual Property

- **Technology and Intellectual Property**: Technological innovation is at the core of BRICS economic development strategies. Promoting effective cooperation in research and development, intellectual property protection and technology transfer is critical to accelerating technological progress within the bloc and beyond. BRICS can work together to develop norms and policies that encourage innovation while ensuring that the benefits of emerging technologies are accessible and fairly distributed.

Development of Fair Business Standards

- **Fairness in Trade Rules**: BRICS have the opportunity to lead the creation of a global trading system that promotes fair and sustainable trade rules. This includes tackling unfair business practices, ensuring that trade rules support sustainable development, and considering the social and economic impact of trade on the most vulnerable countries. The BRICS commitment to fair and sustainable trade can serve as a model for global trade policy reform.

Balancing Growth and Sustainability

- **Economic Growth and Environmental Sustainability**: In pursuing economic growth and the expansion of trade and investment, the BRICS are also faced with the challenge of ensuring that this development is environmentally sustainable. This requires a joint commitment to promote business practices that minimize environmental impact, invest in clean and renewable technologies, and adopt holistic approaches that balance economic growth with environmental protection.

In conclusion, BRICS' trade and investment relations with the rest of the world and with each other reflect a complex network of interactions that are vital for global economic stability and sustainable development. By overcoming the challenges and seizing the opportunities presented by the evolving international environment, BRICS can not only strengthen their economic position but also help shape a fairer, more resilient and prosperous future for the global community. Their ability to promote cooperation, innovation and a balanced approach to development will be crucial to achieving these objectives.

As BRICS navigate the global trade and investment ecosystem, they face the dual task of supporting their growing economies and contributing to the restructuring of global economic dynamics. Their unique position as emerging economies with vast resources, enormous populations, and significant growth potential provides them with unique opportunities to influence international trade and investment in ways that promote greater equity and sustainability.

Expanding the Role in Global Markets

- **Market Penetration Strategies**: BRICS are adopting innovative strategies to expand their role in global markets, exploiting new technologies, developing high-growth sectors such as the digital economy, and increasing their competitiveness in traditional sectors through innovation and chain enhancement. This includes strengthening domestic production capacities, investing in research and development, and adopting brand strategies to position their products and services in global markets.

Development of Economic Corridors

- **Building Economic Corridors**: The BRICS are working on building transnational economic corridors that facilitate trade and investment across regions and continents. These corridors, which include transport, logistics and communication infrastructures, not only improve connectivity between BRICS and other countries but also serve as catalysts for regional economic development, facilitating access to markets and stimulating economic growth in the areas crossed.

Policies for Attracting Investments

- **Attracting Foreign Investments**: BRICS are intensifying efforts to attract foreign direct investment (FDI) by creating attractive business environments, simplifying bureaucratic processes, and ensuring a stable legal and regulatory framework. Through special economic zones, tax incentives and public-private partnerships, they seek to attract foreign investors in key sectors for economic diversification and technological development.

Strengthening Global Food Security

- **Boosting Agriculture and Food Security**: Given their significant agricultural capacity, the BRICS have a crucial role to play in strengthening global food security. By investing in sustainable agricultural technologies, improving water and soil management practices, and promoting international cooperation in the agricultural sector, BRICS can help ensure that global food supply chains are resilient, sustainable and able to meet growing demand.

Green Economy Initiative

- **Promoting the Green Economy**: As part of global efforts to combat climate change and promote sustainable development, the BRICS are exploring ways to catalyze the transition to a green economy. This involves not only investments in renewable energy and clean technologies but also the adoption of policies that encourage sustainable business practices and environmentally friendly production. BRICS cooperation in the green economy sector can stimulate innovation, create market opportunities and promote sustainable economic development models.

Active Participation in Global Economic Governance

- **Influence on Global Economic Governance**: Through active and constructive participation in global economic governance platforms, such as the G20, the WTO and other international financial institutions, the BRICS are seeking to shape a more inclusive and representative world economic order. By working to reform existing institutions and promote fairer rules of the game, they aim to ensure that emerging and developing economies have a stronger voice in global economic decisions. This collective action is essential to address disparities in the international economic system and to promote principles of justice and equity in global economic relations.

Defending Multilaterality in Trade

- **Supporting the Multilateral Trading System**: BRICS emphasize the importance of supporting and strengthening the rules-based multilateral trading system, especially at a time when trade tensions and protectionism threaten to further fragment the global economy. By promoting dialogue and cooperation within the World Trade Organization and other multilateral platforms, BRICS seek to keep international trade channels open, thus facilitating freer and fairer trade that benefits economies at all levels of development.

Investments in Research and Development

- **Promoting R&D for Innovation**: Recognizing the central role of innovation as a driver of economic growth and sustainable development, BRICS invest significantly in research and development (R&D) to empower their high-tech sectors. This commitment to promote innovation through science, technology and higher education not only strengthens their domestic economies but also contributes to the global knowledge pool, offering innovative solutions to global challenges.

Development of Strategic Partnerships

- **Deepening Bilateral and Regional Economic Ties**: While the BRICS continue to consolidate their internal economic cooperation, they also seek to develop strategic partnerships with other regions and countries. Through bilateral trade agreements, regional cooperation initiatives and strategic dialogues, BRICS can access new markets, diversify their external economic relations, and promote mutual economic growth with partners around the world.

Confronting the Challenges of Globalization

- **Navigating the Complexities of Globalization**: The BRICS are in a unique position to address the complexities and contradictions of globalization. While they benefit from global economic integration, they must also manage the challenges it brings, including inequalities, environmental impacts, and vulnerability to global market fluctuations. By adopting holistic approaches and inclusive policies, BRICS can lead to a more equitable and sustainable form of globalization.

Ultimately, BRICS' trade and investment relations with the rest of the world and within their block offer a microcosm of evolving global economic dynamics. By proactively addressing challenges and strategically seizing the opportunities that emerge in this dynamic context, BRICS can not only improve their economic well-being but also contribute significantly to the creation of a more resilient, equitable and inclusive global economic landscape. Their ability to collaborate, innovate and promote sustainable development will be crucial in shaping the future of the world economy.

In the field of international trade and investment, the BRICS are faced with the challenge of balancing the need for global economic integration with the desire to maintain a certain strategic autonomy. The growing economic interdependence between nations requires a holistic approach that considers both economic and social and environmental aspects of development.

Building a Favourable Business Environment

- **Regulatory and Business Innovation**: The creation of a favorable business environment that encourages innovation and competitiveness is essential to attract investment and stimulate economic growth. The BRICS are exploring ways to simplify administrative procedures, improve regulatory transparency, and provide incentives for start-ups and SMEs. The goal is to create an ecosystem that facilitates innovation, attracts talent and capital and promotes the development of new technologies and business models.

Promoting Fair and Sustainable Trade

- **Sustainability in Trade**: While the BRICS are committed to expanding their role in world trade, there is also growing recognition of the importance of promoting fair and sustainable trade practices. This includes supporting responsible supply chains, encouraging sustainable production and consumption, and promoting biodiversity. Through international cooperation, BRICS can guide the development of global standards that promote environmental, social and economic sustainability in international trade.

Integration of Emerging Technologies

- **Digitalization and Emerging Technologies**: The integration of emerging technologies into production processes and business models represents another key area of opportunity for the BRICS. From the Internet of Things (IoT) to artificial intelligence (AI), from robotics to blockchain, the adoption of these technologies can improve efficiency, reduce costs and open up new markets. The BRICS are trying to capitalize on these technologies to promote innovation in key sectors, improve the competitiveness of their economies, and address social and economic challenges.

Strengthening Multilateral Cooperation

- **Multilateral Forums and Dialogue**: Strengthening cooperation and dialogue through multilateral forums is essential to address trade and investment issues in a global context. The BRICS are using platforms such as the G20, the BRICS Summit and other international organizations to promote constructive discussions on global economic issues, from the reform of international financial institutions to the governance of the digital economy. This commitment to multilateralism helps build consensus, promote shared standards, and facilitate international cooperation.

Challenges of Globalization and Economic Diversification

- **Addressing the Challenges of Globalization**: In the context of globalization, BRICS must navigate complex economic dynamics that include market volatility, competition for resources, and cross-border environmental impacts. Promoting economic diversification, investing in sectors with high growth potential, and developing policies that protect the environment and local communities are critical steps to ensure that globalization brings fair and sustainable benefits.

In conclusion, the BRICS journey in international trade and investment illustrates their growing influence in the global economy and their commitment to shaping a future in which economic progress goes hand in hand with environmental sustainability and social justice. As they face the challenges of globalization and seek to exploit the opportunities offered by technological innovation and international cooperation, the BRICS play an increasingly important role in defining the norms and practices that will guide global economic development in the near future. Adopting strategies aimed at promoting fairer trade, responsible investment, and greater multilateral cooperation can not only strengthen their economies but also contribute to a more resilient and inclusive world economic order.

Focus on Economic Inclusion

- **Inclusion and Access to the Global Market**: Promoting economic inclusion represents a fundamental pillar in the BRICS trade and investment strategies. This involves removing barriers that restrict the access of least developed countries to global markets and supporting the efforts of these countries to improve their production capacities. Through capacity-building initiatives and technical assistance programs, BRICS can support wider economic participation and ensure that the benefits of globalization are more equally shared.

Supporting Green Transitions

- **Energy Transitions and Environmental Sustainability**: BRICS are emerging as key players in global discussions on climate and sustainability. Addressing the dual challenge of maintaining economic growth while responding to the urgency of environmental issues requires innovative policies and investments in green technologies. By promoting the transition to clean and sustainable energy sources and supporting sustainable production and consumption practices, BRICS can drive the transformation to a greener global economy.

Investing in Humanity

- **Education, Health and Human Development**: In addition to their emphasis on economic dynamics, BRICS recognize the importance of investing in people as the foundation of sustainable development. Improving access to quality education, promoting public health and supporting skills development are essential to building resilient and inclusive societies. Attention to the formation of human capital and the promotion of social well-being can accelerate progress towards the Sustainable Development Goals (SDGs) and improve the quality of life for all.

Cultural and Social Dialogue

- **Promotion of Dialogue and Cultural Understanding**: BRICS, through their cultural and social diversity, have the opportunity to enrich global dialogue and promote greater mutual understanding. Through cultural, educational and social exchanges, they can contribute to building bridges between the world's diverse communities, strengthening social cohesion and promoting shared values of respect, tolerance and solidarity.

Ultimately, the BRICS approach to international trade and investment, which balances ambitions for economic growth with a commitment to sustainable development and inclusion, offers important lessons for the rest of the world. As they continue to explore new paths of economic cooperation and navigate the challenges of a rapidly changing global landscape, their success in promoting a more just and equitable world economic order will depend on their ability to maintain an open dialogue, to adopt inclusive policies, and to work together to address shared global challenges.

As the BRICS continue their commitment to reform the dynamics of international trade and investment, they face the complexity of a world in which economic issues are inexorably intertwined with social, political and environmental issues. This interconnection requires constant attention to adaptability and innovation in their economic strategies, while ensuring that those strategies are sustainable and beneficial to a wider range of stakeholders.

Collaboration for Supply Chain Resilience

- **Resilient and Diverse Supply Chains**: Recent global challenges have highlighted the importance of building resilient and diverse supply chains. BRICS, with their vast resources and production capacities, can play a crucial role in developing supply chains that are more flexible and less dependent on individual markets or suppliers. Through cooperation and the construction of strategic partnerships, both within the bloc and with global partners, they can contribute to greater global economic stability, while reducing vulnerability to external shocks.

Enhancing the Role of Sustainable Technologies

- **Sustainable Technologies as a Pillar of Development**: Investment in sustainable technologies represents a priority area for BRICS in promoting environmentally friendly economic practices. From renewable energy to electric mobility, from precision agriculture to smart cities, the adoption of technologies that reduce environmental impact and improve efficiency can guide the transition to greener development models. These efforts not only contribute to the fight against climate change but also offer new economic opportunities and stimulate the creation of sustainable jobs.

Strengthening Public Health Systems

- **Public Health and Economic Development**: The
  COVID-19 pandemic has highlighted the interdependence
  between public health and economic stability. The BRICS
  recognize the importance of strengthening health
  systems, both to protect the well-being of the population
  and to ensure economic resilience. By investing in health
  infrastructure, medical research, and capacity to respond
  to health emergencies, BRICS can not only improve
  public health but also minimize the economic impact of
  future health crises.

Promoting Access to Education and Innovation

- **Education, Research and Innovation**: Access to
  quality education and opportunities for research and
  innovation are fundamental for economic and social
  development. The BRICS are investing in education
  systems that promote academic excellence, scientific
  research and technological innovation. By supporting
  education in critical fields such as science, technology,
  engineering, and mathematics (STEM), and by promoting
  collaboration between universities, research institutes,
  and industry, BRICS can cultivate a highly skilled
  workforce and stimulate the development of new
  technologies and industries.

Integration of Equitable Development Strategies

- **Equitable and Inclusive Development**: As the
  BRICS continue to expand on the global stage, it remains
  imperative to ensure that economic development benefits
  all sections of society. This requires policies that address
  inequalities, promote equitable access to economic
  opportunities, and support vulnerable groups. Through
  initiatives that improve financial inclusion, provide social
  safety nets, and promote local development, BRICS can

work toward achieving more balanced and inclusive societies. Their ability to implement reforms that promote equitable redistribution of resources, access to health and education, and social protection for all citizens will have a significant impact on their long-term success and internal stability.

Enhancing Regional Integration

- **Deepening Regional Integration**: For BRICS, regional economic integration offers an opportunity to consolidate their economies, expand domestic markets, and reduce dependence on external business partners. Through the promotion of regional free trade agreements, shared infrastructure and harmonized trade policies, they can facilitate intra-regional trade and investment. This not only stimulates economic growth but also contributes to greater political and social cohesion between countries in the same region.

Environmental Sustainability as an Imperative

- **Priority to Environmental Sustainability**: The commitment to environmental sustainability remains an imperative for BRICS, as they seek to reconcile economic growth with environmental protection. The promotion of circular economies, the sustainable management of natural resources, and investment in clean technologies are all fundamental aspects of their development strategies. Through international cooperation on climate change and commitment to achieving sustainable development goals, BRICS can guide global action towards more sustainable development models.

Expanding Access to Digital Connectivity

- **Digitalization for Development**: Digitalization offers enormous opportunities to improve economic efficiency, access to services and civic participation. The BRICS are exploring ways to expand access to digital connectivity in their societies, through the development of broadband infrastructure, the promotion of digital literacy and support for technology startups. Digitalization can act as a lever for innovation and inclusion, opening new ways for economic and social participation.

Strengthening Global Economic Governance

- **Influence in Global Economic Governance**: As the BRICS consolidate their role in the world economy, they continue to seek greater influence in global economic governance. This includes not only reforming international financial institutions to more fairly reflect the global economic landscape but also taking a leadership role in discussions on global economic issues such as sovereign debt, international taxation and financial regulation. Their ability to contribute to a constructive dialogue and to propose sensible reforms can help ensure a more stable and just global economic system.

In summary, BRICS trade and investment relations reflect the challenges and opportunities of a rapidly changing world, where the search for sustainable and inclusive economic solutions is more critical than ever. By addressing these challenges with a collaborative and future-oriented approach, BRICS can not only ensure their growth and prosperity but also help shape a world economic order that benefits a wider range of nations and communities. Their future trajectory will be a key indicator of the direction of global economic development in the 21st century.

The dynamics of trade and investment relations between the BRICS and the rest of the world, as well as within the group itself, signals a significant change in the global economic architecture towards greater multipolarity and interdependence.

The BRICS economies, characterized by rapid growth, growing political and economic influence, and a commitment to sustainable and inclusive development, are actively reforming the rules of international trade and investment.

Summary of BRICS Trade and Investment Dynamics

- **Intensification of Intra-BRICS Trade**: Intra-BRICS trade has intensified, demonstrating the complementarity of their economies. However, the reduction of trade barriers and the facilitation of trade remain crucial to fully exploit the potential of this economic block.

- **Strategic Investments**: Cross-investment between BRICS is growing, with a particular emphasis on infrastructure, energy, technology and sustainable development, underlining the importance of strengthened economic cooperation.

- **Expanding Global Role**: In global trade, the BRICS are expanding their impact through trade negotiations, reforms of international financial institutions, and investments in emerging technologies, promoting a more balanced trading system.

- **Challenges and Opportunities**: They address common challenges such as protectionism, trade tensions and the need for sustainable energy transitions, but also unique opportunities to drive sustainable development and technological innovation.

Vision for the Future

The future of BRICS' trade and investment relations, in their continued commitment to greater equity and sustainability in the global economy, will depend on their ability to navigate the complex challenges of a rapidly changing world. By maintaining a balance between economic growth and environmental sustainability, social equity and multilateral cooperation, BRICS can not only strengthen their economies but also contribute to a more resilient and inclusive world economic order.

Imperatives for Success

- **Promoting Enhanced Multilateralism**: The BRICS' success in shaping global economic governance will be amplified by their support for a multilateral system that emphasizes cooperation, dialogue, and mutual respect among nations.

- **Innovation and Sustainability**: By investing in research and development, adopting sustainable technologies and promoting innovation, BRICS can lead the transition to a global economy that values both economic growth and environmental responsibility.

- **Economic and Social Inclusion**: By addressing inequalities and promoting economic and social inclusion, BRICS can ensure that the benefits of globalization and technological progress are more widely shared, contributing to global stability and prosperity.

In conclusion, BRICS' trade and investment relations with the world represent a significant barometer of global economic trends, reflecting both emerging challenges and the potential of a new multipolar economic order. With their commitment to reform, cooperation, and sustainable development, the BRICS are well-positioned to play a central role in shaping the global economic future, promoting a growth model that is equitable, sustainable and inclusive. Their trajectory in the coming years will be fundamental in determining the shape of this new global economic landscape, stressing the importance of constructive dialogue, international cooperation and innovation guided by the vision of a shared and prosperous future for all.

6. Innovation and Technology: focus on how the BRICS are driving innovation in key sectors such as technology, renewable energy and space.

The BRICS, consisting of Brazil, Russia, India, China and South Africa, are emerging as significant forces in the global arena of innovation and technology. These countries are investing considerably in research and development (R&D) and adopting proactive policies to promote innovation in key sectors such as information technology, renewable energy and space exploration. These efforts are driven by the awareness that technological innovation is crucial for sustainable economic growth, international competitiveness, and the solution of complex global challenges.

Information and Communication Technology (ICT)

- **Digitalization and Development of ICT Infrastructure**: The BRICS are rapidly expanding their digital infrastructures and promoting the adoption of ICTs in various economic sectors. India, with its 'Digital India' program, aims to transform the entire economy into a digitally enhanced economy, while China is at the forefront of the development of 5G, artificial intelligence (AI) and big data. These countries are also supporting technology startups and business incubators to stimulate innovation.

Renewable Energy

- **Leadership in Renewable Energy**: The BRICS are taking decisive steps to diversify their energy matrices and promote the use of renewable energy. China is the world leader in the production of solar panels and wind turbines, while Brazil is a pioneer in the use of sugarcane bioethanol. Cooperation within the block on renewable energy projects not only reinforces energy security but also contributes to global efforts to mitigate climate change.

Space Exploration

- **Advances in Space Exploration**: The BRICS are also making important progress in space exploration and use. China has recently launched lunar and Martian exploration missions, demonstrating advanced capabilities in space technologies. India has gained global attention with the cost-effective Chandrayaan space program for lunar exploration and the Mars Orbiter mission. Russia, with its historic legacy of space exploration, continues to be a key player in space, while Brazil and South Africa are developing their capabilities in satellite technologies and space applications.

Global Challenges and Innovative Solutions

- **Contributions to Solving Global Challenges**: The BRICS focus on innovation extends to the search for innovative solutions to address global challenges such as food security, health and climate change. The use of advanced technologies in precision agriculture, personalized medicine and environmental monitoring are just a few examples of how innovation in the BRICS is helping to improve the quality of life and promote sustainable development.

Promoting Innovation through Cooperation

- **International Cooperation for Innovation**: Recognizing that innovation is often fueled by transnational collaboration, BRICS are promoting international cooperation in research and development. Through joint initiatives, such as technology parks, academic exchange programs and partnerships between universities and industries, the BRICS aim to create a global innovation ecosystem that facilitates the transfer of knowledge and technologies. Space exploration not only strengthens their economies and increases their global competitiveness but also helps to shape the future of technological innovation worldwide. This commitment to technological advancement and sustainable innovation highlights the BRICS vision of a world in which economic growth is closely linked to technological progress and environmental sustainability.

Collaboration for Research and Development

The collaboration between the BRICS in the field of research and development (R&D) is essential to overcome common technological challenges and accelerate innovation. Through shared platforms and cooperative research projects, BRICS can leverage their diversity of expertise and resources to achieve significant progress in areas such as clean technologies, medicine, and cybersecurity. International collaboration in R&D not only improves efficiency and reduces costs, but also opens up new avenues for technology transfer and the commercialization of innovations.

Challenges and Opportunities in Technological Adoption

As BRICS move rapidly to adopt and develop new technologies, they also face significant challenges, including the need to improve the education and technical skills of their workforce, protect intellectual property, and ensure equitable access to technological innovations. Managing these challenges requires well-designed policies that promote STEM education, entrepreneurship and innovation, while ensuring that the benefits of technological innovation are shared fairly within societies.

Global Impact of BRICS Innovation

The BRICS approach to innovation and technology has an impact that goes beyond their national borders. Through their growing contribution to global science, technology and innovation, they are becoming essential partners in the search for solutions to global challenges. The impact of their innovations in sectors such as renewable energy, ICT and space exploration not only demonstrates their potential for technological leadership but also offers replicable models and lessons learned that can benefit other nations and communities around the world.

Towards an Innovative and Sustainable Future

Ultimately, the BRICS focus on innovation and technology reflects a shared commitment to building a future in which economic development is driven by sustainable innovation, international collaboration, and equitable access to technologies. By proactively addressing the challenges and seizing the opportunities presented by technological evolution, BRICS can lead the way to a more connected, resilient and sustainable world. Their success in innovation and technology will not only strengthen their position in the global economy but will also contribute significantly to technological progress and sustainability at an international level.

As the BRICS advance in the field of innovation and technology, they are also opening new frontiers in international collaboration, demonstrating how the sharing of knowledge and resources can accelerate scientific and technological progress for global benefit. Their innovation strategy, which emphasizes key sectors such as digital technologies, clean energy and space exploration, aligns with global sustainable development goals, offering valuable lessons on how to face contemporary challenges in a collaborative and innovative way.

Valorization of Scientific Cooperation

Scientific cooperation between the BRICS is becoming increasingly crucial in dealing with complex global issues such as climate change, pandemics and food security. Through joint research networks and multilateral initiatives, BRICS can combine their expertise and resources to accelerate the development of innovative solutions. This type of collaboration not only strengthens the research capacities of each member country but also promotes a more inclusive and holistic approach to science and technology, overcoming geographical and disciplinary barriers.

Impulse to the Digital Economy

With the acceleration of global digitalization, the BRICS are placing particular emphasis on the development of the digital economy as an engine of growth and innovation. By investing in digital infrastructure, such as broadband connectivity and data centers, and by promoting digital entrepreneurship, the BRICS are facilitating an environment in which technology startups can thrive. The adoption of policies that support the digital economy not only stimulates internal innovation but also opens the door to greater participation in the global technology market.

Sustainable Development and Green Technologies

Recognition of the importance of sustainable development is driving the BRICS towards the adoption and development of green technologies. Investment in renewable energy, energy efficiency and climate change mitigation technologies are key examples of how the BRICS are trying to balance economic growth with environmental protection. These efforts not only contribute to the reduction of greenhouse gas emissions but also offer new market opportunities and create jobs in the clean technology sector.

Strengthening Access to Technology

A fundamental aspect of the BRICS approach to innovation is the strengthening of access to advanced technologies for a larger segment of the population. Through initiatives that promote digital inclusion and technological literacy, BRICS are working to ensure that the benefits of technological progress are shared fairly. This not only improves the quality of life of citizens but also stimulates greater economic and social participation, contributing to the construction of more informed and resilient societies.

Future Perspectives

Looking to the future, the BRICS journey in the arena of innovation and technology is imbued with potential to catalyze positive change, not only within their borders but around the world. As they continue to explore new horizons in science and technology, their commitment to cooperation, sustainability, and inclusion will be crucial in determining the impact and durability of their innovations. The BRICS' ability to act as pioneers in the field of innovation offers a promising vision of a future in which technology and international collaboration are at the service of wider and more sustainable human progress.

As the BRICS advance on the path of innovation and technology, their strategy increasingly emphasizes the importance of building synergies between different sectors to maximize the impact of their initiatives. The integration between research, industry and public policies is essential to transform innovative ideas into tangible solutions that can benefit society as a whole. This multidisciplinary approach to innovation opens new ways to address some of the most pressing challenges of our time, from energy security to public health, from social inclusion to environmental resilience.

Synergies between Research and Industry

The close collaboration between the academic world and the industrial sector in the BRICS is accelerating technology transfer and applied innovation. Through strategic partnerships and incentives for joint research and development, BRICS are facilitating an ecosystem where universities and research institutions can collaborate directly with businesses to commercialize new discoveries. This link between research and the market is crucial to reduce the development time of innovations and to stimulate knowledge-based economic growth.

Open and Collaborative Innovation

The adoption of open innovation models in the BRICS is promoting an environment in which companies, start-ups, researchers and even end users collaborate in the development of new products and services. This collaborative approach not only accelerates innovation but also ensures that technological solutions are better suited to meeting the real needs of society. The sharing of knowledge and resources, together with the promotion of open innovation platforms, could drive a new wave of technological progress in the BRICS and beyond.

Policies for Sustainable Innovation

The BRICS are also developing policies that encourage the development of sustainable and environmentally friendly technologies. From renewable energy to sustainable agriculture, from green buildings to smart cities, the emphasis is on developing solutions that not only stimulate economic innovation but also promote environmental sustainability. These policies are supported by funding for research in green technologies, tax incentives for sustainable businesses, and awareness programs that promote environmental awareness.

Role of Artificial Intelligence and Digitalization

The BRICS are actively exploring the potential of artificial intelligence (AI), big data, and the Internet of Things (IoT) to drive innovation in various sectors. The application of AI to healthcare, precision agriculture, natural resource management and logistics is radically transforming these industries, making them more efficient and sustainable. Digitalization, in particular, is becoming a fundamental tool for social inclusion, offering access to essential services to previously marginalized populations.

Future Challenges and Opportunities

Looking to the future, the BRICS are facing significant challenges, but also immense opportunities, in their commitment to innovation and technology. The key to their success will lie in their ability to maintain a balance between economic growth, technological progress and environmental and social sustainability. By tackling these challenges with a holistic and collaborative approach, BRICS can not only cement their role as a leader in global innovation but also contribute to building a fairer, more sustainable and prosperous future for all. Their trajectory in the coming years will continue to be a crucial observation area for the world, as it offers valuable insights into how emerging economies can navigate the complex landscape of global innovation, simultaneously facing their internal challenges and helping to solve global problems.

Priority to International Collaboration

As the BRICS advance, their emphasis on international collaboration proves essential to overcome technical and logistical barriers to innovation. Through participation in global research consortia, the development of shared technological standards, and engagement in multilateral dialogues on the ethics and governance of AI, BRICS can promote an innovation environment that respects the principles of equity and accessibility. This openness to dialogue and collaboration helps ensure that the innovative solutions developed respond to a wide range of global needs and priorities.

Capacity Development and Training

Another key area of focus for the BRICS is local capacity development and training in advanced technological fields. Investing in STEM education, promoting professional training programs, and facilitating access to online learning platforms are crucial strategies for building a workforce ready for the future. These efforts not only help bridge the technological skills gap but also encourage innovation from within, allowing local entrepreneurs and researchers to actively contribute to technological progress.

Emphasis on Governance and Security

As technology adoption accelerates, BRICS also face the challenge of ensuring that innovation proceeds responsibly and safely. The governance of emerging technologies, the protection of personal data and cybersecurity have become central themes on their political agendas. By developing robust regulatory frameworks and promoting digital security awareness, BRICS can mitigate the risks associated with digitalization and ensure that technologies are used ethically and productively.

Orientation towards Inclusion and Equity

Finally, the BRICS orientation towards innovation places a strong emphasis on inclusion and equity. Recognizing that the benefits of technological progress are not always distributed equally, they are taking steps to ensure that technological innovations are accessible to all segments of society. This includes developing assistive technologies for people with disabilities, promoting access to digital financial services in rural areas, and supporting businesses led by women and minorities in the technology sector. Through these initiatives, BRICS strive to build a future where innovation leads to tangible improvements in the lives of all citizens.

Overall, the BRICS approach to innovation and technology represents a dynamic model for sustainable progress, balancing aspirations for economic growth with imperatives of social and environmental sustainability. As they continue to explore new horizons of innovation, their trajectory offers inspiration and insights into how nations can collaborate to address the challenges of the 21st century, while promoting development that is inclusive, equitable and beneficial to the entire global community.

As the BRICS advance further in the field of innovation and technology, it is evident that their impact extends beyond national borders, affecting the very fabric of the global economy and society. Their aspiration to lead in sectors such as AI, renewable energy, and space technologies not only positions the BRICS as pioneers of global innovation but also opens up new possibilities to address transnational issues through technology.

Technological Integration and Urban Development

The integration of advanced technologies into urban development and city planning becomes another arena in which the BRICS are making significant progress. The adoption of smart city solutions, which use AI, IoT and big data to optimize urban services such as transportation, waste management and energy, can radically transform urban life, making it more sustainable, efficient and comfortable for citizens. This not only improves the quality of life in BRICS metropolises but also provides replicable models for cities around the world that face similar challenges.

Biotechnology and Food Safety

Biotechnology emerges as another critical sector in which the BRICS are exploring new frontiers. Through the development of advanced genetic engineering techniques and bioprocesses, they are trying to revolutionize agriculture, food production and medicine. These innovations have the potential to improve food security, combat previously incurable diseases, and reduce the environmental impact of agriculture. The focus on research and development in the field of biotechnology underlines the BRICS commitment to sustainable solutions to global food and health problems.

Technologies for Adaptation and Mitigation of Climate Change

The BRICS also recognize the crucial importance of tackling climate change through technological innovation. Investment in adaptation and mitigation technologies, such as carbon sequestration, next-generation solar energy, and climate resilient infrastructure, demonstrates their commitment to combating climate change. By promoting research and the adoption of these technologies, BRICS not only aim to protect their countries from the impacts of climate change but also contribute to global efforts for a more sustainable future.

Digital and Technological Inclusion

Digital and technological inclusion remains a fundamental objective for BRICS, which seek to ensure that the advantages of the digital age are accessible at all levels of society. Initiatives aimed at expanding Internet access, promoting digital literacy and supporting entrepreneurship in the technology sector are essential to building resilient and inclusive societies. Through these initiatives, the BRICS aim to bridge the digital divide and create economic opportunities for everyone, emphasizing the role of technology as a tool for social empowerment.

Ethical and Regulatory Challenges of Innovation

While pursuing the vanguard of innovation, the BRICS are also confronted with the complex ethical and regulatory issues that emerge. AI regulation, personal data protection, and cybersecurity require thoughtful approaches that balance innovation with the protection of individual rights and collective security. The development of regulatory frameworks that promote the responsible and ethical use of new technologies is crucial to ensure that innovation proceeds in a way that benefits society as a whole without compromising the fundamental values of privacy, security and fairness.

Global Research Collaborations

The expansion of global research collaborations represents another vital step for the BRICS in their march towards innovation. By forming international partnerships with universities, research institutions, industries, and governments around the world, BRICS can tap into a diversity of talents, resources, and perspectives. These cross-cutting collaborations are essential to address complex global challenges that require innovative and multidisciplinary solutions, from global pandemics to food security, from climate change to environmental sustainability.

Promoting STEM Education

A renewed commitment to promote education in STEM (science, technology, engineering and mathematics) disciplines is essential to support continuous innovation in the BRICS. By investing in STEM education and encouraging young people, especially girls and women, to pursue careers in these fields, BRICS can ensure a constant flow of innovative minds ready to contribute to technological development and problem solving. Initiatives that link STEM education with industry and research can also provide valuable practical experiences and stimulate interest in innovation and scientific discovery.

Sustainability and Responsible Innovation

The BRICS are also emphasizing the importance of sustainability and responsible innovation in their technological development efforts. This approach seeks to ensure that new technologies not only drive economic growth and competitiveness but are also designed and implemented in a way that respects the environment, promotes social justice and improves human well-being. The integration of sustainability principles in the initial stages of the innovation process is essential to achieve these ambitions.

Overcoming Barriers to Innovation

Finally, overcoming systemic barriers to innovation remains a critical challenge for BRICS. This requires an environment that fully supports innovation through effective public policies, adequate legal and regulatory systems, access to capital for startups and SMEs, and a culture that values and celebrates entrepreneurship and creativity. By tackling these barriers, BRICS can create fertile ground for innovation, allowing them to play an even more significant role in global technological development.

As the BRICS advance in their path of innovation and technology, their success will depend on their ability to navigate these complexities, while promoting innovation that is inclusive, sustainable and beneficial to the entire world. With the right balance between technological ambition and social responsibility, BRICS can lead the way to a future in which technology elevates humanity, preserving the planet for future generations.

As the BRICS continue their commitment to innovation and technology, they face the need to further integrate ethical and sustainability considerations into their technological development strategies. The approach they take to navigate issues of digital equity, the technological gap between and within countries, and the environmental impact of emerging technologies will have significant repercussions not only for their societies but for the global innovation landscape.

Digital Equity and Reducing the Technology Divide

A fundamental challenge for the BRICS in promoting technological innovation concerns digital equity. The need to ensure that emerging technologies, such as artificial intelligence and blockchain, are accessible to all sections of the population is crucial. This involves targeted investments in digital infrastructure, especially in rural areas and disadvantaged communities, and the development of policies that facilitate equitable access to digital services. Through such initiatives, BRICS can work to reduce the technological divide and promote innovation that benefits all of society.

Environmental Sustainability of Technologies

The adoption of a sustainable approach in the development and implementation of new technologies is another crucial aspect. The BRICS are in a unique position to lead research and innovation in technologies that minimize the ecological footprint, promote the efficient use of resources, and contribute to the global energy transition. Investing in research on sustainable materials, renewable energy and circular economy solutions can not only help mitigate the negative effects of technological development on the environment but also open up new economic opportunities in the green sector.

Inclusive and Participatory Innovation

Promoting inclusive and participatory innovation, involving a wide range of stakeholders in the technological development process, is essential to ensure that technological solutions are equally distributed and respond to different needs. BRICS can encourage co-creation platforms and feedback mechanisms that allow communities to contribute to the design and prototyping phases of technologies. By facilitating the participation of traditionally underrepresented groups, such as women, youth, and indigenous peoples, BRICS can enrich the innovation process with a variety of perspectives and experiences.

Governance and Regulation of Emerging Technologies

Creating regulatory and governance frameworks for emerging technologies represents another key challenge. While BRICS seek to maintain an environment that fosters innovation, they must also ensure that new technologies are developed and used in ways that respect human rights, privacy, and security. Drafting laws and regulations that balance these objectives can help establish trust in emerging technologies and ensure that their development proceeds in a responsible and ethical manner.

Global Collaboration for Innovation

Finally, strengthening global collaboration to address transnational challenges through innovation remains a central objective. BRICS have the opportunity to assume a leadership role in promoting an international dialogue on innovation that transcends political and sectoral boundaries. Through joint research initiatives, exchange programs and multilateral partnerships, they can foster a global innovation ecosystem that addresses issues such as climate change, global health, and food security. International collaboration not only accelerates technological progress but also facilitates the sharing of best practices and lessons learned, promoting innovative solutions that can be adapted and implemented in different geographical and socio-economic contexts.

Priority to Education and Technological Training

A renewed commitment to education and technological training is essential to support continuous innovation. The BRICS are expanding educational programs that not only provide the necessary technical skills but also encourage critical thinking, creativity, and ethics in technology. Investing in technological education from childhood to adulthood prepares future generations to navigate and shape the evolving technological landscape, while ensuring that a qualified workforce supports the BRICS innovation ambitions.

Ethics and Responsibility in Innovation

The consideration of ethical issues is becoming increasingly important in the context of BRICS-led innovation. As they explore the frontiers of science and technology, integrating ethical reflection into the innovation process ensures that emerging technologies promote the common good and respect fundamental principles of justice and human rights. The creation of ethical councils, public consultation, and the adoption of universal ethical principles in innovation can help navigate the moral complexities posed by new technologies such as artificial intelligence and genetic engineering.

Supporting Local Innovation and Technology Transfer

As the BRICS continue to emerge as leaders in global innovation, it is crucial to support local innovation and facilitate technology transfer within their countries and to other developing nations. Through policies that encourage innovation at the local level, support for business incubators and accelerators, and programs that facilitate access to technologies and knowledge, BRICS can ensure that the benefits of innovation are widely shared. This will help to reduce the global technological gap and promote sustainable development around the world.

Looking to the Future with Optimism and Prudence

In conclusion, while the BRICS are following the path of innovation and technology, their journey is imbued with optimism and prudence. Their ability to address ethical challenges, promote inclusion and sustainability, and collaborate globally for innovation will define not only their success but also their contribution to global progress. The approach they will adopt to innovation, characterized by responsibility, collaboration and a commitment to the common good, could offer a model for how nations around the world can harness the power of technology to face contemporary challenges and build a brighter future for all.

The BRICS commitment to innovation and technology is also a reflection of their desire to define new trajectories for economic and social progress that are resilient to global changes and capable of facing emerging challenges. As they explore new horizons in innovation, these countries are also establishing fertile ground for exploring how technology can be used to promote greater harmony between human development and environmental sustainability.

Promoting Technological Convergence

The convergence between different technologies — such as artificial intelligence, robotics, biotechnology and nanotechnologies — offers immense possibilities for tackling complex transdisciplinary challenges. BRICS, through the promotion of centers of excellence and technological clusters, can facilitate technological convergence, thus accelerating the creation of innovative solutions that can range from personalized medicine to sustainable production and beyond. Encouraging environments where technological convergence is possible not only stimulates innovation but also promotes holistic approaches to global problems.

Reorientation towards the Circular Economy

The adoption of circular economy principles represents another area in which BRICS can drive innovation. Through the development and implementation of technologies that minimize waste and promote the reuse and recycling of resources, BRICS can contribute significantly to reducing the ecological footprint of human activity. The circular economy not only offers a path to greater environmental sustainability but also opens up new economic opportunities and stimulates the creation of green jobs.

Artificial Intelligence for Social Good

Artificial intelligence (AI) holds the potential to transform sectors and societies, and the BRICS are exploring ways to use AI to address pressing social issues. Whether it's improving access to education through personalized learning platforms, optimizing the distribution of health resources, or increasing agricultural efficiency to ensure food security, AI can play a crucial role in promoting social good. The emphasis placed on social AI underlines the importance of guiding technological innovation not only towards economic success but also towards social and ethical progress.

International Collaboration on Standards and Regulations

As the BRICS advance in the field of innovation, it becomes increasingly important to collaborate internationally on standards and regulations that guide the development and use of emerging technologies. By setting common standards and promoting regulations that reflect shared values of fairness, security, and sustainability, BRICS can help shape a global technological environment that is both innovative and responsible. This joint effort not only facilitates cross-border trade and investment but also promotes an ethical and safe use of technologies around the world.

Focus on Resilience and Adaptability

Finally, as the BRICS explore the future of innovation and technology, an emphasis on resilience and adaptability becomes critical. In a world characterized by rapid changes and uncertainties, the development of technological systems that are able to adapt and respond to unexpected conditions is vital. This includes the creation of resilient digital infrastructures, the development of agricultural technologies capable of withstanding extreme climatic variations, and the implementation of public health systems capable of dealing with future pandemics. By investing in resilience and adaptability, BRICS can not only safeguard their technological advances against future shocks but also offer replicable models for other nations trying to navigate their own sustainable development challenges.

Accelerating the Energy Transition

A critical part of the BRICS commitment to innovation concerns accelerating the transition to cleaner and renewable energy sources. The adoption of advanced energy technologies, from solar and wind energy to new forms of energy storage and smart grids, can help reduce dependence on fossil fuels and mitigate the impact of climate change. Promoting research and development in these areas, together with the implementation of policies that encourage the use of renewable energy, will not only benefit the environment but may also stimulate economic innovation and create new job opportunities.

Enhancing Technologies for Global Health

Innovation in the BRICS is also taking a central role in the development of technological solutions to improve global health. From developing more effective vaccines and treatments to creating digital health systems that improve access to care, BRICS can play a key role in responding to global health needs. The adoption of innovative health technologies not only improves outcomes for patients but also contributes to building more resilient and responsive health systems.

Harnessing the Potential of Blockchain Technology

Blockchain technology offers a unique opportunity for BRICS to innovate in sectors such as finance, logistics and governance. By using blockchain to create more transparent, secure and efficient systems, BRICS can drive digital transformation in these fields. Whether it's simplifying cross-border financial transactions, ensuring the origin of goods in the supply chain, or improving the integrity of electoral processes, blockchain has the potential to offer revolutionary solutions to long-standing problems.

Reorientation towards Open Innovation

Finally, a growing orientation towards open innovation could serve as a catalyst for further technological advances in the BRICS. By adopting an approach that encourages knowledge sharing and collaboration between public, private and academic sectors, BRICS can accelerate the development of new technologies and solutions. Open innovation not only fosters a more dynamic and collaborative environment for technological progress, but it also helps to ensure that innovations are widely accessible and have a positive social impact.

Through these strategies and initiatives, the BRICS are laying the groundwork for a future in which innovation and technology play a crucial role in promoting sustainable development, social inclusion and global resilience. As they navigate the challenges and opportunities presented by the evolving global technological landscape, their collective commitment to responsible and sustainable innovation will be critical in shaping a more equitable, resilient and prosperous world.

In conclusion, the BRICS commitment to innovation and technology represents a fundamental pillar for their future development and for their role in the global economy. Through a strategic focus on key sectors such as renewable energy, artificial intelligence, space exploration, and blockchain technology, these countries are not only advancing their technological capabilities but also helping to shape global innovation trends. Their approach, which balances economic growth with environmental sustainability and social equity, offers a model for how innovation can be guided in a responsible and inclusive way.

International collaboration emerges as a recurring theme in BRICS innovation strategies, underlining the importance of sharing knowledge, resources and best practices to address complex global challenges. Their ability to form effective partnerships, both within the bloc and with other nations and international organizations, will be crucial to the success of their innovation initiatives.

Investing in education, especially in STEM disciplines, and promoting digital inclusion are recognized as key elements for building societies capable of fully exploiting the benefits of technological innovation. These efforts aim to prepare a qualified and innovative workforce that can actively contribute to technological development and social progress.

The governance and regulation of emerging technologies represent another critical area of focus for BRICS. The creation of regulatory frameworks that promote the ethical and responsible use of new technologies is essential to ensure that innovation proceeds in a way that respects human rights and security, while promoting an environment favorable to research and development.

The focus on resilience and adaptability, together with the promotion of the circular economy and sustainable development, demonstrates the BRICS' commitment to ensuring that technological innovation advances in harmony with the environment and contributes positively to society. Their vision of open and collaborative innovation not only accelerates technological progress but also ensures that the benefits of that progress are widely shared.

In short, as the BRICS follow their trajectory of innovation and technology, they face challenges with a holistic approach that integrates economic development, sustainability and social equity. Their strategy emphasizes the importance of international collaboration, skill development, responsible governance, and the promotion of equitable access to technologies. Looking to the future, BRICS have the unique opportunity to drive global innovation that not only promotes technological progress but also contributes to building a more sustainable and just world for everyone.

7. Environmental Challenges and Sustainability: exploration of environmental policies and initiatives for sustainable development in BRICS countries.

The BRICS countries (Brazil, Russia, India, China, and South Africa) are facing significant environmental challenges that reflect both global pressures and those specific to their national contexts. As these nations continue to experience rapid economic growth, they are increasingly called upon to balance that growth with the need to promote sustainability and environmental protection. Their response to these environmental challenges is manifested through a series of policies, initiatives and commitments that aim to ensure more sustainable development.

Brazil

Brazil, with its vast Amazon rainforest, plays a crucial role in regulating the global climate and conserving biodiversity. The country's environmental policies are therefore of fundamental importance not only regionally but also globally. In recent years, Brazil has faced significant challenges related to deforestation, which have raised international concerns. To respond, Brazil has implemented initiatives to promote sustainable forest management, reforestation, and conservation of protected areas. In addition, it is exploring the development of renewable energy, such as hydroelectric, wind and solar energy, to reduce its dependence on fossil fuels.

Russia

Russia, with its vast land area and its rich natural resources, is committed to tackling climate change and improving energy efficiency. It has ratified the Paris Agreement and is working to reduce greenhouse gas emissions through a series of measures, including the modernization of industrial and energy infrastructure and the development of renewable energy sources. Russia is also addressing issues related to air and water pollution in urban and industrial areas, promoting cleaner and more sustainable production practices.

India

India is facing multiple environmental challenges, including air pollution, water resource management, and waste management. To address these issues, India has adopted the International Solar Initiative, aiming to become a global leader in the development of solar energy. In addition, it is promoting the use of electric vehicles and the implementation of more effective waste management technologies. Its emphasis on universal access to clean sanitation and on increasing urban green areas also demonstrates a commitment to environmental sustainability and public health.

China

China has embarked on an 'ecological revolution' to address its serious environmental challenges, including air pollution, soil degradation and habitat loss. It has set ambitious goals to reduce the intensity of carbon emissions, increase the share of renewable energy in its energy mix, and improve energy efficiency. China is also a leader in developing green technologies, such as solar panels and electric cars, and is investing in green infrastructure projects, such as urban forest parks and sustainable public transport systems.

South Africa

South Africa faces environmental challenges that include water scarcity, soil degradation, and dependence on coal for energy. It is adopting an energy transition to cleaner and renewable sources, with the aim of reducing its greenhouse gas emissions and improving energy security. South Africa is also implementing conservation programs to protect its rich biodiversity and sustainably manage natural resources. Key initiatives include projects to restore degraded landscapes and the promotion of sustainable agriculture to ensure food security while maintaining the integrity of the ecosystem. A further commitment is aimed at improving the management of water resources, through technological innovation and regional cooperation, to address its critical water situation.

Common Initiatives and Collaborations

Beyond individual actions, BRICS collaborate on environmental and sustainable development issues through shared platforms and multilateral initiatives. This includes dialogue and the exchange of best practices on issues such as climate change, the conservation of biodiversity and the development of clean energy. Cooperation within the block aims to strengthen the collective response to environmental challenges, promoting an approach that balances economic growth with environmental protection.

Challenges and Opportunities

BRICS environmental strategies represent a complex set of challenges and opportunities. As they seek to address their development needs, they must also navigate global pressures to reduce emissions and protect natural ecosystems. The balance between economic development and environmental sustainability requires innovative policies, investments in clean technologies and a commitment to international cooperation.

Sustainability initiatives in the BRICS have the potential to drive change not only nationally but also globally, given their significant impact on the world economy and the environment. The success of these initiatives will depend on their ability to effectively implement environmental policies, mobilize sufficient resources for sustainable development, and actively involve all sectors of society in the ecological transition process.

Looking to the Future

Looking to the future, BRICS have the opportunity to position themselves as a leader in promoting global sustainable development. Through continuous innovation, international collaboration and the adoption of a holistic approach to sustainability, they can offer innovative solutions to the environmental challenges we face today. The BRICS commitment to sustainability will not only improve the quality of life of their populations but will also contribute significantly to global efforts to build a greener and more sustainable future.

In summary, while the BRICS face unique environmental challenges, their collective response through proactive environmental policies and initiatives for sustainable development highlights a growing commitment to protecting the environment and promoting sustainability. Their role in innovation and international cooperation will be crucial to overcome today's environmental challenges and guide the world towards long-term sustainability goals.

The BRICS approach to sustainability and managing environmental challenges continues to evolve, reflecting a growing awareness of their global responsibility and the crucial role they can play in promoting sustainable development practices. These countries, through their collaboration and individual initiatives, are exploring new paradigms for an economy that is not only dynamic and growing but also environmentally friendly and promotes social justice.

Valorization of Biodiversity and Conservation

The conservation of biodiversity is emerging as a priority issue for the BRICS, given their possession of some of the regions with the greatest biodiversity in the world. Initiatives aimed at protecting natural habitats, maintaining endangered species and promoting agricultural practices that support species diversity are gaining momentum. These actions not only aim to preserve natural wealth for future generations, but they also contribute to maintaining the ecosystems on which food security and global climate stability depend.

Innovation for Waste Reduction

The BRICS are also innovating in the field of waste management, seeking solutions to reduce waste production, promote recycling and improve resource efficiency. Technology plays a key role in this area, with the development of new biodegradable materials, more efficient recycling processes and circular economy systems that transform waste from a problem to a resource. These initiatives help not only to reduce the environmental impact of waste but also stimulate industrial innovation and can create economic opportunities.

Challenges of Sustainable Urbanization

Rapid urbanization represents another critical challenge for BRICS, requiring innovative strategies to build more sustainable and resilient cities. Efforts are underway to integrate green urban planning, improve the energy efficiency of buildings, develop sustainable public transport, and promote urban green spaces. These initiatives not only aim to reduce the environmental impact of growing urban areas but also seek to improve the quality of urban life, tackling problems such as air pollution and congestion.

Education and Environmental Awareness

A fundamental element of BRICS sustainability strategies is education and environmental awareness. Recognizing that lasting change requires collective commitment, they are promoting educational programs that encourage sustainable practices among citizens of all ages. From the integration of sustainability in school curricula to the organization of public awareness campaigns, the goal is to build a culture of sustainability that guides individual and collective choices.

Multilateral Collaboration for Climate Action

Finally, the BRICS recognize that effectively tackling environmental challenges, in particular climate change, requires multilateral collaboration. By actively participating in international environmental dialogues and supporting global agreements such as the Paris Agreement, they are seeking to contribute to and shape global responses to environmental crises. Their collaboration can not only accelerate the adoption of sustainable practices but also ensure that climate mitigation and adaptation strategies take into account different economic and social realities.

In conclusion, while the BRICS navigate the complex landscape of environmental challenges and sustainability, their multidimensional approach, which includes technological innovation, conservation, management

sustainable resources, sustainable urbanization, environmental education and international collaboration, offers a holistic vision to address these issues. The BRICS commitment to integrate economic development with environmental sustainability and social justice represents not only a necessity for their long-term well-being but also a significant contribution to global efforts to create a more sustainable future.

Achieving these ambitions will require ongoing commitment, significant resources, and a willingness to face internal and external resistance. However, through knowledge sharing, technological cooperation, and mutual support, BRICS can overcome these obstacles. Their ability to effectively implement environmental policies and initiatives will not only determine their resilience and future prosperity but will also impact the world's ability to address environmental challenges on a global scale.

As they advance, the BRICS have the opportunity to demonstrate how innovation, both technological and in governance, can drive progress towards sustainability. Their strategies can serve as an example for other nations seeking to balance economic growth with environmental protection. In addition, their growing role in the global economy and geopolitics provides BRICS with a unique platform to influence the direction of environmental policies and sustainable development at the international level.

By successfully tackling environmental challenges through innovative policies and sustainable practices, BRICS can help shape a new development paradigm that values the balance between economic, social and environmental needs. Their future trajectory will offer valuable lessons on how emerging economies can pursue growth while remaining committed to safeguarding the environment for future generations.

The approach adopted by the BRICS in facing environmental challenges and promoting sustainability is further enriched when we consider the intersection between technology, social policy and international cooperation. The adoption of green technologies and the circular economy, for example, not only responds to environmental needs but also creates new jobs, stimulates innovation and opens ways for inclusive and sustainable economic growth.

Strengthening Climate Resilience

Strengthening resilience to climate change is a growing priority for BRICS, which are faced with increasingly frequent and devastating extreme weather events. Investing in climate resilient infrastructure, promoting sustainable agriculture and developing early warning systems are just some of the measures taken to protect vulnerable communities and ensure food and water security. These actions, combined with the conservation of natural ecosystems that act as barriers against climate impacts, are essential for building societies capable of resisting and adapting to future climate challenges.

Promotion of Sustainable Cities

With increasing urbanization, the BRICS are also placing special emphasis on creating sustainable and livable cities. This includes implementing green mobility solutions, efficient waste management, expanding urban green spaces, and improving air quality. These sustainable cities not only provide a healthier and more pleasant environment for citizens, but they also serve as laboratories for sustainable innovations that can be replicated and adapted in other parts of the world.

Cooperation for Global Environmental Governance

The BRICS' position as influential global players places them in a unique position to promote more effective and inclusive global environmental governance. Through dialogue and collaboration with other nations and international organizations, BRICS can help shape a world order that recognizes and addresses environmental challenges in a fair and sustainable manner. The commitment to multilateral agreements, the exchange of good practices and the promotion of international standards can strengthen global efforts to protect the environment.

Investment in Education and Sustainable Innovation

Finally, the BRICS recognize the importance of investing in education and innovation as keys to promoting sustainability. By instituting educational programs that emphasize environmental sustainability, ethics, and social responsibility, BRICS can prepare future generations to become conscious and committed citizens and leaders. In addition, by supporting innovation in clean technologies and sustainable practices, they can guide the transition to a global economy that is not only dynamic and innovative but also environmentally friendly and socially equitable.

As the BRICS continue their commitment to sustainable development and the management of environmental challenges, their integrated and holistic strategy offers hope and direction for a future in which economic progress goes hand in hand with the protection of the environment and the promotion of social justice. Their trajectory in promoting sustainable and innovative practices provides a model full of ideas for other nations that aspire to achieve sustainable development in the context of the complex global challenges of the 21st century.

In pursuing sustainability strategies, BRICS address the need to integrate environmental initiatives with economic growth and social equity, setting the stage for an approach to progress that fully respects the principles of sustainable development. This balance is proving crucial not only to mitigate the effects of climate change and protect the environment but also to ensure that the benefits of growth and innovation are accessible at all levels of society.

Innovation in Sustainability Financing

A significant challenge for BRICS in the field of sustainability is innovation in the financing of environmental projects. The creation of innovative financial mechanisms, such as green bonds, climate funds and venture capital investments for green start-ups, offers ways to mobilize significant resources for the green transition. These tools not only attract investments in the environmental sector but also encourage companies to integrate sustainable practices into their business models.

Strengthening Climate Change Adaptation Policies

While the mitigation of climate change remains a central objective, the BRICS are also strengthening their adaptation policies to manage the inevitable impacts of climate change. The development of robust adaptation strategies, which include raising critical infrastructure, protecting vulnerable communities and adapting agricultural systems, is essential to minimize the economic and social damage caused by extreme climate events. This commitment reflects the understanding that a proactive approach to adaptation can significantly reduce the long-term costs associated with climate change.

Capacity Development and Knowledge Exchange

The importance of capacity building and knowledge exchange between BRICS and with other nations cannot be stressed enough. Sharing experiences, successes and lessons learned in the field of environmental sustainability can accelerate the adoption of best practices and strengthen global responses to environmental challenges. Through collaboration platforms and training programs, BRICS can not only improve their resilience and capacity for innovation but also contribute to building a more informed and prepared global community on the front of sustainability.

Promoting Environmental Justice

Environmental justice emerges as a guiding principle in BRICS sustainability policies, recognizing that environmental challenges often have a disproportionate impact on the poorest and most vulnerable communities. Promoting equitable access to natural resources, protecting the rights of indigenous communities, and ensuring that the benefits of sustainable development are shared fairly are all crucial aspects of this commitment. This emphasis on environmental justice not only aims to reduce inequalities but also reinforces social support for environmental initiatives.

Integrating Sustainability into Education

Finally, the integration of sustainability principles into education is recognized by the BRICS as fundamental to promote responsible and informed global citizenship. By incorporating environmental education into school curricula and promoting university research on sustainability issues, BRICS can prepare future generations to contribute effectively to environmental protection and sustainable development. This long-term vision for education underlines the need for collective commitment and information to address environmental challenges in a sustainable and responsible manner.

Valorization of Green Technologies and Innovation

A constant drive towards the adoption and development of green technologies represents another fundamental pillar of the BRICS approach to sustainability. By investing in research and development for renewable energy, energy efficiency, carbon capture and storage technologies, and sustainable mobility solutions, BRICS can reduce their ecological footprint and promote sustainable consumption and production patterns. Innovation in these areas not only contributes to the fight against climate change but also opens up new paths for economic growth, creating emerging industries and green jobs.

Public-Private Partnerships for Sustainability

Collaboration between the public and private sectors is essential to achieve ambitious sustainability goals. Through public-private partnerships, BRICS can mobilize the skills, resources and technologies of both sectors to address environmental challenges. These collaborations can accelerate the transition to sustainable practices in key sectors such as energy, industrial production and agriculture, while promoting innovation and economic development.

Improving Environmental Governance

An effective and transparent environmental governance system is essential to successfully implement sustainability policies. The BRICS are working to strengthen their environmental institutions, improve legislation and regulations, and promote public participation in environmental decisions. This effort aims to ensure that policies are well coordinated, based on solid scientific evidence and able to adapt to evolving needs and priorities.

Involving Local Communities

The active involvement of local communities in sustainability initiatives is crucial to ensure that environmental policies are rooted in the local context and respond effectively to the needs of the most vulnerable populations. The BRICS are promoting participatory approaches that allow communities to have a voice in decisions that affect their environment and way of life. This involvement not only improves the effectiveness of policies but also strengthens the link between sustainability and social development.

Global Vision for the Future

As the BRICS continue to advance on their path to sustainability, their collective and individual approach offers important insights to address global environmental challenges. Their ability to balance economic growth, social justice and environmental protection will be decisive in shaping a sustainable future not only for their countries but for the entire planet. Looking ahead, BRICS' commitment, innovation and cooperation in the field of sustainability can serve as a catalyst for broader global actions, underscoring the importance of international solidarity and working together for a greener, fairer and more resilient world.

In the field of sustainability, the approach adopted by the BRICS expands further towards the integration of innovative strategies to address environmental issues and promote equitable development. The geographical and socioeconomic diversity of these countries provides fertile ground for experimenting with unique solutions that can be adapted and implemented in varied settings.

Intensification of the Use of Circular Economies

An emerging aspect of the BRICS sustainability agenda is the adoption of circular economy principles. This model focuses on the reduction, reuse and recycling of materials to minimize waste and optimize the use of resources. Adopting this model requires a systematic change in industrial production, consumer habits, and government policies. The BRICS are exploring the potential of the circular economy to stimulate industrial innovation, reduce pressure on natural resources and create new sustainable economic opportunities.

Promotion of Agroecology and Food Sovereignty

Agroecology emerges as a significant approach to simultaneously address the challenges of food security, the protection of biodiversity and the fight against climate change. By promoting agricultural practices that work in harmony with natural ecosystems, BRICS can support sustainable food production and the resilience of rural communities. Food sovereignty, which emphasizes the right of peoples to define their own agricultural and food policies, becomes a key objective, ensuring that agricultural development is equitable and accessible to all.

Integrated Approaches to Water Management

The sustainable management of water resources is another critical area of intervention. The BRICS face different challenges in terms of access to water, pollution, and water stress. The adoption of integrated approaches to water resource management, which consider the interconnection between water, food and energy, is essential to ensure water security. This includes investments in desalination technologies, efficient irrigation systems, rainwater collection practices, and policies for the protection of surface and groundwater.

Involving the Private Sector in Green Initiatives

The active involvement of the private sector is essential to accelerate the transition to sustainability. The BRICS are encouraging businesses to integrate environmental considerations into their operations through incentives, regulations and public-private partnerships. This not only stimulates green innovation but also helps to create a more resilient and low-carbon economy. Corporate social responsibility becomes a key tool for promoting sustainable business practices that respond to the needs of communities and the environment.

Strengthening Community Resilience

The resilience of local communities in the face of climate change and environmental shocks is a central theme in the BRICS sustainability agenda. By developing programs that strengthen communities' capacity to adapt to change, manage natural resources sustainably, and protect biodiversity, BRICS can contribute to building stronger and more resilient societies. The empowerment of local communities, in particular through education and active participation in environmental management, is fundamental to realizing the vision of sustainable development rooted in the territory.

> Ultimately, the BRICS approach to environmental challenges and sustainability reflects a holistic understanding of the interdependencies between economic development, social equity, and environmental protection. Recognizing that these challenges are interconnected, BRICS are exploring innovative ways to promote development that does not compromise the ability of future generations to meet their needs. Their strategy includes a wide range of initiatives, from the promotion of renewable energy and clean technologies to the strengthening of environmental governance and the enhancement of natural and human capital.

Development of International Frameworks

In the global arena, the BRICS are working to influence the creation of international frameworks that promote more effective and just sustainable development practices. Through active participation in climate and environmental negotiations and support for international treaties, they seek to ensure that the concerns and priorities of developing countries are adequately represented and considered. This commitment reflects the understanding that only through a cooperative and inclusive approach is it possible to address environmental challenges on a global scale.

Technology and Innovation for Sustainability

The emphasis placed on technology and innovation represents a cornerstone of BRICS sustainability strategies. Through research and development in key sectors such as sustainable agriculture, clean energy and resource efficiency, they are not only addressing their environmental challenges but also contributing to the global pool of sustainable solutions. The spread of these technologies, especially in developing countries, is essential to accelerate the global transition to more sustainable development models.

Investments in Green Infrastructure

The BRICS recognize the importance of investing in green infrastructure as a key component of their sustainable development strategy. This includes the development of environmentally friendly public transport systems, the construction of energy-efficient buildings, and the implementation of waste and water management systems that minimize environmental impact. These investments not only help to reduce the ecological footprint but also improve the quality of urban life, promoting cleaner, safer and more livable cities.

Sustainability Education and Community Involvement

Sustainability education and active community involvement are recognized as fundamental elements for building widespread environmental awareness and promoting long-term behavioral change. Through educational programs, awareness campaigns and community participation initiatives, BRICS aim to instill values of environmental responsibility and to encourage sustainable lifestyles among citizens of all ages. This commitment reinforces the link between sustainable development and active citizenship, underlining the crucial role that each individual can play in protecting the environment.

Towards a Sustainable Future

Ultimately, while the BRICS continue to face complex environmental challenges, their holistic, multilateral approach to sustainability offers hope for a greener and more just future. Their ability to successfully implement these strategies, to innovate in ways that respect the environment, and to actively engage communities in protecting our planet will be critical to the success of their sustainable development efforts. Looking ahead, the example of the BRICS can serve as an inspiration for other nations seeking to balance economic growth with environmental sustainability, highlighting the power of cooperation

international and innovation guided by the vision in building a more sustainable world.

Integrating Biodiversity into Economic Decisions

An emerging element in BRICS sustainability strategies is the integration of biodiversity conservation into economic decisions. Recognizing that biodiversity is critical to human well-being and economic livelihood, BRICS are exploring ways to evaluate and incorporate the value of ecosystem services into their economies. This includes initiatives for the payment of ecosystem services, which encourage the conservation and sustainable use of natural resources, and the development of financial instruments that support conservation projects.

Innovation in Water Resources Management

Faced with growing challenges related to water resources management, BRICS are innovating with new technologies and approaches to ensure equitable and sustainable access to water.

This includes promoting the efficient use of water in agriculture, the adoption of advanced technologies for wastewater treatment and recycling, and the development of resilient water infrastructure that can withstand the impacts of climate change. Such measures are essential to prevent water scarcity, protect water quality and support access to drinking water for everyone.

Building Climate-Resilient Economies

The BRICS are working to build climate resilient economies that can withstand and adapt to the impacts of climate change. This involves a rethinking of industrial practices, the adoption of low-carbon technologies and the promotion of sustainable consumption models. Through collaboration with the private sector and civil society, they are seeking to reduce greenhouse gas emissions, increase energy efficiency and support the transition to a green economy that not only mitigates the impacts of climate change but also offers opportunities for sustainable growth.

Promoting Sustainable Mobility

In the area of sustainable mobility, the BRICS are adopting innovative policies and technologies to reduce urban air pollution and greenhouse gas emissions from transport. This includes investing in environmentally friendly public transport systems, encouraging the use of electric vehicles and promoting shared mobility models. These initiatives not only help to create cleaner and more livable cities but also to stimulate innovation in the transport sector, paving the way for a more sustainable and accessible future of mobility.

Expanding International Dialogue and Collaboration

Finally, expanding international dialogue and collaboration remains a key component of the BRICS approach to sustainability. Through multilateral forums, global partnerships and knowledge exchange platforms, BRICS can share their experiences, learn from other successful models, and promote collective action against environmental challenges. Their active participation in shaping the global agenda for sustainable development underlines their role as key players in promoting a greener and more just future worldwide.

Continuing on this trajectory, BRICS can not only achieve their sustainable development goals but can also inspire and guide other nations and communities towards more sustainable practices. The balance between economic growth, social equity and environmental protection that they seek to achieve offers a valuable model for tackling some of the most pressing global challenges of our time.

In conclusion, the BRICS approach to environmental challenges and sustainability illustrates a deep and multifaceted commitment to achieving development that is balanced, just and sustainable in the long term. Through a series of policies, initiatives and collaborations, these countries are proactively addressing the complexities related to protecting the environment, managing resources, climate change, and promoting resilient and inclusive economies.

BRICS strategies for sustainability are characterized by several fundamental pillars: innovation in green technologies, the development of sustainable infrastructure, the promotion of education and environmental awareness, the adoption of circular economy models, and the strengthening of environmental governance. These efforts are further amplified by a commitment to international cooperation, multilateral dialogue, and the exchange of knowledge and good practices, reflecting the awareness that environmental challenges require coordinated global responses.

The BRICS, through their path to sustainability, demonstrate how it is possible for rapidly growing economies to pursue the goal of economic development without neglecting environmental and social responsibility. Their initiatives offer valuable insights on how to effectively integrate sustainability into national development plans and how environmental policies can contribute not only to the protection of the ecosystem but also to the creation of economic opportunities, innovation and the improvement of the quality of life.

Important is the role of education and environmental awareness, which paves the way for a cultural change towards more sustainable practices and responsible consumption. The investment in the formation of a globally aware and responsible citizenship is essential to guarantee the support and active participation of communities in sustainability initiatives.

The BRICS experience also highlights the importance of creating partnerships between the public sector, the private sector and civil society to mobilize the resources, skills and technologies necessary to achieve the transition to sustainability. The adoption of inclusive and participatory approaches ensures that the solutions developed are balanced, effective and capable of responding to the diverse needs of populations.

Ultimately, the BRICS are forging a path that could redesign global narratives on growth and sustainability, showing that economic progress can be achieved while maintaining a deep commitment to environmental protection and social justice. As they continue to face the challenges inherent to their rapid development, their journey to sustainability remains an important example of how vision, collaboration and innovation can drive a more sustainable and resilient future for all.

8. Population and Social Dynamics: Demography, Urbanization, and Social Issues in the BRICS.

The BRICS countries (Brazil, Russia, India, China and South Africa) represent a significant portion of the world's population and experience unique social and demographic dynamics that influence and are influenced by their economic and social development paths. These dynamics include demographic trends, processes of urbanization, and a variety of social issues ranging from economic inequality to migration, education, and public health.

Demography

The demography of the BRICS is characterized by significant differences in terms of population size, growth rates, and age structure. For example, while China and India together make up nearly 40% of the world's population, with India expected to overtake China as the most populous country in the next decade, Russia is facing a declining population due to low birth rates and high mortality. Brazil and South Africa, on the other hand, show different demographic patterns, with a relatively young population but with distinct challenges in terms of public health and education.

Urbanisation

Urbanization is a key trend in the BRICS, with a rapid growth of cities bringing challenges and opportunities. Urban expansion requires adequate infrastructure, public services, housing and employment opportunities, but it also offers possibilities for economic innovation and sustainable development. The effective management of urbanization, including the planning of smart and sustainable cities, is crucial to address problems such as congestion, pollution and social disparities in urban areas.

Economic and Social Inequality

BRICS face significant levels of economic and social inequality, with wide gaps between rich and poor, urban and rural areas, and ethnic and gender groups. These inequalities can undermine social cohesion, restrict access to opportunities and aggravate social tensions. Addressing these inequalities requires inclusive policies that promote equity, quality education, access to health services, and social protection for all.

Migration

Migration is another important social dynamic in the BRICS, both within countries and internationally. People are moving in search of better economic opportunities, education or security. These migratory flows present challenges, such as social integration and border management, but they also offer opportunities for demographic renewal and the development of human capital. Effective migration management requires policies that balance security, human rights and integration.

Education and Public Health

Education and public health are central issues for social development in the BRICS. Access to quality education and health care are essential for improving well-being, supporting economic growth and promoting social equity. However, BRICS face challenges such as disparity in access to education, quality of education, disease prevention, and the provision of health services. Investing in education and public health is fundamental to building more just, healthy and informed societies.

Towards More Inclusive and Sustainable Societies

In short, as the BRICS navigate the complex dynamics of population and society, their challenge is to transform these trends into opportunities for inclusive and sustainable development. By proactively addressing issues such as inequality, urbanization, migration, education, and public health, BRICS can promote more resilient, dynamic and balanced societies. The key to success in these areas lies in implementing informed, flexible, and inclusive policies that recognize and respond to the specific needs of diverse populations within their borders.

Strengthening Social Protection Systems

Strengthening social protection systems is essential to ensure a safety net for vulnerable populations, including the poor, the elderly, the unemployed and migrants. Well-designed social protection policies can help mitigate the effects of poverty and inequality, provide access to essential services such as education and health, and support social and economic inclusion.

Investment in Infrastructure and Public Services

Investing in adequate infrastructure and public services is crucial to supporting sustainable urbanization and ensuring equitable access to economic opportunities, quality education and healthcare. This includes the development of affordable housing, efficient transportation systems, drinking water and healthcare networks, and education services that can accommodate the growing urban population and improve the quality of life in cities.

Promotion of Social and Cultural Integration

The promotion of social and cultural integration is essential to address the challenges posed by migration and ethnic and cultural diversity in the BRICS. Creating inclusive societies that value diversity and promote mutual respect and understanding can help prevent social conflicts and strengthen the social fabric. This requires policies that facilitate the integration of migrants, support the conservation and promotion of indigenous cultures and languages, and combat discrimination and xenophobia.

Supporting Innovation in the Education and Health Sector

Innovation in the education and health sector is vital to improving the quality and accessibility of these essential services. Using technology, such as e-learning and telemedicine, BRICS can overcome some of the geographical and socioeconomic barriers that limit access to education and health care. At the same time, investment in research and development can lead to new solutions for persistent public health problems and help raise educational standards.

Transnational Collaboration to Address Common Challenges

Finally, transnational collaboration between BRICS and with other countries and international organizations is crucial to address common challenges related to demography and social dynamics. Through the exchange of knowledge, experience and good practices, BRICS can learn from each other and work together to develop innovative solutions to shared problems such as urbanization, migration, education and public health.

In summary, dealing with the complex dynamics of population and society requires a holistic approach that considers the interdependencies between various sectors and the specific realities of each BRICS country. By adopting inclusive and innovative policies, supporting social integration and promoting international collaboration, BRICS can successfully navigate the challenges posed by their demography and social dynamics, helping to build more just, resilient and sustainable societies.

As the BRICS continue on their development path, their response to complex population and society dynamics will continue to evolve, facing new challenges and exploiting emerging opportunities. A fundamental aspect in this context is the ability to adapt and innovate in the face of rapid demographic changes, social movements and the constantly evolving needs of their populations.

Accentuating Equity in Technological Progress

Technological progress offers enormous potential to improve the quality of life, but it also presents the risk of increasing inequalities if the benefits are not equally distributed. The BRICS are trying to ensure that technological innovation is accessible at all levels of society, reducing the digital divide and promoting technological skills that allow wider participation in the digital economy. Initiatives such as providing low-cost Internet access in rural and remote areas, digital literacy programs, and incubating local tech startups can play a crucial role in ensuring that technological progress fosters greater social equity.

Strengthening Social Cohesion

Social cohesion is essential to maintain stability and promote prosperity within BRICS countries, in the face of challenges such as internal and external migration, inequalities and social tensions. The BRICS are working to strengthen the social fabric through policies that promote integration and dialogue between different communities, the celebration of cultural diversity and support for vulnerable groups. Programs that facilitate access to education, affordable housing, and employment opportunities can help reduce social friction and build more harmonious and inclusive societies.

Sustainable Management of Natural Resources

The sustainable management of natural resources is another critical area, given the rapid urbanization and industrialization in the BRICS. These countries are exploring strategies to balance resource exploitation with environmental conservation, through responsible extraction practices, innovative water management policies and the protection of vulnerable ecosystems. Initiatives aimed at promoting sustainable agriculture, water conservation and responsible forest management are essential to ensure that natural resources can support future generations.

Priority to Health and Wellbeing

The health and well-being of the population remain fundamental priorities for BRICS, especially in light of recent global challenges such as the COVID-19 pandemic. These countries are investing in more robust, accessible and resilient health systems, promoting disease prevention, improving access to health services, and strengthening medical research. Attention to mental health and well-being, in particular, is emerging as a critical area of intervention, recognizing its significant impact on quality of life and productivity.

Collaboration to Address Demographic Challenges

Finally, international collaboration remains a key component of the BRICS approach to their population and society dynamics. By sharing knowledge, resources and best practices, BRICS can more effectively address common demographic challenges, such as an ageing population, migration flows and managing urbanization. Cooperation in the field of demographic research, urban development policies and social planning can help to develop more informed and sustainable strategies for the future.

In conclusion, the BRICS are tackling their complex population and social dynamics with a mix of proactive policies, innovation and collaboration. These strategies not only aim to mitigate immediate challenges but also seek to establish the foundations for resilient, inclusive and sustainable societies capable of navigating future changes. Their collective and individual commitment to address issues such as technological equity, social cohesion, resource management, public health, and demographic challenges reflects a deep understanding of the interconnection between social well-being, economic development, and environmental sustainability.

The emphasis placed on transnational collaboration further underlines the awareness that many of the challenges faced are global in nature and require joint responses. Through forums such as BRICS, these countries can not only share lessons learned but also work together to influence the global agenda on key issues affecting population and social dynamics.

By investing in education, health, social protection and infrastructure, BRICS are creating the conditions for all citizens to realize their potential and contribute to the collective progress of their societies. The promotion of integration and cultural diversity further enriches the social fabric, encouraging a sense of belonging and reducing divisions.

The BRICS' multifaceted approach to managing their population and social dynamics serves as an important example of how emerging economies can address complex challenges through innovation, informed politics, and international cooperation. As they continue to evolve and adapt to future changes, their efforts can offer valuable insights for other countries facing similar issues, highlighting the importance of sustainable and inclusive solutions to build a fairer and more prosperous future for all.

As the BRICS move through the complex landscape of population and social dynamics, it becomes apparent that the approach required to address these challenges is as dynamic as the challenges themselves. Their ability to adapt, innovate and collaborate not only defines progress within individual countries but also helps to shape global responses to constantly evolving demographic and social issues.

Adapting to Demographic Changes

Demographic changes present both challenges and opportunities for BRICS. For example, the rapid aging of the population in some of these countries requires innovative policies for managing health and social care, supporting the elderly and renewing the workforce. At the same time, a young and growing population in other BRICS members offers a demographic potential that, if well managed with investments in education and economic opportunities, can serve as an engine of growth and innovation.

Integration of Migrants and Refugees

The management and integration of migrants and refugees remain a major challenge. The BRICS, being both a destination and a source of significant migratory flows, are in the unique position of having to develop policies that not only address the root causes of forced migration but also guarantee the effective integration of migrants into their societies. This requires a delicate balance between protecting migrants' rights, maintaining national security and promoting social harmony.

Promoting Universal Access to Education and Health

Universal access to education and health services is a fundamental pillar for building balanced and advanced societies. The BRICS are experimenting with various models to expand access to these essential services, from the digitalization of education to the promotion of public health and universal health insurance programs. These efforts are crucial not only to improve the quality of life of citizens but also to ensure that all segments of society can fully participate in economic and social development.

Addressing Inequality through Social Innovation

Inequality remains one of the most persistent and pervasive challenges. The BRICS are seeking to use social innovation to create more inclusive and equitable solutions that address the roots of economic and social inequality. This includes the development of technological platforms for financial inclusion, skills and entrepreneurship development programs for disadvantaged communities, and the implementation of universal basic income policies to combat poverty.

Recognition and Protection of Cultural Diversity

Cultural diversity in the BRICS is an invaluable resource that enriches the social fabric and promotes creativity and innovation. The protection and promotion of cultural diversity, including the rights of indigenous peoples and ethnic minorities, are essential for maintaining social cohesion and building inclusive societies. Policies that support cultural expression, heritage conservation, and multicultural education can help cultivate mutual respect and intercultural understanding.

Environmental Sustainability and Social Justice

Environmental sustainability and social justice are deeply intertwined in issues of population and social dynamics. The BRICS recognize that the responsible management of natural resources and the protection of the environment are fundamental to ensuring a sustainable future for all. Through policies that promote green economic practices, conservation of biodiversity, and environmental justice, BRICS aim to create a balance between economic development and the protection of the rights of current and future generations. Initiatives that aim to reduce the environmental impact of industrial and urban activities, together with support for communities most vulnerable to the effects of climate change, reflect an integrated approach to sustainability that takes into account both the environment and social justice.

Building Sustainable Cities and Communities

Rapid urbanization presents both challenges and opportunities for BRICS. The construction of sustainable cities and communities, which promote quality life, access to essential services, and social inclusion, is at the center of their urban development strategies. By investing in green infrastructure, environmentally friendly public transport, and public spaces that encourage community cohesion, BRICS are committed to making their cities engines of sustainable growth and centers of social innovation.

Valorization of Work and Social Protection

Changes in the work landscape, accelerated by automation and digitalization, require innovative policies to protect workers and promote equity in the labor market. The BRICS are exploring new models of social protection and welfare systems that respond to the needs of an evolving workforce. This includes supporting retraining and upgrading skills, expanding social security networks to cover the self-employed and informal workers, and implementing policies that promote decent work for all.

Promoting Public Health and Food Safety

Public health and food security are critical priorities, with BRICS facing complex challenges such as communicable diseases, lifestyle-related health issues, and food insecurity. Promoting sustainable food systems, investing in accessible public health services, and research to address emerging threats to public health are essential to ensure the well-being of their populations. The focus on disease prevention, nutrition and universal access to care represents a holistic approach to health that considers the interdependencies between health, environment, and economic development.

Strengthening Crisis Response Capacities

The ability to respond effectively to crises, whether health, economic or environmental, is crucial for social resilience in the BRICS. By developing flexible crisis response mechanisms, which quickly mobilize resources and coordinate actions between different levels of government and sectors of society,

BRICS can improve their ability to deal with future shocks and stresses. This includes preparing for emergency management, supporting research and innovation for crisis solutions, and building informed and resilient communities able to adapt and recover from adversity.

In conclusion, the BRICS approach to their population and social dynamics reflects an understanding that sustainable progress requires active and coordinated engagement across various sectors and levels of society. As they face unique challenges, their collective efforts to promote social innovation, environmental justice, and inclusive development offer important lessons on how emerging and developing economies can navigate the complex landscape of the 21st century, pursuing sustainable development goals and building a fairer and more resilient future for all.

The BRICS commitment to address complex population and social dynamics is further complicated by the intersection of these issues with global challenges such as climate change, digitalization and geopolitical tensions. Their response to these questions not only reflects the search for innovative solutions but also the recognition of the need to adapt and react to a rapidly changing environment.

Integration of Digitalization into Social Strategies

Digitalization presents unique opportunities for BRICS to address some of their most pressing demographic and social challenges. By using digital technology, they can improve access to public services, facilitate education and vocational training, and promote financial inclusion. Initiatives that leverage artificial intelligence, big data, and online platforms to provide personalized health services, distance education, and support for small businesses can help bridge disparities and stimulate social innovation.

Addressing the Social Implications of Climate Change

Climate change represents an imminent threat to BRICS populations, especially the most vulnerable. The search for solutions to mitigate the impacts of climate change and to adapt to it requires an integrated approach that takes into account social implications. This includes developing climate adaptation strategies that protect at-risk communities, promote climate-resilient agricultural practices, and ensure food and water security. Investing in climate-resilient research and infrastructure can reduce the risk of natural disasters and ensure that societies are better prepared to face future challenges.

Strengthening Inclusion and Diversity Policies

Inclusion and diversity policies are fundamental to BRICS as they navigate their population and social dynamics. By recognizing and valuing cultural, ethnic and social diversity within their populations, they can build more cohesive and resilient societies. This requires an active commitment to combat discrimination, promote gender equality, and support the rights of minorities and indigenous communities. Through open dialogue and community participation, BRICS can address social tensions, build mutual understanding, and promote a sense of belonging.

Global Collaboration for Crisis Management

Managing crises, from pandemics to conflicts, requires robust global collaboration. BRICS, through the sharing of resources, expertise and capacities, can play a key role in responding to global crises. Cooperation in areas such as health research, humanitarian assistance and conflict resolution can help mitigate the impacts of these crises on vulnerable populations and promote global stability and peace.

Supporting Innovation for Social Sustainability

Finally, supporting innovation for social sustainability is crucial for BRICS as they face challenges inherent to their population and social dynamics. This involves investing in research and development for sustainable solutions that address issues such as poverty, education, health and inequality. Promoting social entrepreneurship, encouraging startups that solve social and environmental problems, and integrating sustainability into business models can drive progress towards fairer and more resilient societies.

Navigating these complex challenges, BRICS not only address their own internal issues but also contribute to global dialogue and solutions. Their ability to innovate in social policies and to adapt to changes can offer replicable models for other nations facing similar challenges. International cooperation plays a fundamental role in this context, allowing an exchange of knowledge and best practices that transcend national borders.

Development of an Adaptable and Competent Workforce

A well-educated and adaptable workforce is crucial to meeting future economic and social challenges. The BRICS are therefore focusing resources on education and vocational training, aiming to equip citizens with the skills necessary to navigate a rapidly changing labor market. This includes encouraging STEM (science, technology, engineering, and mathematics), digital skills, and lifelong learning as key components of the education system.

Focus on Mental Health

Mental health has become a topic of increasing importance in the BRICS, recognizing that psychological well-being is as important as physical health for social and economic development. The integration of mental health into public health programs, the development of accessible services and the reduction of the stigma associated with mental illness are essential steps towards building more inclusive and supportive societies.

Improving Food and Nutrition Security

Food and nutrition security remains a pre-eminent challenge, with BRICS exploring ways to ensure that all citizens have access to sufficient, safe and nutritious food. This involves supporting local agriculture, developing resilient and sustainable supply chains, and promoting healthy and balanced diets. Addressing the root causes of food insecurity, including poverty and inequality, is critical to ensuring that no one is left behind.

Enhancing Civic Participation

Finally, civic participation and citizen empowerment are essential to address population and social dynamics in the BRICS. By encouraging active involvement in governance, decision-making processes, and community initiatives, BRICS can promote a sense of belonging and shared responsibility among citizens. This not only strengthens social cohesion but also facilitates the adoption of sustainable policies and practices at the local level.

By navigating these interconnected challenges, BRICS demonstrate that adaptability, innovation and cooperation are fundamental to addressing population issues and social dynamics in the 21st century. Their strategies offer important lessons on how informed, inclusive and proactive policies can promote social, economic and environmental well-being, not only within their borders but around the world.

The BRICS complex and layered approach to population dynamics and social issues highlights a deep awareness of the need for holistic and sustainable solutions that embrace the multidimensionality of current challenges. As they continue to adapt and respond to global and local changes, the importance of integrated policies that take into account the cultural, economic and social specificities of each country clearly emerges.

Priority to Community Resilience

Building resilience at the community level is increasingly becoming a priority, recognizing that strong and cohesive communities are better equipped to deal with shocks and stress, whether they are natural disasters, economic crises or pandemics. The BRICS are exploring ways to empower communities through access to essential services, strengthening social ties, and supporting local security networks. This includes encouraging the social and solidarity economy, supporting basic entrepreneurship and investing in public spaces that promote social interaction and a sense of belonging.

Integration of the Sustainable Development Goals (SDGs)

The adoption of the United Nations Sustainable Development Goals as a framework for national policies highlights the BRICS' commitment to promoting equitable and sustainable development. This involves integrating the SDGs into planning and development strategies, ensuring that objectives related to poverty reduction, health and well-being, quality education, and gender equality are at the center of public policies. Collaboration between the public and private sectors, together with the involvement of civil society, is essential to achieve these objectives at national and local levels.

Promoting Gender Equality and Women's Empowerment

Gender equality and women's empowerment are recognized as key elements for sustainable development and the construction of equitable societies. The BRICS are implementing policies aimed at eliminating barriers to education and employment for women, promoting women's participation in all sectors of society, and combating gender-based violence. Programs that support female entrepreneurship, access to economic resources, and women's political representation are vital to ensure that female voices are heard and valued.

Youth Capacity Development and Leadership

Young people in the BRICS represent a significant resource for the future. Investing in capacity development, education and professional training is essential to prepare them to become leaders and innovators in their society. Programs that promote youth leadership, civic engagement, and entrepreneurship can help unlock the potential of young people and ensure that they are able to actively contribute to economic and social development.

Adaptation to the New Work Realities

The evolution of the work landscape, influenced by technology, globalization and demographic changes, requires flexible and proactive policies to ensure that workers are protected and that new job opportunities are accessible. The BRICS are addressing these challenges by reforming labor laws, supporting the transition to greener and more digital economies, and developing training programs that respond to the needs of the modern labor market.

As the BRICS continue their path of responding to population and social dynamics, the need emerges for an even more flexible and adaptive approach, capable of anticipating future trends and responding with innovative policies. This implies not only a continuous commitment to the research and development of sustainable solutions but also the will to explore new forms of governance that facilitate collaboration between different sectors of society.

Active Involvement of Civil Society

The active involvement of civil society, including voluntary groups, non-governmental organizations and local communities, becomes crucial to ensure that policies and initiatives are rooted in local realities and respond effectively to the needs of populations. Through dialogue platforms and public participation mechanisms, BRICS can benefit from a wide range of perspectives and expertise, thus strengthening the effectiveness of their social development strategies.

Harnessing Technology for Social Inclusion

The adoption of advanced technologies provides BRICS with powerful tools to promote social inclusion and improve access to essential services. From mobile applications that facilitate access to healthcare and education, to digital platforms that support social innovation and entrepreneurship, technology can help overcome traditional barriers and create equitable opportunities for all citizens.

Integration of Climate Adaptation Strategies

As the BRICS adapt to the new realities of work and to the impacts of climate change, the integration of climate adaptation strategies into social development policies becomes increasingly important. Addressing climate-related risks, such as rising temperatures, extreme weather events and rising sea levels, requires an approach that considers both environmental resilience and social sustainability, ensuring that communities are prepared and protected from the changes taking place.

Promotion of the Circular and Sustainable Economy

The adoption of the circular economy in the BRICS represents an opportunity to simultaneously address environmental challenges and those related to social development. By promoting sustainable consumption and production models that minimize waste and enhance resources, BRICS can stimulate economic innovation, create green jobs and reduce inequalities, while promoting environmental protection.

Strengthen International Collaboration

Finally, strengthening international collaboration remains a fundamental aspect for BRICS, allowing them to deal more effectively with global challenges affecting population and social dynamics. By sharing knowledge, resources and good practices, they can not only accelerate their progress towards more inclusive and equitable societies but also contribute significantly to global efforts to promote sustainable development.

In conclusion, the BRICS commitment to navigating population dynamics and social issues reflects a complex and constantly evolving approach that recognizes the need for integrated and sustainable solutions. As they face the challenges inherent to their social and economic transition, the emphasis on flexibility, innovation, and cooperation remains essential to achieve their goal of building resilient, just and prosperous societies, capable of facing the uncertainties of the future.

In conclusion, the BRICS commitment to navigating and managing complex population dynamics and social issues is manifested through a multilevel approach that integrates innovation, proactive policies and international collaboration. Their experience reflects a deep understanding that demographic and social challenges are intrinsically linked to the wider context of sustainable development, requiring solutions that embrace social equity, economic resilience and environmental sustainability.

Holistic Policy Integration

The key to success in the BRICS lies in their ability to integrate social, economic and environmental policies in a holistic manner, ensuring that initiatives in one sector support and reinforce objectives in others. This holistic approach allows not only to address immediate issues but also to position these countries for a more resilient and sustainable future, in which economic growth goes hand in hand with social progress and environmental protection.

Community Engagement and Empowerment

A crucial aspect of the BRICS approach is the recognition of the importance of empowerment and the active involvement of local communities in decisions that influence their future. Through open dialogue, civic participation, and the promotion of education and awareness, these countries are working to ensure that policies are inclusive and rooted in local realities, thus increasing the effectiveness of social development initiatives.

Innovation and Adaptability

Innovation is at the heart of BRICS strategies to address population dynamics and social issues. Through the adoption of new technologies, the exploration of alternative economic models such as the circular economy, and investment in research and development, the BRICS are trying to find sustainable solutions to complex problems, while ensuring that their economies and societies can adapt and prosper in the context of a rapidly changing world.

Global Collaboration for Shared Challenges

Finally, the BRICS recognize that many of the challenges they face are global in nature and require collaborative responses. Through international cooperation, knowledge exchange and the construction of strategic partnerships, they are seeking to contribute and shape global solutions to issues such as climate change, inequalities, migration and public health. Their active participation in multilateral forums and global initiatives demonstrates a commitment to go beyond national borders and work together to address the common challenges of humanity.

In summary, the BRICS approach to their population dynamics and social issues embodies a balance between the need for immediate answers and the vision of a sustainable and inclusive future. As they continue to navigate these complex waters, the lessons learned and the strategies adopted offer valuable insights into how emerging and developing economies can address their demographic and social challenges, while contributing to global sustainable development goals. The BRICS commitment to innovation, equity and international collaboration sets the stage for building more resilient, just and prosperous societies for all.

9. Culture and Soft Power: BRICS cultural influence at a global level.

The BRICS (Brazil, Russia, India, China and South Africa) represent not only emerging economic powers but also centers of rich cultural diversity with growing global influence. The concept of 'soft power', coined by Joseph Nye, describes a country's ability to persuade and attract other countries through culture, political values and foreign policies, rather than through military or economic means. The BRICS are effectively using their soft power to build bridges, influence global public opinion and promote their interests on a global scale.

Brazil: The Joy of Cultural Diversity

Brazil exercises its soft power through its lively music, soccer and carnival, which have a global appeal and represent the joy and diversity of its culture. Samba and bossa nova, for example, have become ambassadors of Brazilian culture around the world. In addition, Brazil's reputation in soccer and its commitment to sport as a means of unity and peace between peoples further reinforce its global cultural influence.

Russia: Cultural Heritage and Innovation

Russia exploits its rich cultural heritage, which includes literature, classical music, ballet and theater, to project its soft power. The works of Tolstoy, Dostoevsky, Tchaikovsky and numerous other Russian artists are celebrated internationally. Russia also organizes global cultural events, such as the St. Petersburg International Music Festival and the Moscow Biennial, which attract a worldwide audience, showing its commitment to innovation in arts and culture.

India: The Rise of Cinema and Spirituality

India exercises its soft power through Bollywood, its film industry, which is one of the largest in the world, and its spiritual and philosophical heritage. Indian films, music and traditional dances have found audiences around the world, creating a deep cultural connection. In addition, spiritual practices such as yoga and meditation have taken on a global resonance, positioning India as a center of spiritual and physical well-being.

China: Dissemination of Language and Culture

China has invested significantly in promoting its language and culture through the establishment of Confucius Institutes around the world. These centers not only teach the Chinese language but also organize cultural events to showcase the richness of Chinese culture. China also uses its film industry and media to project its narrative and values globally, increasing its cultural influence.

South Africa: Voice of Africa

South Africa, with its history of overcoming apartheid and its vibrant art and music scene, plays a key role in increasing global awareness and appreciation of African culture. Through music, art, literature and cinema, South Africa shares stories of resilience, diversity and innovation, acting as a voice for the African continent on the world stage.

Cultural Cooperation between BRICS

In addition to their individual initiatives, the BRICS also collaborate to promote cultural cooperation between their countries. This includes cultural exchanges, joint art festivals, and educational initiatives that aim to build mutual understanding and respect. These activities not only strengthen the ties between the BRICS but also help to project a collective narrative that underlines their importance as emerging cultural forces in the world.

In conclusion, the BRICS are effectively exploiting their soft power to increase their cultural influence globally, demonstrating how culture, art, music, cinema and traditions can serve as powerful tools for diplomacy and international dialogue. Through these cultural expressions, they not only share the richness and diversity of their heritages with the world but they also facilitate intercultural understanding and strengthen international ties.

Future Strategies for the Expansion of Soft Power

Looking to the future, the BRICS are likely to continue to broaden and refine their soft power strategies to address emerging global challenges and navigate the complex geopolitical landscape. This could include:

- **Digital Innovation**: Leveraging digital platforms and social media to reach wider global audiences, sharing cultural content that resonates with younger generations and promoting intercultural dialogue across virtual borders.

- **Cultural and Educational Diplomacy**: Expanding programs such as Confucius Institutes and similar cultural and educational initiatives that promote language, art and history, to build bridges of understanding and stimulate interest and appreciation for different cultures.

- **Transnational Creative Collaborations**: Encouraging collaborations between artists, writers, musicians and content creators from BRICS and other countries, to produce works that mix different cultural elements and speak to a global audience with universal messages of hope, resilience and innovation.

- **Cultural Tourism**: Promoting cultural tourism as a way for people to directly experience the richness of BRICS cultures, while supporting local economies and promoting heritage conservation.

- **Sustainability and Social Responsibility**: By integrating issues of sustainability and social responsibility into their expressions of soft power, BRICS can not only strengthen their global image but also promote important messages regarding environmental protection, social equity and sustainable development.

Through these and other initiatives, BRICS have the opportunity not only to enrich global cultural dialogue but also to shape international narratives so that they reflect a wider range of voices and perspectives. In an increasingly interconnected world, the power to influence through culture and shared values is a fundamental aspect of global leadership, and the BRICS are uniquely positioned to play a significant role in this dynamic context.

As the BRICS continue to strengthen their global cultural influence through soft power, the emphasis is shifting toward a deeper integration of their cultural narratives into the fabric of global diplomacy and international cooperation. This process is not limited to the simple export of culture but also involves the creation of an intercultural dialogue that promotes peace, understanding and mutual respect at the world level.

Emphasis on Cultural Co-creation

A key strategy for BRICS in strengthening their soft power could be to emphasize cultural co-creation, facilitating projects involving artists, thinkers and content creators from different countries in joint initiatives. This approach would not only enrich the global cultural landscape with works that reflect a fusion of different perspectives but would also strengthen interpersonal and intercultural ties, promoting a sense of global unity through diversity.

Recognition and Promotion of Intangible Cultural Heritage

UNESCO stresses the importance of intangible cultural heritage as a carrier of cultural diversity and guarantor of sustainable development. BRICS can play a crucial role in recognizing, cataloguing and promoting the oral traditions, performing arts, social rituals and craft techniques that constitute the intangible cultural heritage of their nations. This would not only help preserve these practices for future generations but would also help raise global public awareness of the richness and variety of BRICS cultures.

Integration of Culture into Sustainable Development Policies

The BRICS are exploring ways to integrate culture into their sustainable development policies, recognizing that culture is both an engine and a facilitator of sustainable development.

Initiatives that use art and culture to raise awareness of environmental issues, promote education and gender equity, and stimulate social innovation can have a significant impact locally and globally. Art and culture offer powerful tools for engaging communities, promoting social change, and catalyzing collective action toward sustainable goals.

Expanding Access to Culture through Technology

Digital technology offers unprecedented opportunities to expand access to culture and promote intercultural dialogue. BRICS can exploit digital platforms, virtual reality and other emerging technologies to make their cultural heritages accessible to a global audience, offering immersive experiences that overcome geographical and socio-economic barriers. This not only democratizes access to culture but also opens up new avenues for creative expression and international collaboration.

Supporting Linguistic Diversity

Promoting and supporting linguistic diversity is another important aspect of BRICS soft power, recognizing that language is a fundamental vehicle of culture and identity. Initiatives aimed at safeguarding and promoting minority and indigenous languages, together with the dissemination of the main BRICS languages through education and the media, can help maintain global linguistic heritage and promote intercultural understanding.

In short, the potential of the BRICS to influence the global cultural scene through soft power is vast and diverse. As they continue to navigate the challenges and opportunities of the 21st century, the deep integration of culture into their strategies of global diplomacy and sustainable development will not only enrich intercultural dialogue but will also help to forge a more connected, comprehensive and resilient world. The adoption of an approach that values cultural co-creation, the promotion of intangible cultural heritage, the integration of culture into sustainable development policies, the expansion of access to culture through technology and the support of linguistic diversity represents not only a strategy to increase the soft power of the BRICS but also a commitment to building a more inclusive and supportive global community.

As the BRICS advance, their role as emerging cultural actors on the world stage is expanding, offering new perspectives and enriching international dialogue with their unique traditions, innovations and visions. Their ability to weave together internal cultural diversity with common global goals uniquely positions them to lead by example, showing how culture can be a bridge to mutual understanding and transnational cooperation.

The challenge for BRICS in the near future will be to maintain this balance between preserving their unique cultural identities and promoting an inclusive narrative that embraces global diversity. It will be essential to promote policies that facilitate cultural exchanges, enhance creativity and innovation, and recognize the fundamental role of culture in promoting peace, justice and sustainable development.

In addition, BRICS must continue to explore how culture can contribute to solving pressing global problems, such as climate change, inequality and public health, integrating the cultural dimension into solutions to these challenges. By promoting open cultural dialogue, supporting diversity and inclusion, and investing in cultural initiatives that promote sustainability, BRICS can further strengthen their soft power and help shape a global future that values and celebrates the richness of human diversity.

In conclusion, the soft power of the BRICS, rooted in their rich cultural heritage and projected through innovative and collaborative strategies, offers a powerful and positive vision for the future of international relations. With their continuous commitment to the promotion of culture as a vehicle of diplomacy and development, the BRICS not only increase their influence on the world stage but also actively contribute to the creation of a more connected world, capable of facing together the challenges of our time.

10. Defense and Security: analysis of defense policies and initiatives for regional and global security.

The BRICS countries (Brazil, Russia, India, China and South Africa) are taking an increasingly significant role in regional and global defense and security issues. Each of these states has specific defense policies and security approaches that reflect their geopolitical positions, perceived threats and strategic objectives. However, through the BRICS forum, they also seek to coordinate their positions on international security issues, promote regional stability, and influence the world order in ways that reflect their collective and individual interests.

Brazil: A Peace-Oriented Approach

Brazil has traditionally adopted an approach to defense and security focused on international cooperation, regional stability, and support for peace missions under the aegis of the United Nations. Its defense policy emphasizes the defense of sovereignty, the protection of its vast natural resources, and the promotion of peace and security in South America. Brazil is actively engaged in peace-keeping operations and seeks to promote diplomatic solutions to regional conflicts.

Russia: Reaffirming its Global Role

Russia pursues a defense policy that aims to reaffirm its role as a global power, with a significant emphasis on strengthening its military capabilities and modernizing its armed forces. Its security strategy focuses on deterring potential threats along its borders and protecting Russian interests worldwide. Russia is actively involved in various regions, seeking to exert influence through military cooperation and participation in regional security organizations.

India: Tackling Complex Challenges

India faces a complex security environment, characterized by regional challenges, in particular tensions with Pakistan and China, and the threat of terrorism. Its defense policy focuses on strengthening defense capabilities, modernizing armed forces, and developing credible deterrence. India also stresses the importance of security cooperation with other countries, actively participating in regional and global dialogues and developing strategic partnerships.

China: Expanding Security and Influence

China is rapidly expanding its military capabilities and strategic influence, with the goal of protecting its national interests, upholding its territorial claims, and increasing its role in global security issues. Its Belt and Road Initiative and its growing involvement in security organizations and multilateral forums demonstrate China's desire to promote a new world order that reflects its interests and values. China also emphasizes maritime security, the development of cyber and space capabilities, and supports a vision of common, cooperative and sustainable security.

South Africa: Promoter of Peace and Security in Africa

South Africa sees itself as a promoter of peace and stability in Africa, actively engaging in peace and security initiatives on the continent. Its defense policy emphasizes conflict prevention, support for peace operations, and the promotion of African security cooperation through regional mechanisms such as the African Union. South Africa is also committed to strengthening its defense capabilities to protect its borders and contribute to peacekeeping missions.

BRICS Cooperation in Defense and Security

In the context of BRICS cooperation in defense and security, members seek to expand their dialogue and cooperation on issues affecting regional and global stability. This joint effort reflects a desire to contribute to a more multipolar world order, where the voices of emerging countries are more influential in international security decisions. Cooperation between BRICS occurs in various forms, including information exchanges, joint military exercises and security dialogues, aimed at strengthening mutual trust and promoting shared understanding on critical security issues.

Joint Military Exercises

One of the most visible manifestations of defense cooperation between the BRICS is the organization of joint military exercises. These activities not only serve to strengthen operational capacities and compatibility between member countries' armed forces, but they also represent a symbolic demonstration of unity and common intent in matters of security. These exercises help to improve collective readiness to face threats such as terrorism, piracy and humanitarian emergencies.

Security Dialogues and Conferences

The BRICS regularly organize security dialogues and conferences that offer platforms for the discussion of strategic issues, from non-proliferation to cybersecurity, from the fight against terrorism to regional stability. These meetings allow members to coordinate their positions on global security issues and to explore areas for practical cooperation, including the joint response to emerging challenges.

Cooperation in the Field of Computer Security

Recognizing the growing importance of cybersecurity in the digital age, the BRICS are deepening their cooperation in this field. By sharing experiences, policies and best practices, they aim to strengthen national defenses against cyber threats and promote a secure, stable and peaceful cyberspace. Collaboration in this area is critical to protecting critical infrastructure, fighting cybercrime, and ensuring information security globally.

Promoting Peace and Regional Stability

The BRICS are actively engaged in promoting peace and stability in their respective regions and at the global level, supporting conflict resolution initiatives, participating in peace-keeping operations and providing humanitarian assistance where necessary. Through their joint commitment, they aim to contribute to a more peaceful international environment, which facilitates sustainable development and cooperation between nations.

Future Challenges and Opportunities

Despite progress, BRICS defense and security cooperation faces several challenges, including strategic differences, regional tensions, and the need to balance national interests with collective objectives. However, opportunities for further collaboration remain significant, especially in areas such as managing global crises, defending against climate change, and developing international standards for cybersecurity and space.

In conclusion, BRICS cooperation in defense and security highlights the potential of emerging countries to work together to address global challenges, promote stability and contribute to a more balanced and just world order. As the BRICS continue to develop their strategic partnership, their ability to translate dialogue into concrete actions and effectively coordinate defense and security policies will be crucial to their long-term impact on global security.

As the BRICS continue to explore and strengthen their defense and security collaborations, attention is expanding to new horizons that include unconventional security and collective resilience. Evolving global dynamics and emerging challenges require a broader and more innovative approach that goes beyond traditional military and geostrategic issues.

Focus on Human Security

A critical dimension that emerges in defense and security cooperation between BRICS is the emphasis on human security. This concept broadens the notion of security to include issues such as food security, health security, environmental protection and economic security. Recognizing that threats to human security transcend national borders, BRICS are exploring ways of collaboration that aim to ensure that populations are protected from interconnected global threats, such as pandemics, natural disasters, and transnational crime.

Expanding Cooperation in Disaster Management

Disaster management is another area where the BRICS are intensifying their cooperation, sharing knowledge, technologies and resources to respond more effectively to catastrophic events.

Establishing rapid response mechanisms and platforms for sharing information in real time can improve member countries' capacity to mitigate the impacts of disasters, safeguard human lives and protect critical infrastructure.

Cooperation in the Field of Defense Technology

Technological innovation in the military and security fields represents an additional area of cooperation between the BRICS. The development and sharing of advanced technologies, from satellite surveillance to cyber-defense, can strengthen each country's capacity to protect its national interests and contribute to collective security. In addition, collaboration in research and development can facilitate access to new technologies, reducing dependence on external suppliers and promoting technological autonomy.

Energy Security Strategies

Energy security has become a central concern for the BRICS, given their growing role as global energy consumers and producers. Cooperation in this area focuses on ensuring stable and secure access to energy resources, the diversification of energy sources and the development of clean and renewable energy technologies. By collaborating on energy security issues, BRICS can improve their resilience to global energy shocks and promote sustainable energy transitions.

Dialogue on International Norms and International Law

Finally, the BRICS are trying to influence the formation of international norms and international law on security and defense. Through constructive dialogue and active participation in international forums, they aim to promote a fairer world order that reflects the principles of multilateralism, sovereignty and non-interference. This commitment not only aims to protect their common interests but also to contribute to global peace and stability.

As the BRICS move forward in consolidating their defense and security cooperation, their ability to collectively face traditional and unconventional challenges will be critical to their long-term impact on regional and global security. Their initiative in promoting innovative and inclusive approaches to security can offer new perspectives in global discussions, establishing a model of multilateral cooperation that could be emulated by other regions and international coalitions.

Promoting Cooperation in the Space Sector for Security

Space exploration and use offer new frontiers for defense and security cooperation between BRICS. By collaborating in the development of space technologies for surveillance, communication and navigation, BRICS countries can significantly improve their capabilities to monitor and respond to global threats, from environmental surveillance to the monitoring of military movements. Space cooperation can also facilitate the joint development of standards and practices to ensure the safety and sustainability of space activities.

Strengthening Maritime Security Capabilities

Given the importance of maritime routes for global trade and energy security, another area of interest to BRICS is the strengthening of maritime security. By collaborating in developing maritime surveillance capabilities, in sharing information on threats to maritime security, such as piracy and smuggling, and in coordinating patrol operations, BRICS can contribute to the security and stability of critical maritime routes, while promoting freedom of navigation in accordance with international law.

Intelligence Sharing and Countering Terrorism

One area in which cooperation between the BRICS is particularly critical concerns the fight against terrorism and the fight against violent radicalization. Through shared mechanisms for intelligence exchange and law enforcement cooperation, BRICS can improve their ability to prevent terrorist attacks, dismantle transnational terrorist networks, and counter terrorist financing. Collaboration in this area underlines the importance of a holistic approach that also includes strategies to address the root causes of terrorism, such as poverty, inequality and social exclusion.

Development of Rapid Response Mechanisms to International Crises

The BRICS are also exploring the development of rapid response mechanisms to deal with international crises, from managing refugees and humanitarian crises to responding to pandemics. These collective efforts aim to coordinate quick and effective actions in emergency situations, maximizing the use of available resources and ensuring that assistance quickly reaches those who need it.

Dialogue on Ethics and Regulations for Defense and Security

Finally, dialogue on ethical principles and regulations governing the use of new technologies in the field of defense and security represents an important dimension of BRICS cooperation. This includes discussions on the ethical implications of artificial intelligence and autonomous systems in military operations, regulations for cyberspace, and arms control. Through an open and inclusive dialogue, BRICS can contribute to the development of an international regulatory framework that balances security needs with respect for human rights and the principles of international law.

Defense and security cooperation between BRICS, addressing traditional and emerging challenges with a collaborative and multidimensional approach, not only strengthens regional and global security but also contributes to the construction of a more just and resilient international order. As these collaborations deepen and expand, the BRICS' ability to positively influence global security dynamics will be an important factor in shaping the future of international governance and security cooperation. The growing interdependence between States requires a renewed commitment to transnational collaboration, and the BRICS, with their resources, diversity and strategic capabilities, have a unique role to play in this context.

Integrating Cybersecurity Capabilities

In the digital age, cybersecurity has become a top priority for national and international security. The BRICS are expanding their cooperation in this area through the development of shared capacities, the formation of cyber-incident response teams, and the development of common strategies to deal with threats such as cyber terrorism and cyber espionage. The goal is to create a secure cyberspace that supports economic development and protects critical infrastructure and sensitive information.

Collaboration for Global Financial Stability

The BRICS also recognize the importance of global financial stability as a key component of security. Collaboration through multilateral financial institutions, such as the BRICS New Development Bank, aims to provide financial support to members in times of crisis, promote sustainable development projects and offer an alternative to existing global financial structures. This approach not only contributes to the economic security of member countries but also promotes greater equity and inclusion in the global economy.

Support for Peace and Mediation Initiatives

Another important dimension of BRICS cooperation in the field of defense and security is joint support for peace and mediation initiatives in conflict zones. Through joint diplomatic missions, dialogue initiatives, and support for peace processes, BRICS can play a significant role in facilitating conflict resolution and promoting regional stability. This commitment not only demonstrates their willingness to contribute to global peace but also reinforces their soft power and diplomatic influence.

Research and Shared Development in Defense Technologies

Innovation continues to shape the defense and security landscape, and the BRICS are seeking to enhance their cooperation in the field of research and development of new defense technologies. This includes missile defense systems, unmanned vehicles, advanced surveillance technologies, and futuristic combat systems. Sharing knowledge and resources in this area can accelerate the development of defensive capabilities and improve preparedness for emerging threats.

Challenging Monopolistic Narratives in Global Security

Finally, the BRICS are challenging monopolistic narratives in global security by promoting a more multipolar approach to international governance. Through dialogue and cooperation, they seek to ensure that security decisions reflect a wider range of interests and perspectives, counteracting the dominance of any single actor or coalition. This effort not only promotes principles of justice and fairness but also encourages more creative and inclusive solutions to global problems.

BRICS cooperation in the field of defense and security, therefore, extends far beyond traditional military issues, embracing a holistic vision that encompasses economic, human and environmental security. As they continue to navigate the complexities of the global landscape, the BRICS' commitment to deeper and more strategic collaboration in these areas will be crucial to shaping a safer, more stable and just world for everyone.

As the BRICS consolidate their cooperation on defense and security, new perspectives are opening up to address emerging global challenges. The complexity of the world order requires increasing attention to the synergy between development, security and human rights, underlining the need for a more integrated and holistic approach.

Integrating Environmental Issues into Safety

The integration of environmental issues into security strategies represents a field of increasing importance. Climate change, loss of biodiversity and limited natural resources require reflection on how environmental issues affect national and global security. BRICS are exploring ways to incorporate climate resilience and sustainable resource management into their defense and security plans, recognizing that environmental stability is inherently linked to human security and sustainable development.

Capacity Development for the Management of Health Emergencies

Recent pandemics have highlighted the importance of international cooperation in managing health emergencies. The BRICS are expanding their collaboration in the field of public health to include pandemic preparedness and response, the exchange of information and research on vaccines and treatments, and the strengthening of national health systems. This approach not only improves the ability to respond to health crises but also contributes to global security by improving the resilience of societies.

Strengthening Economic Security

Economic security has become a central concern, with BRICS seeking to diversify their economies, protect critical supply chains, and develop strategies to address economic vulnerabilities. Collaboration in this area may include sharing economic intelligence, developing financial crisis response mechanisms, and joint investment in strategic sectors. Promoting greater economic security helps stabilize vulnerable regions and contributes to global peace and security.

Deepening Cooperation in the Fight against Terrorism and Radicalization

The fight against terrorism and radicalization remains a priority for BRICS, which seek to deepen their cooperation through the sharing of intelligence, joint operations and programs to counter radicalization. Recognizing that terrorism has no borders, this cooperation extends beyond BRICS members, seeking to involve other countries and international organizations in a united front against threats to global security.

Promotion of International Norms and International Law

The BRICS continue to support the development and adherence to international norms and principles of international law that govern conduct in common global spaces, such as the sea, space and cyberspace. Through multilateral dialogue and diplomacy, they seek to contribute to the creation of a security framework that is fair, rules-based and capable of dealing with emerging challenges, while ensuring that the interests and concerns of developing countries are adequately represented.

As BRICS advance their collective commitment to address defense and security issues, their ability to act cohesively and to articulate a shared vision for global security will be critical. The challenge is twofold: to strengthen internal cooperation between

BRICS members, while ensuring that their approach to security is inclusive, sustainable and based on mutual respect. In this way, the BRICS will not only help to shape a more stable and just international security environment but will also promote a model of global cooperation that recognizes the complexity of contemporary challenges and the need for collective and multidimensional responses.

Consolidating Multilateral Governance

In the defense and security arena, the BRICS emphasize the importance of strengthening multilateral institutions and global governance mechanisms. Through their engagement with the United Nations and other international organizations, they seek to promote a more inclusive world order that reflects the aspirations and concerns of emerging and developing countries. The objective is to ensure that international standards and principles in global security management are fair, transparent and based on consent.

Promoting Stability through Sustainable Development

The BRICS recognize that security and development are interconnected and that promoting sustainable development is critical to long-term stability. Through joint initiatives that aim to reduce poverty, improve education and health, and support economic development, they work to address some of the root causes of instability and conflict. By promoting inclusive and sustainable growth, BRICS contribute not only to the well-being of their populations but also to building more resilient and peaceful communities globally.

Strengthening Cooperation in Non-Traditional Security

Non-traditional security, which includes challenges such as climate change, pandemics, transnational crime, and water security, requires innovative and collaborative responses. The

BRICS are expanding their cooperation in these areas, recognizing that threats to non-traditional security can have profound impacts on national and regional stability. Through the sharing of best practices, cooperation in research and development, and the implementation of joint projects, they work to strengthen their collective resilience to these emerging threats.

Commitment to Conflict Resolution and Peacebuilding

Active engagement in conflict resolution and peacebuilding represents another crucial dimension of the BRICS approach to global security. Through diplomatic and mediation initiatives, contributions to United Nations peacekeeping operations and support to national reconciliation processes, the BRICS seek to promote peaceful solutions to conflicts and to support the transition to stable and peaceful societies.

Future Challenges and Perspectives

In pursuing these objectives, the BRICS face several challenges, including the need to coordinate security and defense policies between members with different interests and priorities, managing regional tensions, and responding to criticism regarding respect for human rights and fundamental freedoms. However, the opportunities for a positive impact are significant. By deepening cooperation, adapting strategies to changing realities, and promoting an open and inclusive dialogue, BRICS can play a key role in shaping a more equitable, stable and resilient global security landscape.

In conclusion, the evolution of defense and security cooperation between the BRICS reflects a shared commitment to collectively address global challenges, promote peace and stability, and contribute to a more just and multipolar world order. As they continue to adapt and respond to the complexities of the international context, BRICS cooperation in defense and security offers a unique opportunity to develop new paradigms of multilateral collaboration. These paradigms not only aim to strengthen collective security but also to address global issues through lenses of sustainable development, social justice and respect for diversity and sovereignty.

Intensifying Efforts in Preventive Diplomacy

The adoption of stronger and more proactive preventive diplomacy represents a key area in which the BRICS could intensify their efforts. By focusing on the root causes of conflicts, such as economic disparities, ethnic and religious tensions, and competition for natural resources, BRICS can work together to develop strategies that prevent tensions from escalating into open conflicts. This approach would not only help maintain regional peace and stability but would also promote deeper understanding and mutual respect between different communities and nations.

Expansion of Cooperation in the Digital Domain

With digitalization continuing to shape every aspect of modern society, the expansion of cooperation in the digital domain emerges as another critical area. This includes not only cybersecurity but also the use of digital technologies to promote peace, facilitate diplomacy, and support development efforts. For example, the BRICS could collaborate in the development of digital platforms for conflict mediation, the sharing of knowledge on sustainable development, and the promotion of culture and peace education.

Supporting Innovation for Peace

Technological innovation offers new opportunities to support peace and security efforts. BRICS could explore collaboration in developing emerging technologies, such as artificial intelligence, to monitor and prevent conflicts, manage humanitarian crises, and contribute to disarmament and non-proliferation. The adoption of such technologies must be guided by strong ethical principles and an in-depth understanding of the potential security and human rights implications.

Strengthening Peacebuilding Capacity

In addition to conflict resolution, strengthening peacebuilding capacities is essential to ensure lasting peace. BRICS can work together to develop programs that support post-conflict reconstruction, reconciliation, and the strengthening of democratic institutions. This could include support for peace education, leadership training and economic development, thus contributing to building resilient and inclusive societies.

Expansion of the Dialogue on Security and Development

Finally, an expanded and in-depth dialogue between BRICS on how security and development influence each other could lead to a more holistic understanding of the strategies needed to address contemporary challenges. Recognizing that security goes beyond military issues and includes economic development, social justice, public health, and environmental protection, BRICS can promote a more integrated approach to global security.

As the BRICS continue to expand and deepen their defense and security cooperation, their collective approach to managing global challenges could serve as a model for other regional and international coalitions. Their ability to balance national interests with collective objectives, to navigate geopolitical complexities and to promote innovative and inclusive solutions could contribute significantly to the creation of a more stable, just and resilient global security landscape. By expanding cooperation in new areas, adopting holistic approaches to security and development, and strengthening dialogue and mutual trust, BRICS can play a crucial role in shaping international security dynamics.

Valuing Global and Regional Partnerships

A promising direction for the BRICS is to further enhance global and regional partnerships, extending the collaboration network beyond five member countries. By creating strategic alliances with other nations, regional blocs, and international organizations, BRICS can amplify their voice and increase their impact on global security issues. These partnerships can facilitate knowledge exchange, promote wide-scale cooperation in response to crises, and strengthen support for a multipolar security architecture.

Implementing Hybrid Capacity Initiatives

The implementation of hybrid capability initiatives, which combine military, civil, economic, technological and information resources, represents an additional strategy to address security challenges more effectively. This approach allows for a flexible and adaptable response to emerging threats, maximizing the use of the different skills and abilities present within the BRICS. The development of hybrid strategies requires a high level of coordination and cooperation but can offer innovative solutions to protect peace and stability.

Deepening National Resilience Strategies

BRICS can also benefit from deepening national resilience strategies, ensuring that their countries are prepared to face a range of security threats, from natural disasters to armed conflicts, from pandemics to economic crises. National resilience, built through investment in critical infrastructure, economic diversification, emergency preparedness and social cohesion, is critical to mitigate the impact of crises and accelerate recovery.

Development of Early Warning and Conflict Prevention Mechanisms

Establishing early warning and conflict prevention mechanisms is essential to anticipate and mitigate potential threats before they turn into open crises. The BRICS, using their intelligence networks and monitoring capabilities, can develop shared systems for the early identification of risks and the timely activation of preventive measures. These systems, backed by a strong diplomatic commitment, can play a crucial role in maintaining regional and international peace and security.

Recognition and Support for New Security Threats

Finally, the recognition and support of new security threats, such as the challenges posed by artificial intelligence, biotechnology, climate change and data security, require a prospective vision and the adoption of innovative policies. BRICS must remain at the forefront in identifying potential future challenges and developing collaborative strategies to address them, while ensuring that the solutions adopted respect human rights and promote sustainable development.

In conclusion, as the BRICS continue to strengthen and diversify their defense and security cooperation, their ability to implement integrated approaches and shared visions will be critical to address the complexities of the contemporary security landscape. Through a commitment to collaboration, innovation, and collective responsibility, BRICS can play a significant role in promoting a safer, more stable and just global environment. Their success in this endeavor will depend on their ability to navigate geopolitical challenges, to adapt to emerging threats and to promote solutions that respect and enhance the diversity and needs of all peoples.

Encouraging a Culture of Peace and Security

Further development could see the BRICS actively promote a culture of peace and security that transcends military issues and extends to values, education and social practices. This cultural commitment to peace can help mitigate tensions before they escalate into conflicts, promoting mutual understanding and respect between different communities and nations.

Strengthening the Links Between Security and Human Rights

Strengthening the link between security and respect for human rights is essential, since sustainable security can only be achieved in a context that values and protects fundamental rights. BRICS have the opportunity to take the lead in demonstrating how security policies can be implemented in a way that promotes justice, freedom and dignity for all, while addressing national and global security concerns.

Collaboration for Global Economic Stability

Given their growing importance in the world economy, BRICS can play a key role in promoting global economic stability. Through collaboration in international financial institutions and the promotion of inclusive and sustainable economic policies, they can help create a more resilient global economic environment, capable of resisting and recovering from crises.

Exploring New Security Domains

As the security landscape evolves, BRICS can actively explore new security domains, such as outer space security and water security. Cooperation in these unconventional sectors can lead to new understandings and strategies to collectively address future challenges, ensuring that the BRICS remain at the forefront of the global security agenda.

Development of Flexible Cooperation Platforms

Finally, the development of flexible cooperation platforms that allow variable and tailored participation in security projects can offer BRICS and their partners the opportunity to collaborate on specific initiatives based on shared interests. This flexibility can increase the effectiveness of defense and security cooperation, allowing countries to engage more meaningfully based on their capabilities and priorities.

In summary, the future trajectory of BRICS cooperation in the field of defense and security presents itself full of challenges but also significant opportunities. Through an ongoing commitment to innovation, collaboration and respect for the principles of multilateralism and global justice, BRICS can not only strengthen their collective security but also contribute to building a more equitable and peaceful world order.

In conclusion, BRICS cooperation in the field of defense and security represents a fundamental component of their commitment to a more balanced and multipolar world order. This collaboration extends beyond traditional military and strategic concerns, embracing a holistic vision that links security to sustainability, development, human rights, and economic stability.

BRICS, through their innovative and collaborative approach, have the unique opportunity to shape global security dynamics in ways that reflect the diversity of their experiences and perspectives. By focusing on areas such as human security, the management of health emergencies, economic security, the fight against terrorism, environmental security, and the promotion of peace, BRICS can contribute significantly to solving the most pressing global challenges.

The intensification of preventive diplomacy efforts, the expansion of cooperation in the digital domain, the support for innovation for peace, the strengthening of peacebuilding capacities and the deepening of the dialogue on security and development are just some of the ways through which the BRICS can strengthen their cooperation and their impact on the global security landscape. These actions, together with the encouragement of a culture of peace and security, the strengthening of the links between security and human rights, and the exploration of new security domains, outline a promising path for the BRICS.

The creation of flexible cooperation platforms that facilitate variable and tailored participation in security projects, together with the recognition and support for new security threats, highlights the need for an adaptable and proactive approach. This flexibility is crucial to address the wide spectrum of security challenges in a rapidly changing world, allowing BRICS to respond effectively to emerging crises and to promote innovative and inclusive solutions.

The challenge for BRICS in the future will be to maintain a balance between the individual aspirations of the members and the collective objectives of the group, navigating complex geopolitical issues and promoting an open and inclusive dialogue. Their ability to successfully implement the strategies discussed, to adapt to changing global dynamics, and to promote a more stable and just security environment will have a significant impact not only on regional security but also on the global security architecture.

In short, while the BRICS continue to develop and deepen their cooperation in the field of defense and security, their collective vision and shared actions can make vital contributions to building a more secure, resilient and peaceful world, in which security is understood in holistic and inclusive terms, reflecting the interconnected realities of the 21st century.

11. Education and Research: state of higher education and scientific research.

Higher education and scientific research are fundamental pillars for the social and economic development of every nation. They play a crucial role in innovation, in technological progress, and in the formation of a qualified workforce capable of facing contemporary challenges. The BRICS countries (Brazil, Russia, India, China, South Africa) have made significant investments in these sectors, recognizing their strategic value for improving global competitiveness and for sustainable development.

Brazil

Brazil has made significant efforts to expand access to higher education, with initiatives such as the University for All Program (ProUni) and the Unified Selection System (SiSU), which facilitate entry into higher education institutions. However, the country faces challenges related to the quality of education and inequality in access. Scientific research in Brazil is internationally recognized in areas such as agriculture, renewable energy and medicine, but it suffers from unstable funding and a brain drain to countries with greater research opportunities.

Russia

Russia has a robust higher education system, with a strong emphasis on science and technology education. The country has traditionally excelled in fields such as engineering, physical sciences and mathematics. In recent years, it has launched the 5-100 project, aimed at bringing at least five Russian universities to the top 100 in the world. Russia is also a leader in scientific research, especially in the nuclear, space and applied sciences, although it faces the challenge of modernizing its research infrastructure and increasing international collaboration.

India

India has one of the largest higher education systems in the world, with an impressive number of engineering and technology graduates each year. The Indian government is seeking to improve the quality of higher education through the National Initiative for World-Class Universities (Institutions of Eminence) and increasing funding for research. India stands out in sectors such as information technology, pharmaceuticals and space technologies, but it faces challenges related to the quality of education in many institutions and the need for more basic research.

China

China has made extraordinary progress in higher education and scientific research, becoming one of the world leaders in terms of the number of scientific publications and patents. Through initiatives such as Project 985 and Project 211, it has invested significant resources in strengthening its flagship universities. China excels in fields such as artificial intelligence, genetics and renewable energy, and is actively promoting international collaboration in research and attracting foreign talent through programs such as the Thousand Talents Plan.

South Africa

South Africa, the leader of higher education on the African continent, focuses on improving access to higher education for all communities and strengthening research and innovation. It has areas of excellence in research such as HIV/AIDS, climate change and astronomy. The country is also a key member of global science initiatives such as the Square Kilometre Array (SKA). However, South Africa's higher education system faces challenges related to inequality, funding, and the need to improve the connection between higher education and the labor market.

Common Challenges and Opportunities

The BRICS, despite their different trajectories and national contexts, share common challenges in higher education and scientific research, including the need to improve the quality of education, ensure stable funding for research, and promote greater equity and inclusion. At the same time, they represent significant collaborative potential in research and innovation, being able to share knowledge, resources and best practices to address global challenges such as climate change, emerging diseases and food security. Cooperation between BRICS in higher education and research can therefore serve not only to strengthen their national systems but also to contribute significantly to global scientific and technological progress.

As the BRICS commit to strengthening their cooperation in the field of higher education and scientific research, a unique opportunity emerges for these countries to position themselves as leaders in global innovation and sustainable development. Collaboration between these countries can catalyze significant progress in various sectors, while simultaneously addressing inequalities and promoting inclusion in the global research and education landscape.

Synergies in Research to Address Global Challenges

The establishment of joint research networks between universities and research institutes in BRICS countries can accelerate the development of innovative solutions for global challenges such as food security, public health, climate change and energy sustainability. These collaborations can exploit the different skills and resources of each country, while at the same time promoting cultural and academic exchanges that enrich the research environment.

Expanding Access and Equity in Higher Education

A common challenge faced by the BRICS is expanding access to higher education, while ensuring equity and quality. Scholarship and exchange programs, university partnerships, and the use of educational technologies can play a key role in making higher education more accessible to a wide range of populations. In addition, these initiatives can promote the mobility of students and researchers between BRICS countries, enriching the educational experience and stimulating intercultural understanding.

Investments in Research Infrastructure

To support research and innovation, it is essential to invest in cutting-edge research infrastructure. BRICS can collaborate in the development of joint research structures, such as laboratories and data centers, that serve as platforms for large scale collaborative research projects. These investments would not only strengthen the research capacities of the BRICS but would also promote the sharing of resources and expertise, maximizing the impact of the research carried out.

Development of Inclusive Educational and Research Policies

Designing educational and research policies that are inclusive and respect diversity is essential to promote an equitable and productive learning and research environment. BRICS, through dialogue and collaboration, can develop regulatory frameworks that encourage the inclusion of underrepresented groups in higher education and research, ensure gender equity, and promote academic freedom. This approach would not only enrich the academic and research environment but would also help to stimulate innovation.

Valorization of Multilingualism in Research and Education

Recognizing and valuing multilingualism in academic and research settings can enrich the learning process and promote greater participation. BRICS can adopt policies that support the publication of research in different languages, in addition to English, and encourage the development of multilingual educational materials. This would not only facilitate access to education and research for a wider audience but would also promote the respect and enhancement of cultural and linguistic diversity.

Promoting Industry-University Collaboration

Stimulating collaboration between the industrial sector and higher education institutions is crucial to ensure that research and innovation are aligned with market needs and contribute to economic development. BRICS can encourage industry-university partnerships that facilitate knowledge transfer, promote applied innovation, and support the creation of academic start-ups and spin-offs. These synergies between the academic world and the private sector can accelerate the commercialization of innovations and stimulate economic growth.

In summary, the BRICS, through a strategic and focused collaboration in the field of higher education and scientific research, have the opportunity to drive global progress in key areas of sustainable development and technological innovation. By strengthening cooperation and promoting inclusive and equitable policies, they can contribute significantly to building a more connected, resilient and informed global community.

As the BRICS continue to strengthen their cooperation in the field of higher education and scientific research, the creation of innovative ecosystems that connect universities, industry, governments and civil society becomes increasingly important.

These ecosystems can act as catalysts for technology transfer, social innovation, and sustainable economic development, while offering solutions to emerging global challenges.

Focus on Sustainability and Green Solutions

An emerging priority for BRICS collaboration in higher education and research is sustainable development and the search for green solutions. Focusing on research projects that address climate change, the loss of biodiversity, the sustainable management of water resources and the production of clean energy can not only generate innovative technologies but also train a new generation of leaders aware of environmental issues. Collaboration in these essential areas stimulates knowledge sharing between BRICS countries and promotes holistic approaches to environmental challenges.

Strengthening Online Learning Platforms

The expansion of online learning platforms and the adoption of advanced educational technologies represent another significant area of cooperation. The digitalization of education offers the opportunity to overcome geographical and socio-economic barriers, making higher education and continuing training more accessible to a global audience. BRICS can collaborate in the development of open and massive online courses (MOOCs), virtual learning platforms and online laboratories, which can enrich the educational experience and promote lifelong learning.

Intensification of Academic Mobility and Research

Academic and research mobility is essential to stimulate innovation and strengthen international cooperation. By creating joint exchange programs for students and researchers between BRICS countries, it is possible to promote the sharing of ideas, access to different research cultures and exposure to new contexts and challenges. Such programs not only enrich the academic experience but also contribute to building international professional networks that can support future collaboration.

Development of Common Research Standards

To facilitate transnational collaboration in research, the development of common standards for conducting and evaluating scientific research is essential. BRICS can work together to establish ethical guidelines, quality standards, and evaluation protocols that ensure research integrity and excellence. This would not only strengthen mutual trust between researchers but would also promote greater consistency and comparability between research results.

Encouraging Entrepreneurship and Innovation

Finally, encouraging entrepreneurship and innovation through higher education and research is crucial to transform ideas into practical solutions and business opportunities. BRICS can set up business incubators, accelerators, and mentorship programs that connect students, researchers, and entrepreneurs with the industrial sector and venture capital. These initiatives not only promote the commercialization of innovations but also stimulate the creation of jobs and contribute to economic growth.

Through these and other initiatives, BRICS can not only address their national needs in terms of higher education and scientific research but also contribute significantly to the global community. By promoting excellence in research, equitable access to education, and sustainable innovation, BRICS can play a key role in shaping a future in which knowledge and innovation are at the service of global development and the well-being of all.

In the field of higher education and scientific research, the BRICS are trying to address global challenges through innovation and collaboration, underlining their growing role as centers of excellence and engines of technological progress. Their cooperation extends in multiple directions, reflecting the complexity and interconnectedness of contemporary challenges, as well as the diversity of their resources and capabilities.

Support for Interdisciplinary Research

Promoting interdisciplinary research is crucial to address complex issues that extend beyond the traditional boundaries of academic disciplines. BRICS can promote research programs that combine social, natural, engineering and humanities sciences to explore innovative solutions to problems such as poverty, inequalities, climate change and food security. This holistic approach not only broadens understanding of issues but also promotes more effective and sustainable solutions.

Strengthening the Links Between Education and Industry

Strengthening the links between higher education institutions and industry is crucial to ensure that training and research are aligned with labor market needs and development priorities. Through strategic partnerships, internships, apprenticeship programs, and collaborative research initiatives, BRICS can facilitate knowledge and technology transfer, prepare students for the global labor market, and stimulate economic innovation.

Enhancing Cultural Diversity in Research and Education

The enhancement of cultural diversity in higher education institutions and research programs enriches the learning environment, promotes intercultural understanding and stimulates innovative approaches to problem solving. The BRICS, with their rich cultural heritages, have the unique opportunity to pioneer the creation of global campuses that celebrate diversity and prepare students to operate in an interconnected global environment.

Encouraging Open Access and Knowledge Sharing

Open access and knowledge sharing are critical to accelerating scientific progress and ensuring that the benefits of research are widely available. BRICS can promote open access policies for publications and research data, thus facilitating the exchange of scientific and technological information between researchers, policy makers and the public. This approach not only democratizes access to knowledge but also stimulates further innovations and practical applications.

Investments in STEAM Education

Investing in STEAM (Science, Technology, Engineering, Art and Mathematics) education prepares students to face the challenges of the 21st century, combining technical rigor with creativity and critical thinking. BRICS can develop curricula that integrate art and design into STEM fields, promoting holistic education that values both technological innovation and humanistic and social understanding.

Development of Leadership Skills in Research

Finally, developing leadership skills among researchers is essential for leading multidisciplinary teams, managing complex projects, and navigating the global research landscape. BRICS can offer training programs in leadership, research management, and scientific communication, preparing researchers to become leaders in their field and to contribute significantly to global scientific debate and policy.

Through these initiatives, BRICS not only strengthen their higher education and research systems but also contribute to forming a global community of scholars, innovators and leaders capable of facing the challenges of our time with creative and sustainable solutions. The commitment to inclusive education, the promotion of interdisciplinary research, and the enhancement of diversity and international collaboration are essential to achieve these objectives.

Creation of International Centers of Excellence

The creation of international centers of excellence in BRICS countries can serve as catalysts for advanced research and innovation. These centers, specialized in key areas such as emerging technologies, environmental sustainability, and public health, can attract talent from around the world, promoting intercultural and interdisciplinary collaboration. By facilitating access to advanced resources and creating opportunities for exchanges and partnerships, centers of excellence can become global benchmarks in their field.

Promoting Transcontinental Collaboration

As the BRICS strengthen their internal cooperation networks, there is also a significant opportunity to extend this collaboration beyond their borders, establishing transcontinental partnerships with other nations and regional blocs. This approach can enrich scientific and academic dialogue, offering new perspectives and resources. Transcontinental collaboration can also help overcome global disparities in research and education, promoting fairer access to knowledge and opportunities.

Encouraging Social Innovation

Social innovation, which aims to develop sustainable solutions for social, economic and environmental problems, is another area in which the BRICS can make a difference. By encouraging social innovation in universities and research centers, BRICS can help solve critical problems such as inequality, access to education, and sustainable resource management. This requires an approach that values social entrepreneurship, facilitates collaboration between different sectors and promotes inclusive and sustainable business models.

Development of Holistic Assessment Tools

The evaluation of higher education and research requires tools that reflect the complexity and multidimensional impact of these sectors. BRICS can guide the development of assessment systems that consider not only academic productivity but also the social, economic and environmental impact of research and education. These tools can help to reorient academic and research priorities towards sustainable development and inclusivity goals.

Supporting the Formation of Young Researchers' Networks

Finally, supporting the training and consolidation of networks of young researchers in BRICS countries is essential to build the next generation of scientific leaders. These networks can offer platforms for sharing ideas, collaborating on research projects, and access to mentorship and funding opportunities. By promoting the engagement of young talents internationally, BRICS can help to forge a resilient, collaborative and innovative global research community.

The BRICS' continued commitment to higher education and scientific research not only strengthens their national capacities but also contributes to the creation of a more equitable, inclusive and sustainable global knowledge ecosystem. Through cooperation and innovation, BRICS can play a key role in shaping solutions to global challenges, while promoting the development and well-being of their societies and the international community as a whole.

As the BRICS advance in promoting higher education and scientific research, the importance of adapting and responding proactively to the rapid transformations of the global education and innovation landscape becomes increasingly evident. Their ability to anticipate and shape future trends in these fields will be crucial to maintaining the relevance and long-term impact of their joint initiatives.

Adapting to Technological Changes

The ongoing technological revolution offers both challenges and opportunities for higher education and research. BRICS have the opportunity to be pioneers in the adoption and integration of new technologies such as artificial intelligence, big data, and augmented and virtual reality in learning and research processes. By facilitating access to these technologies in their institutions, they can not only improve the effectiveness of education and research but also prepare students and researchers to navigate and contribute to the technologically advanced world of tomorrow.

Emphasis on Flexibility and Lifelong Learning

Higher education is increasingly becoming a continuous process rather than a linear path. Recognizing this trend, BRICS can develop programs that promote educational flexibility and support lifelong learning. This includes offering modular learning paths, transferable academic credits, and professional training and retraining opportunities. These approaches can help ensure that the workforce is able to adapt to the changing needs of the global labor market.

Promotion of South-South and Triangular Cooperation

As the BRICS strengthen their bilateral and domestic cooperation, there is also significant potential to expand South-South and triangular collaboration, involving other developing countries and advanced partners. These forms of cooperation can further enrich the higher education and research landscape, offering new perspectives, resources and knowledge networks.

South-South and triangular cooperation can also facilitate the exchange of lessons learned and good practices adapted to development contexts.

Sustainability as a Guiding Principle

Sustainability should be a guiding principle in BRICS education and research strategies, reflecting the urgent need to address global environmental challenges and to promote equitable and inclusive development. By integrating the principles of sustainability into the curricula, research programs and operations of institutions, BRICS can contribute to the formation of a generation that is aware and committed to building a sustainable future.

Recognition of the Role of Culture and the Arts

Finally, the role of culture and the arts in higher education and research deserves greater recognition. In addition to promoting creativity and innovation, culture and the arts can facilitate intercultural understanding and offer unique approaches to problem solving. BRICS can encourage the integration of cultural and artistic dimensions into their educational and research programs, stressing the value of cultural diversity and creative expression in promoting social and scientific progress.

In short, as the BRICS navigate the complex landscape of higher education and scientific research, their commitment to collaboration, innovation, and inclusivity can serve as a model for tackling global challenges. Through continuous adaptation to emerging trends, the promotion of flexibility and lifelong learning, and an emphasis on sustainability and cultural diversity, BRICS can play a significant role in shaping education and research for an equitable and sustainable future.

As the BRICS move to face and shape the future of higher education and scientific research, the importance of an ongoing commitment to adaptability, innovation and a shared vision is clearly evident. This path to excellence in education and research is not without challenges, but it also offers unprecedented opportunities for joint and individual progress.

Encourage the Integration of New Disciplines

Within the rapidly evolving landscape of higher education and research, BRICS can benefit from integrating new disciplines that reflect social, technological and economic changes. This could include emerging areas such as the ethics of artificial intelligence, bioinformatics, urban sustainability, and climate change studies. By promoting interdisciplinary programs that combine science, technology, engineering, arts, and mathematics (STEAM) with these new disciplines, BRICS can better prepare students for the challenges and opportunities of the future.

Development of Innovative Teaching Methodologies

The adoption and development of innovative teaching methods can significantly improve learning effectiveness and student engagement. This could include problem-based learning, educational games, simulation, and blended learning that combines online and in-person lessons. Through experimentation and the implementation of new teaching methods, BRICS can offer richer and more engaging educational experiences, preparing students to think critically, solve complex problems and adapt to changes.

Enhancing International Collaboration in Research

International collaboration in scientific research is essential to address global issues. BRICS can act as promoters of international research networks, facilitating cooperation between researchers, sharing infrastructure and data, and coordinating efforts to address common challenges such as pandemics, food security and climate change. Through joint research funds, researcher exchange programs, and international conferences, BRICS can strengthen their influence in the global research world and contribute to significant advances in multiple fields.

Promoting Equity and Inclusion in Access to Education

Another critical area of focus is equity and inclusion in access to higher education. BRICS may adopt policies aimed at reducing barriers to education for students from disadvantaged backgrounds, including scholarship programs, additional academic support, and outreach initiatives. By promoting fairer access to education, BRICS will not only contribute to the socio-economic development of their countries but also to the construction of more just and inclusive societies.

Exploring Education as a Global Common Good

Finally, BRICS can explore the concept of education as a global common good, recognizing education and knowledge as shared resources that benefit all of humanity. This approach can encourage international cooperation in the field of higher education and research, promote open knowledge sharing, and support the development of educational policies that take into account the collective needs of humanity, as well as national needs.

As BRICS continue to evolve and adapt to the needs of 21st century higher education and scientific research, their shared commitment to innovation, inclusivity, and global collaboration places them in a unique position to positively influence not only their national development but also global progress and well-being. The key to their success will lie in their ability to maintain an open dialogue, to support excellence and to promote policies that reflect a commitment to a sustainable and inclusive future.

In summary, collaboration between BRICS countries in the field of higher education and scientific research represents a fundamental and constantly evolving dynamic in the global context. This group of emerging nations, through their joint commitment and individual initiatives, has the potential not only to transform their education and research systems but also to contribute significantly to knowledge and innovation worldwide.

The future of higher education and scientific research in the BRICS depends on the ability of these countries to navigate a global environment characterized by rapid technological change, complex socio-economic challenges, and a growing need for sustainability. The adoption of interdisciplinary approaches, the integration of new teaching methods, the enhancement of international collaboration, the support for equity and inclusion, and the conception of education as a global common good are all key elements in realizing this vision.

Addressing these challenges will require a constant commitment to innovation, both in terms of educational content and teaching and research methods. The promotion of open access to knowledge, the encouragement of entrepreneurship and social innovation, and the development of common standards for research will help create a more open, collaborative and productive global education and research ecosystem.

Cooperation between BRICS should also extend beyond academic boundaries, actively involving the private sector, non-governmental organizations and civil society in building innovative partnerships that can transform ideas into concrete solutions for global problems. This holistic approach will not only improve the quality and relevance of higher education and research but will also promote sustainable development and the resilience of societies globally.

In addition, BRICS have the opportunity to guide examples of South-South cooperation and transcontinental collaboration, acting as bridges between different regions of the world and promoting a more balanced and multipolar dialogue on the global education and research scene. Through shared initiatives that reflect diversity and common priorities, BRICS can help reduce the knowledge gap between countries and build a future where innovation and learning are accessible to everyone.

In conclusion, higher education and scientific research in the BRICS are at a turning point, with enormous potential to positively influence not only their national development but also global progress. By maintaining a commitment to innovation, inclusivity, and international collaboration, BRICS can successfully navigate the challenges of the 21st century, helping to shape a world characterized by shared knowledge, sustainable progress, and equally distributed opportunities.

12. Infrastructure and Urban Development: significant infrastructure and urban development projects.

The BRICS countries (Brazil, Russia, India, China and South Africa) have initiated and completed numerous significant infrastructure and urban development projects, reflecting their rapid economic growth and urban expansion. These projects not only aim to improve the quality of life of citizens but also to stimulate economic growth, facilitate trade and promote environmental sustainability. Some of the most significant projects in the BRICS countries are listed below:

Brazil

- **The Porto Maravilha Urban Transport Project in Rio de Janeiro**: An ambitious urban redevelopment project that transformed a large, degraded port area into a vibrant space, with new infrastructure, public spaces, access to the sea and venues for the 2016 Olympics.

- **The Growth Acceleration Program (PAC)**: A multi-year initiative aimed at stimulating investment in key infrastructure such as roads, railways, airports, and water treatment systems across the country.

Russia

- **Crimean Bridge: A** 19-kilometer-long bridge that connects the Crimean Peninsula to mainland Russia through the Kerch Strait. It is the longest bridge in Europe and aims to facilitate transport and trade.

- **Development of the Far East Federal District**: A project that aims to promote the economic development of the Russian Far East, improving transport infrastructure and encouraging investments in key sectors such as energy, natural resources and tourism.

India

- **DMIC (Delhi-Mumbay Industrial Corridor)**: One of India's most ambitious infrastructure projects, it aims to develop a high-tech industrial and urban corridor between the cities of Delhi and Mumbai, encouraging economic growth and sustainable development.

- **Smart Cities Mission**: A revolutionary initiative aimed at developing 100 cities across India as smart cities, with the goal of promoting sustainable and financially inclusive cities that use technology to improve urban quality and the lives of citizens.

China

- **The South-North Water Transfer Project**: One of the largest water projects in the world, designed to transfer water from water-rich regions of southern China to arid northern regions, improving access to drinking water and supporting agricultural and industrial development.

- **Zhongguancun**: Often referred to as China's 'Silicon Valley', this tech district in Beijing is a center of innovation and research, hosting thousands of tech startups, research centers, and universities.

South Africa

- **Gautrain**: A rapid rail system connecting Johannesburg, Pretoria, and O.R. Tambo International Airport, aimed at reducing road traffic, promoting the use of public transport and stimulating regional economic development.

- **Coega Industrial Development Zone (IDZ)**: One of the largest industrial development projects in South Africa, located in the Eastern Cape province, aimed at attracting investments in sectors such as energy, automotive and agribusiness.

These projects highlight the importance that the BRICS attach to the development of modern and sustainable infrastructure as pillars of economic growth and urban development. However, they also face challenges, including the need to balance economic growth with environmental sustainability and social equity. Cooperation between BRICS countries and with other international partners can play a crucial role in overcoming these challenges and in promoting innovative and sustainable development practices at a global level.

While infrastructure and urban development projects in BRICS countries highlight their ambition to modernize and expand their capabilities, it is crucial that these efforts continue to evolve to address the changing needs and challenges of the 21st century. Sustainability, technological innovation, social inclusion and urban resilience emerge as central themes that require constant attention and strategic innovations.

Integrating Environmental Sustainability

The concept of sustainable development is driving a new wave of infrastructure projects that not only aim at efficiency and economic growth but also at minimizing environmental impact. BRICS can take a leading role in implementing green technologies and nature-based solutions in future projects, such as the use of sustainable building materials, the integration of renewable energy systems, and the creation of green urban spaces that enhance biodiversity and provide recreational areas for citizens.

Promoting Social Inclusion and Connectivity

Another critical dimension of infrastructure development concerns the promotion of social inclusion and connectivity. Projects must be designed with particular attention to the needs of underrepresented and marginalized communities, ensuring that all citizens have equal access to services and opportunities. This includes the development of accessible public transport systems, the provision of affordable housing, and the implementation of digital infrastructures that guarantee universal access to information and online services.

Strengthening Urban Resilience

The increase in extreme weather events and environmental challenges requires cities to become more resilient and able to adapt to changes. BRICS must integrate principles of urban resilience into the planning and development of new infrastructure, ensuring that cities can withstand, adapt and recover quickly from adversity. This could involve strengthening critical infrastructure, planning advanced urban drainage systems, and developing emergency and crisis response plans.

Harnessing Emerging Technologies

Emerging technologies offer unprecedented opportunities to make infrastructures more efficient, sustainable and responsive to the needs of citizens. BRICS can explore the use of big data, Internet of Things (IoT), artificial intelligence (AI), and blockchain to improve urban infrastructure management, optimize energy consumption, improve public services, and facilitate citizen participation in urban governance. The adoption of these technologies can lead to smarter and more connected cities, where the quality of life is constantly improved through innovation.

International Collaboration for Financing and Expertise

Finally, large scale projects require not only significant financial investments but also a wide range of technical and management skills. International collaboration between BRICS countries and with other global partners can facilitate the sharing of knowledge, resources and good practices. Through mechanisms such as the BRICS New Development Bank, it is possible to mobilize funding for critical infrastructure projects, while international partnerships can offer the expertise needed to address complex technical and planning challenges.

As the BRICS continue to pursue ambitious infrastructure and urban development projects, the adoption of a holistic and sustainable approach, taking into account the environment, social inclusion, resilience and technological innovation, will be crucial to ensure that development brings lasting benefits for all citizens and contributes to global sustainable development goals.

As the BRICS advance in infrastructure and urban development, it becomes essential to emphasize the ability of these projects to adapt and react not only to current needs but also to future projections of urban and demographic growth. Urban expansion and population density require innovative solutions that can support the environment, promote social cohesion and stimulate the economy, while maintaining the flexibility to evolve as society's needs change.

Enhancing Sustainable Mobility

Sustainable mobility emerges as a fundamental aspect for urban development, addressing growing concerns related to traffic congestion, air pollution and quality of life in metropolitan areas. BRICS can invest in efficient public transport systems, cycle networks, walking paths and shared mobility solutions that reduce dependence on private vehicles and promote a more active and sustainable lifestyle. The integration of intelligent technologies to optimize routes, manage traffic flow and improve the user experience can transform the way people move in cities, making it more efficient and pleasant.

Integrated Approaches to Urban Planning

Integrated urban planning becomes crucial for balancing economic development, environmental sustainability and social well-being. This involves considering factors such as access to green spaces, the availability of public services, the quality of housing and the cohesion of communities in the elaboration of urban plans. BRICS can adopt "compact city" models that promote functional density and diversity, while reducing the need for long-distance travel and preserving surrounding natural resources.

Investing in Climate-Resilient Infrastructure

With climate change posing an increasingly tangible threat, investment in climate resilient infrastructure is essential to protect cities and their populations from extreme weather events and their impacts. This includes the construction of flood barriers, the improvement of urban drainage systems, the design of buildings capable of withstanding severe weather conditions, and the creation of urban areas that can adapt and recover quickly from natural disasters.

Promoting Innovation in Housing Construction

Addressing the challenge of housing in rapidly expanding urban environments requires innovative solutions that can offer quality, accessible and sustainable housing. BRICS can explore the use of environmentally friendly building materials, modular and prefabricated construction techniques, and flexible housing concepts that can adapt to the changing needs of families. The integration of green spaces, rainwater collection systems and renewable energy solutions can further improve the sustainability of urban housing.

Community Involvement and Participatory Governance

Finally, the success of infrastructure and urban development projects depends on the active participation and engagement of local communities. BRICS can encourage an approach to participatory governance that involves citizens in the planning, decision and implementation phases of projects. This not only ensures that developments reflect the needs and priorities of communities, but it also promotes a sense of belonging and collective responsibility for the urban future.

As BRICS move toward building infrastructure and urban developments that are resilient, sustainable, and inclusive, their commitment to innovation, collaboration, and community involvement will be critical. By adopting holistic approaches and anticipating future urban needs, they can act as leaders in creating cities that not only support economic growth but also promote a high quality of life for all their citizens.

As the BRICS continue to develop infrastructure and urban projects that aim at sustainability, resilience and inclusion, the importance of fully integrating advanced technologies and data to optimize urban planning and management emerges. The digitalization of cities and the use of intelligent platforms can radically transform the efficiency of urban services, the management of resources and the quality of life of citizens.

Implementation of Intelligent City Management Systems

The adoption of intelligent city management systems, which exploit artificial intelligence, the Internet of Things (IoT) and the analysis of big data, makes it possible to monitor and manage in real time various aspects of the urban environment, such as traffic, air quality, energy consumption and public services. These systems not only improve operational efficiency but also provide valuable data to support evidence-based decision-making, contributing to more responsive and adaptable urban planning.

Development of Integrated Green Infrastructure

In parallel with technological solutions, the development of green infrastructure plays a crucial role in improving urban sustainability. This includes the creation of urban parks, green roofs, vertical gardens and ecological corridors that not only enrich biodiversity and provide recreational spaces for citizens but also contribute to the mitigation of climate change, the improvement of air quality and the management of rainwater. By integrating these green solutions with smart technologies, BRICS can create urban ecosystems that are both technologically advanced and in harmony with the natural environment.

Promoting Accessibility and Digital Equity

In the era of the smart city, ensuring that all citizens have access to digital technologies becomes essential to avoid the creation of new forms of inequality. BRICS must therefore commit to promoting accessibility and digital equity, ensuring universal access to high-speed internet, developing digital skills through educational programs, and ensuring that digital services are inclusive and accessible to people of all ages and abilities.

Strengthening Collaboration between the Public and Private Sectors

The success of infrastructure and urban development projects often depends on effective collaboration between the public and private sectors. Through public-private partnerships (PPPs), BRICS can harness innovation, efficiency, and private sector capital to complement public sector efforts in implementing complex infrastructure projects. These collaborations can also open up new opportunities to finance and implement advanced and sustainable technological solutions in the urban environment.

Integrating Citizen Participation in Urban Planning

Finally, a key element for creating truly resilient, sustainable and inclusive cities is the active integration of citizen participation in urban planning and decision-making processes. Using digital platforms for civic engagement, BRICS can encourage residents to share ideas, feedback, and preferences, ensuring that urban development reflects the needs and aspirations of the community. This participatory approach not only increases transparency and accountability but also promotes a sense of belonging and care for shared urban space.

Through the adoption of these strategies and the implementation of infrastructure and urban projects that embrace technological innovation, environmental sustainability, social inclusion and citizen participation, BRICS can lead the transformation towards cities of the future that are resilient, livable and prosperous for all their inhabitants.

The continuous evolution of infrastructure and urban development in BRICS countries underlines the importance of adapting to emerging trends and to the evolving needs of urban populations. As these nations move towards achieving smarter, more sustainable and inclusive cities, it becomes crucial to integrate principles of climate resilience, social equity and digital innovation into every phase of project planning and implementation.

Focus on Climate Resilience

The integration of climate resilience into infrastructure and urban development projects is of increasing priority, given the urgency of climate change and its wide-scale impacts. BRICS can take a pioneering role in designing and building infrastructures that are not only resistant to current climate impacts but also adaptable to future changes. This includes the creation of cities capable of absorbing and recovering quickly from extreme events, such as floods, heat waves and droughts, through the flexible design of urban spaces, the conservation and restoration of natural ecosystems and the implementation of nature-based solutions.

Innovation for Social Equity

Social equity must be at the heart of infrastructure and urban development projects, ensuring that the benefits of progress and innovation are shared equally among all segments of society. BRICS have the opportunity to explore and implement urban development models that promote economic accessibility, social mobility, and equity in access to essential services. This can be achieved through inclusive planning that considers the needs of vulnerable and marginalized communities and the adoption of policies that encourage affordable housing, quality education and equitable access to healthcare.

Exploiting Digital Technologies for Urban Innovation

The strategic use of digital technologies can transform the way in which cities are planned, built and managed. BRICS can exploit artificial intelligence, the Internet of Things (IoT), geolocation systems and augmented reality to improve urban infrastructure management, optimize the provision of public services, and increase citizen participation in urban governance. The implementation of open and interoperable urban data platforms can also facilitate innovation and the development of new applications and services that improve the daily lives of citizens.

Promotion of Sustainable Development Practices

Sustainability must be a fundamental consideration in all aspects of urban development. This means not only minimizing the environmental impact of new infrastructure projects but also promoting practices that support long-term economic development and social well-being. BRICS can lead by example by investing in renewable energy, promoting the circular economy, encouraging clean transport and creating urban spaces that promote sustainable lifestyles.

Collaboration and Knowledge Sharing

Finally, collaboration between BRICS countries and the sharing of knowledge and best practices can accelerate progress towards common goals of sustainable and resilient urban development. Through shared forums, networks and platforms, synergies can be explored in areas such as research and innovation, capacity building, financing sustainable projects and mobilizing investments for resilient and low-carbon infrastructure.

As BRICS move towards implementing these strategies, their ability to adapt to the ever-changing needs of urban societies, to integrate sustainable innovation, and to promote an inclusive and participatory approach to urban development, will be crucial in defining the long-term success of their efforts. In this dynamic context, BRICS can not only improve the quality of life in their cities but can also offer models and inspiration for global urban development in the 21st century.

Cooperation between BRICS countries in the field of infrastructure and urban development represents a strategic initiative that reflects a shared understanding of the challenges and opportunities related to rapid urbanization and economic growth. These countries, through their significant projects, demonstrate a commitment to innovation, sustainability, social inclusion and resilience, crucial elements for dealing with the complexities of the 21st century.

Infrastructure and urban development projects in the BRICS encompass a wide range of initiatives, from advanced transportation systems and sustainable resource management to innovative housing solutions and the development of livable public spaces. These projects not only aim to improve the quality of urban life but also to promote growth models that are ecologically responsible and socially equitable. Bridging the gap between immediate development needs and long-term goals of sustainability and climate resilience is critical to ensuring that BRICS cities are places where future generations can thrive.

The adoption of intelligent technologies and data-based systems offers the opportunity to transform urban infrastructures into dynamic systems that can respond in real time to the needs of citizens and environmental challenges. This digitalization of the urban environment, however, requires a strong commitment to ensure accessibility and digital equity, ensuring that the benefits of innovation are shared by all segments of society.

The active participation of the community and the involvement of citizens in planning and decision-making processes are essential to create cities that reflect the needs and aspirations of those who live there. This participatory approach reinforces the sense of belonging and collective responsibility towards shared urban space, while at the same time promoting innovative solutions that emerge from below.

In addition, international collaboration and knowledge sharing between BRICS countries and beyond can accelerate the adoption of sustainable and resilient practices in urban development. Through dialogue and cooperation, these countries can not only address their challenges but also help to define new global standards for sustainable urbanization.

In conclusion, the BRICS countries are uniquely positioned to lead the transformation towards smarter, more sustainable and inclusive cities. Through their ongoing commitment to innovation, equity and cooperation, their infrastructure and urban development projects can serve as models for the world, demonstrating how today's planning and investment can create an urban future that values quality of life, environmental sustainability and social cohesion. The lessons learned and experiences shared from these efforts have the potential not only to shape the future of BRICS cities but also to inspire global solutions to contemporary urban challenges.

13. Energy and Natural Resources: management of natural resources and energy policies

The BRICS countries (Brazil, Russia, India, China, South Africa) represent significant emerging economies with a great influence on the global management of natural resources and on energy policies. Their growing demand for energy and natural resources, combined with their commitment to sustainable development, places them at the center of important discussions and actions concerning energy security, energy efficiency, renewable sources and sustainable resource management.

Brazil

Brazil has abundant natural resources, including significant oil and gas deposits, as well as enormous hydroelectric capacity and potential for wind and solar energy. The country's energy policy has historically focused on hydroelectric power, which accounts for the majority of its energy production. However, in recent years, Brazil has increased investment in renewable sources, such as wind and solar, and has adopted policies to reduce dependence on fossil fuels. The country is also a world leader in the production of biofuels, especially ethanol from sugar cane.

Russia

Russia is an energy superpower, with vast resources of natural gas, oil and coal. Its economy and state budget depend to a large extent on exports of these resources. Despite its dependence on fossil fuels, Russia has begun to explore the potential of renewable energy, although the latter's share of total energy production remains low. Russia also has significant water and forest resources, whose sustainable management is essential for the conservation of the global environment.

India

India faces significant challenges in terms of energy security due to its rapid economic growth and energy demand. It is actively investing in renewable energy sources to diversify its energy mix and reduce its dependence on coal, which currently dominates its energy production. The Indian government has set ambitious goals for solar and wind energy, and is promoting energy efficiency and the adoption of electric vehicles. Managing water resources and reducing air pollution are other key priorities.

China

China is the world's largest energy consumer and the largest emitter of greenhouse gases, with a strong dependence on coal. However, it is also a world leader in investment in renewable energy, with significant developments in solar, wind and hydroelectric energy. China is trying to improve energy efficiency, reduce carbon emissions and promote the energy transition to a more sustainable model. The management of water resources and the fight against desertification and pollution are also crucial for the country.

South Africa

South Africa is heavily dependent on coal for its energy production, but it is trying to diversify its energy mix through investments in renewable energy such as solar and wind. The country faces significant challenges related to energy security and the need to provide access to energy for the entire population. The sustainable management of its abundant mineral resources and the conservation of biodiversity are also important issues on South Africa's political agenda.

Towards a Sustainable Future

BRICS countries play a crucial role in the global management of natural resources and energy policies, facing the challenges of ensuring energy security, promoting sustainable development and mitigating climate change. Through internal cooperation and with the international community, they can share experiences, technologies and best practices to address these challenges. The transition to a cleaner and more sustainable energy future requires innovative policies, strategic investments and a shared commitment to transformative change.

In the area of natural resource management and energy policies, BRICS countries face the common challenge of balancing economic growth with environmental sustainability. This balance is crucial not only for the health of the planet but also for ensuring a sustainable quality of life for future generations. As they continue to explore and implement strategies for sustainable resource management and for the adoption of innovative energy policies, some key approaches emerge as particularly promising.

Expansion of the Circular Economy

A circular economy, in which resources are reused and recycled to the maximum, while minimizing waste, offers a promising model for sustainable resource management. BRICS can promote circular economy practices through incentives for companies that adopt sustainable business models, investments in recycling and reuse infrastructure, and policies that encourage responsible consumption among citizens. This approach not only contributes to environmental protection but can also stimulate innovation and create economic opportunities.

Enhancing Energy Efficiency

Improving energy efficiency is critical to reducing overall energy demand and greenhouse gas emissions. BRICS can adopt stricter standards for energy efficiency in the industrial, residential and transportation sectors, as well as promote technologies that reduce energy consumption. Incentive programs for the adoption of high-efficiency equipment and the renovation of existing buildings to make them more energy efficient are measures that can have a significant impact.

Development of Renewable Energy Sources

The adoption of renewable energy sources is crucial to reduce dependence on fossil fuels and mitigate climate change. BRICS have the potential to become global leaders in renewable energy, given their abundance of solar, wind, water and biomass resources. Investing in research and development to improve the efficiency and reduce the costs of renewable technologies, together with the construction of infrastructures for their integration into national energy systems, are essential steps towards a sustainable energy transition.

Integrated Water Resources Management

The sustainable management of water resources is another critical area, especially for BRICS countries that face challenges related to water scarcity, pollution and the need for irrigation for agriculture. Adopting integrated water resource management practices, which consider the entire water cycle and its link with the ecosystem, can help ensure water security. This includes investments in technologies for wastewater treatment and reuse, water conservation policies, and programs for the sustainable management of agricultural water resources.

International Collaboration for Research and Innovation

International collaboration plays a key role in tackling global challenges related to natural resources and energy. BRICS can strengthen cooperation in research and innovation with other nations and international organizations to share knowledge, technologies and good practices. This collaboration can accelerate the development of sustainable solutions and help overcome technical and economic barriers to the energy transition.

By adopting these and other strategic approaches, BRICS countries can not only successfully navigate the challenges associated with natural resource management and energy policies but also assume a leadership role in promoting sustainable development globally. Their ability to implement effective policies, promote sustainable innovation and foster international cooperation will be critical to realizing long-term visions of prosperity, equity and environmental sustainability.

As the BRICS continue their commitment to the sustainable management of natural resources and the adoption of innovative energy policies, it is essential to consider additional layers of complexity and opportunities that emerge in the current global context. Geopolitical dynamics, technological innovations, and social pressures continue to shape the landscape in which these efforts take place, requiring constant adaptation and responsiveness.

Integrating the Geopolitical Dimension

Natural resources and energy are often at the center of geopolitical issues, with countries competing for access and control. The BRICS, thanks to their growing economic and political influence, have the opportunity to promote a more balanced and collaborative international dialogue on these issues. Through multilateral platforms and energy diplomacy initiatives, they can work to ensure that natural resource management and energy transitions take place in a way that respects the principles of equity, national sovereignty, and international cooperation.

Exploiting Technological Innovations

The advent of new technologies offers extraordinary possibilities to transform the way in which natural resources are managed and energy is produced, distributed and consumed. From carbon capture and storage to distributed generation of renewable energy, from precision agriculture to water desalination, BRICS can invest in research and development of technologies that promote the sustainable use of resources and energy efficiency. The creation of innovation ecosystems involving universities, startups, businesses and governments can accelerate technology transfer and the adoption of sustainable solutions.

Listening to Communities and Promoting Inclusion

Decisions related to natural resource management and energy policies have a direct impact on local communities, especially indigenous and rural communities that are closely dependent on the natural environment. It is crucial that BRICS adopt participatory and inclusive approaches, listening to the voices of communities and ensuring that their rights and well-being are protected. Co-creating solutions with communities can not only lead to fairer and more sustainable results, but it can also enrich decision-making with local knowledge and perspectives.

Promoting Public Knowledge and Awareness

Education and public awareness on the issues of natural resources and energy are essential to support sustainable policies and encourage responsible behavior. BRICS can invest in educational campaigns, school programs and media initiatives that increase awareness of environmental problems, the benefits of renewable energy and the importance of saving energy and conserving resources. Informing and involving citizens can strengthen public support for sustainable initiatives and stimulate the adoption of more sustainable practices at individual and community levels.

Strengthening Climate and Environmental Resilience

Finally, in the context of ongoing climate change and the loss of biodiversity, BRICS must strengthen their efforts to increase their countries' climate and environmental resilience. This involves not only reducing greenhouse gas emissions and protecting natural resources, but also preparing infrastructure and communities for the impacts of climate change. Investing in early warning systems, sustainable soil and water management practices, and ecosystem-based adaptation strategies can help mitigate risks and ensure resilient development.

As the BRICS navigate these complex dynamics, their collective and individual commitment to innovative, just and sustainable solutions in the field of natural resources and energy policies will be crucial to address global challenges and promote long-term sustainable development.

In the context of a world facing unprecedented environmental challenges, BRICS countries are uniquely positioned to play a leadership role in developing natural resource management strategies and energy policies that aim at sustainability, equity, and resilience. As they continue to pursue progress in these areas, adopting a holistic and proactive approach becomes increasingly crucial.

Emphasis on Biodiversity and Resource Conservation

The conservation of biodiversity and the sustainable management of natural resources are essential to maintain vital ecosystems on which not only flora and fauna but also human societies depend. BRICS can intensify efforts to protect natural areas, restore degraded ecosystems, and promote sustainable resource use through policies and practices that take biodiversity into account. The creation of ecological corridors, the protection of endangered species and the promotion of sustainable agriculture and forestry are key measures in this direction.

Innovation in the Water Sector

Water is a fundamental natural resource that requires innovative strategies for its sustainable use, given the increasing pressure due to a growing population, urbanization and climate change. BRICS can be pioneers in the development and implementation of advanced technologies for wastewater treatment, desalination, efficient irrigation, and integrated water resource management. This would not only help ensure water security but would also contribute to the protection of aquatic ecosystems.

Fair Energy Transition

A fair energy transition that shifts the focus from fossil fuels to renewable sources is essential to mitigate climate change and promote sustainability. BRICS must ensure that this transition considers social and economic impacts, while supporting communities and workers who may be negatively affected by the change. The development of policies and programs that promote training, professional retraining and access to new job opportunities in the renewable energy sector is vital for an inclusive and equitable transition.

Valorization of Local Communities in Resource Management

Local communities often have valuable traditional knowledge that can enrich natural resource management and conservation strategies. BRICS can strengthen the involvement of local and indigenous communities in planning and managing resources, recognizing and valuing their stewardship role. Collaboration with these communities not only guarantees more sustainable and respectful approaches but also contributes to the preservation of cultural diversity and knowledge.

International Research and Collaboration

Finally, sustained research and development, together with international collaboration, are essential to address complex challenges related to natural resources and energy. BRICS can promote joint research initiatives and global partnerships to explore new sustainable technologies, innovative management models, and strategies for adaptation to climate change. Sharing knowledge and best practices through these collaborative channels can accelerate progress toward common sustainability and resilience goals.

As BRICS advance in these areas, their leadership and collective commitment can offer valuable visions and practical solutions to global challenges, setting a path to a more sustainable and resilient development that benefits not only their economies and societies but also the entire world. The ability to integrate environmental, social and economic considerations into a holistic framework will be crucial to achieve a future in which natural resources are managed sustainably and energy policies promote equity, security and sustainability for all.

As the BRICS proceed on their path to the sustainable management of natural resources and the adoption of innovative energy policies, it becomes crucial to consider the interconnection between global ecosystems and the world economy. This in-depth understanding can guide the implementation of strategies that not only aim to solve local and national issues but also contribute positively to global resilience and sustainability.

Integrated Sustainability in Global Markets

The integration of sustainability principles into global markets represents a significant step towards achieving a long-term positive impact. BRICS can play a critical role in encouraging fair and sustainable business practices, adopting and promoting high environmental and social standards for exports and imports. This includes promoting trade in goods and services that support the conservation of resources, renewable energy and the reduction of emissions, while stimulating innovation and competitiveness in sustainable industries.

Clean Technologies and Green Tech

The advancement and diffusion of clean technologies play a key role in reducing the ecological footprint of human activity, offering solutions for sustainable energy, efficient resource management and the reduction of pollution. BRICS, through targeted investments in research and development and through incentive policies, can accelerate the adoption of green tech in their economies and globally. The establishment of innovation centers dedicated to clean technologies and international collaboration in research projects can increase the reach and effectiveness of these technologies.

Sustainable Forest Management

Deforestation and forest degradation represent critical challenges to biodiversity, climate and the lives of indigenous communities. BRICS can take a leading role in promoting sustainable forest management that balances the use of forest resources with conservation. This includes implementing sustainable forestry practices, combating illegal timber trade, and promoting reforestation and restoration of degraded forest ecosystems. International cooperation for forest monitoring and for the exchange of best practices can strengthen efforts in this area.

Water Conservation and Water Sustainability

Given the vital importance of water for all aspects of life and development, BRICS must implement comprehensive strategies for water conservation and water sustainability. This may include improving water efficiency in agriculture, industry and housing, protecting water sources from contamination, and developing resilient water infrastructure. Collaboration on cross-border water projects and the sharing of technologies and knowledge in the field of sustainable management of water resources can help to resolve water tensions and promote equitable water management.

Multilateral Partnerships for Global Sustainability

Finally, strengthening multilateral partnerships for global sustainability is essential to effectively address transnational environmental challenges. BRICS can work with other nations, international organizations, the private sector, and civil society to promote shared sustainable development goals, address climate change, protect biodiversity, and ensure global food and water security. The creation of platforms for dialogue and joint action can facilitate cooperation, the exchange of knowledge and the mobilization of resources for sustainable initiatives on a global scale.

As the BRICS advance on these paths, their collective leadership in the field of natural resources and sustainable energy policies can offer replicable models and inspiration for other nations and regions, contributing significantly to global efforts to build a more sustainable and resilient future.

The management of natural resources and the implementation of sustainable energy policies represent complex but fundamental challenges for BRICS countries in the context of their development and the wider global landscape. The path they have undertaken, oriented towards innovation, sustainability and collaboration, reflects a growing recognition of the interdependence between economic growth, social well-being and environmental responsibility. This shared commitment to responsible management of natural resources and the adoption of progressive energy policies can not only guide BRICS towards a greener and more inclusive future, but it can also provide leadership and inspiration to the rest of the world.

In conclusion, the main pillars of this commitment include:

1. **Innovation and Green Technology**: Investments in research and development for clean technologies and innovative solutions for renewable energy and energy efficiency are crucial. This not only stimulates economic growth but also contributes to the reduction of the ecological footprint and the achievement of sustainability objectives.

2. **Sustainable Development and Resource Conservation**: The adoption of circular economy practices, the sustainable management of forests and water resources, and the conservation of biodiversity are essential to maintain ecological balance and ensure that natural resources remain available for future generations.

3. **Social Equity and Access to Energy**: Ensuring universal access to clean and reliable energy sources is critical to improving quality of life and promoting social equity. This requires policies that facilitate the energy

transition and support vulnerable communities during this change.

4. **Multilateral Collaboration**: Cooperation between BRICS and with other nations, international organizations, and stakeholders is vital to effectively address global environmental challenges. Multilateral partnerships can facilitate the exchange of knowledge, the harmonization of standards and the mobilization of financial resources.

5. **Community Participation and Inclusive Governance**: The active involvement of local communities and support for participatory governance practices reinforce the legitimacy and effectiveness of sustainability initiatives. Listening to and integrating local wisdom and traditional knowledge can lead to more resilient and socially accepted solutions.

Through the consistent implementation of these strategies, BRICS can address intrinsic challenges in natural resource management and energy policies, while promoting sustainable development, environmental justice, and shared prosperity. Their success in these areas will not only positively affect the well-being of their citizens but will also help define a new paradigm for economic growth and international cooperation in the 21st century, oriented towards resilience, sustainability and inclusion.

14. Agriculture and Food Security: strategies for sustainable agriculture and food security.

Sustainable agriculture and food security represent crucial challenges for BRICS countries, given their large territories, climate and socio-economic diversity, and the significant role they play in global agriculture. With increasing population pressure, climate change and the depletion of natural resources, BRICS are adopting innovative strategies to ensure sustainable food production and improve food security, balancing the need to produce more food with that of protecting the environment and supporting rural communities.

Promotion of Precision Agriculture

Precision agriculture uses advanced technologies, such as IoT (Internet of Things) sensors, big data analysis, drones and satellite positioning systems, to optimize crop yields and reduce the use of water, fertilizers and pesticides. By implementing these technologies, BRICS can improve the efficiency of agriculture, reduce environmental impact and increase productivity, contributing to food security and sustainability.

Development of Resilient Crop Varieties

The genetic improvement of plants, through traditional and biotechnological methods, can lead to the development of varieties of crops that are more resilient to climate change, diseases and parasites, as well as more efficient in the use of water and nutrients. The BRICS are investing in agricultural research to create these innovative varieties, which can play a crucial role in adapting agriculture to climate change and ensuring stable yields.

Integration of Sustainable Agriculture and Agroecological Practices

The adoption of agroecological and sustainable agriculture practices, which encourage crop diversification, rotation, composting, and the use of natural techniques for pest control, can reduce dependence on chemical inputs and improve soil health. BRICS are promoting these practices among small farmers and rural communities, recognizing their potential to improve food security, protect biodiversity, and support rural livelihoods.

Strengthening Food Value Chains

Strengthening food value chains, from production to consumption, is essential to increase efficiency, reduce food losses and waste, and improve market access for small producers. The BRICS are working to improve agricultural and logistics infrastructure, encourage the adoption of innovative post-harvest and conservation practices, and promote access to fair and transparent markets.

Food and Nutrition Security Support

In addition to increasing food production, BRICS focus on food and nutrition security, ensuring that all citizens have access to sufficient, safe and nutritious food. This includes supporting school feeding programs, initiatives to combat malnutrition and obesity, and policies that promote balanced and sustainable diets.

International Collaboration for Agricultural Innovation

Finally, international collaboration plays a key role in promoting agricultural innovation and food security. BRICS can leverage their experiences and resources by sharing knowledge, technologies and good practices, participating in global agricultural research networks, and supporting multilateral initiatives aimed at improving global food security.

By implementing these strategies, BRICS can not only address their domestic challenges in terms of sustainable agriculture and food security, but they can also contribute significantly to global efforts to ensure that the world's food system becomes more resilient, sustainable and capable of feeding a growing population in an equitable and sustainable way.

While the BRICS pursue sustainable agriculture and food security through the strategies mentioned above, it is essential to extend these efforts by considering additional dimensions and innovative approaches that can address emerging challenges and take advantage of new opportunities.

Valuing Water as a Critical Resource

Water is at the heart of agricultural production and food security. BRICS must continue to innovate in sustainable water management, optimizing water use through precision irrigation techniques and promoting the recycling and reuse of wastewater in agriculture. In addition, adopting agricultural practices that improve water retention in the soil can help mitigate the effects of drought and improve crop resilience.

Promoting Agricultural Diversification

Agricultural diversification not only helps to reduce economic risks for growers, but it can also improve biodiversity, soil health and the resilience of agroecosystems. BRICS can encourage crop diversification, integrated agriculture and agroforestry systems, which offer both environmental and economic benefits. This approach can also help preserve local and traditional varieties, which are important for food security and nutrition.

Investments in Rural Infrastructure and Market Access

Improving small farmers' access to markets is critical to food security and rural income. Investments in rural infrastructure, such as roads, warehouses and markets, together with access to financial services and e-commerce platforms, can facilitate this access. BRICS can also promote short supply chains and local food systems that directly connect producers to consumers, reducing waste and improving the freshness and quality of food.

Policies for the Reduction of Food Waste

Food waste represents a significant challenge to food security and the efficient use of resources. BRICS can adopt policies and initiatives to reduce waste along the entire food value chain, from agriculture to consumption. This includes improving collection and postharvest practices, supporting innovation in food packaging and preservation, and promoting greater consumer awareness of food waste.

Supporting Adaptation and Mitigation of Climate Change in Agriculture

Agriculture is both a victim and a contributor to climate change. BRICS must implement strategies that support the adaptation of agricultural systems to climate change and that promote agricultural practices capable of reducing greenhouse gas emissions. This may include supporting conservation agriculture, sustainable pasture management, agroforestry, and the use of renewable energy in agricultural operations.

Strengthening International Cooperation in Agriculture

Finally, given the global nature of the challenges related to agriculture and food security, the BRICS must seek to strengthen international cooperation. This may include active participation in multilateral platforms, the exchange of knowledge and technologies, supporting developing countries through technical assistance, and the development of equitable trade rules that promote market access for small producers.

Through the implementation of these complex and integrated strategies, BRICS can play a leadership role in promoting sustainable agriculture and improving food security not only within their borders but also globally. By tackling challenges with innovative and collaborative actions, they can contribute significantly to building resilient, sustainable and inclusive food systems for future generations.

As the BRICS continue to navigate and address the challenges of sustainable agriculture and food security, the incorporation of additional innovative approaches and holistic strategies proves essential. The complexity of issues related to food and agriculture in a rapidly changing world requires solutions that not only address immediate needs but that also lay the foundation for long-term resilience and sustainability.

Integration of Agricultural Education and Training

A key element in promoting sustainable agriculture among the BRICS is investment in agricultural education and training. By offering educational programs that cover sustainable agricultural practices, resource management, use of agricultural technologies, and understanding the impacts of climate change on agriculture, we can equip the next generation of farmers with the knowledge and skills necessary to face future challenges. In addition, agricultural education can encourage innovation and stimulate the interest of entrepreneurs in the agricultural sector.

Promotion of Food Sovereignty

In addition to food security, food sovereignty — the right of peoples to define their own sustainable policies and strategies for the production, distribution and consumption of food — emerges as a fundamental principle. BRICS can support food sovereignty by promoting local and regional food systems, supporting family and community agriculture, and ensuring that agricultural and food policies are aligned with the needs and aspirations of local communities. This approach can not only improve access to food but also protect biodiversity and cultural traditions related to nutrition.

Development of Agricultural Insurance and Safety Networks

The introduction of agricultural insurance systems and financial safety nets can offer farmers greater protection against risks related to climate, crop diseases and market fluctuations. These measures can help stabilize farmers' incomes, encouraging them to adopt sustainable farming practices without the fear of financial failure in the event of adverse events. BRICS can work together to develop innovative insurance models that are accessible even to small manufacturers.

Implementing Integrated Support Policies

For a significant impact on sustainable agriculture and food security, an integrated approach is needed that links agricultural policies with environmental, water, energy and rural development policies. BRICS can work to create a cohesive political framework that supports multifunctional agriculture, capable of providing not only food but also ecosystem services, conserving natural resources and contributing to the social and economic development of rural communities.

Strengthening Global Collaboration and Knowledge Sharing

Finally, BRICS can play a leading role in promoting collaboration and knowledge sharing globally to address the challenges of sustainable agriculture and food security. Through international platforms, they can facilitate the exchange of innovations, good practices and lessons learned between countries and regions. In addition, they can support multilateral initiatives that aim to improve the global governance of food and agricultural resources, contributing to a shared commitment to a more sustainable and secure food future for all.

Through the adoption of these complex strategies and their consistent implementation, BRICS can address current and future challenges of sustainable agriculture and food security, positioning themselves as a leader in creating resilient and productive food systems that respect ecological balances and promote social justice. The integrated, multifocal approach necessary to achieve these objectives involves a sustained commitment to innovation, community support, and international cooperation.

Encouraging Sustainable Technologies and Innovation

The adoption of sustainable technologies in agriculture represents a powerful lever for increasing productivity while respecting the environment. Biotechnology, robotics, and digital agriculture can offer solutions to improve resource use efficiency and reduce negative impacts on natural resources. BRICS can promote innovation and research centers dedicated to the development and dissemination of these technologies, while facilitating the access of small farmers to these innovative solutions.

Development of Regenerative Agricultural Practices

Regenerative agricultural practices, which go beyond sustainability to actively improve soil health, increase biodiversity and sequester carbon, can play a crucial role in mitigating climate change and strengthening food security. BRICS can support the transition to regenerative agriculture through incentives, training and technical assistance, thus helping to create food systems that are truly capable of regenerating natural resources rather than exhausting them.

Strengthening the Resilience of Rural Communities

Rural communities, often the most vulnerable to climate and economic shocks, need specific support to increase their resilience. This may include access to flexible financial services, adapted insurance systems, and infrastructure that enhances their ability to withstand and recover from adverse events. By developing social safety nets and early warning systems for natural disasters, BRICS can help protect rural livelihoods and ensure the continuity of food production.

Collaboration for Global Standards in Sustainable Agriculture

Given their economic influence and their role in the global market for agricultural products, BRICS can work together and with other international actors to promote global standards for sustainable agriculture. This may include harmonizing pesticide regulations, animal welfare standards, and certifications for sustainable agricultural practices. Promoting these standards can not only improve food security but also facilitate trade in sustainable agricultural products.

Promoting Fair Access to Markets

Finally, ensuring that small farmers and rural communities have equitable access to markets is critical to their economic sustainability and food security. BRICS can take steps to promote inclusive supply chains, support agricultural cooperatives, and facilitate the access of local and sustainable products to national and international markets. This would not only help to ensure fair prices for producers but also to promote diversity and quality in the food supply for consumers.

Through these initiatives, integrated into a coherent framework of agricultural and food policies, BRICS can effectively address challenges related to sustainable agriculture and food security, while promoting food systems that are resilient, productive and just. Commitment to these complex strategies will prove essential in navigating climate change, supporting economic growth, and ensuring the well-being of future generations.

As the BRICS deepen their commitment to sustainable agriculture and food security, it is crucial to recognize and integrate the emerging dimensions that directly influence these sectors. The global context, characterized by rapid technological, demographic and climate changes, requires a continuous evolution of strategies and policies to remain effective and relevant.

Adapting to Evolving Demographic Dynamics

With the increase in the global population and demographic transformations, such as increasing urbanization, the BRICS must face additional pressures on food and agriculture systems. Planning for a future in which cities will continue to expand requires innovations in urban and peri-urban food production, such as vertical gardening and urban agriculture, to complement traditional rural food sources and ensure food security for urban populations.

Improving Soil Health and Water Management

Soil health and sustainable water management are critical to the long-term resilience and productivity of agriculture. Adopting soil management practices that improve fertility, such as land cover, crop rotation, and conservation agriculture, can help maintain and improve soil health. At the same time, innovative strategies for rainwater collection, efficient irrigation and integrated water resource management are essential to optimize water use in agriculture.

Valorization of Traditional and Local Knowledge

Traditional and local knowledge offers valuable insights into sustainable agriculture, resource conservation, and nutrition. BRICS can recognize and integrate this knowledge into agricultural and food development programs, valuing indigenous and local food systems and promoting agricultural and food diversity. This approach not only safeguards cultural heritage but also contributes to more resilient and sustainable food systems.

Development of Integrated Food Policies

To address the complexity of food systems, integrated policy development is needed that connects agriculture, nutrition, health, the environment, and the economy. BRICS can work to formulate national food policies that simultaneously address objectives of sustainable production, access to food, healthy diets and reduction of environmental impact. These policies can facilitate a transition to food systems capable of supporting not only food security but also public health and environmental sustainability objectives.

Promoting Climate Resilience in Agriculture

Faced with the urgent challenge of climate change, promoting climate resilience in agriculture becomes a top priority. BRICS can take steps to reduce the vulnerability of agricultural systems to climate extremes, supporting research on climate-resilient crops, adaptive agricultural practices, and forecasting and early warning systems for agricultural risks. This not only helps protect farmers' livelihoods but also ensures the continuity of food production in the face of climate change.

Strengthening International Cooperation Networks

Finally, international cooperation remains crucial to address the global challenges of sustainable agriculture and food security. BRICS can strengthen cooperation networks with other nations, international organizations and sectors of civil society to exchange knowledge, share good practices, and mobilize resources for research and innovation. A shared commitment to common goals can accelerate progress toward more sustainable and resilient food systems globally.

Through continued commitment to these strategies and the adoption of a holistic and adaptive approach, BRICS can effectively navigate the complexities of modern agriculture and food security, setting examples for sustainable practices and resilience that can be emulated globally.

By further deepening strategies for sustainable agriculture and food security in BRICS countries, it is crucial to explore the synergies between environmental conservation and agricultural practices. The ability to align food production objectives with those of conservation can offer innovative solutions for contemporary challenges, while ensuring the resilience of agricultural landscapes and the sustainability of resources.

Integrating Conservation Practices into Agriculture

Adopting agricultural practices that incorporate environmental conservation elements, such as buffer belts, water and soil conservation, and the maintenance of wildlife habitats, can significantly improve biodiversity and ecosystem health. BRICS can promote agricultural approaches that balance food production with conservation, such as agroecology and organic agriculture, that use natural methods for pest control and soil fertility, while reducing the impact on the environment.

Improving Access to Diverse Genetic Resources

The diversity of genetic resources in crops and livestock is critical for food security and adaptability to changing environments. BRICS can encourage the conservation and sustainable use of agricultural genetic resources, supporting germplasm banks, genetic improvement programs, and the in situ conservation of local and traditional varieties. This not only safeguards agricultural biodiversity but also provides farmers with resilient options in the face of environmental and climate stresses.

Strengthening Local and Regional Food Systems

Promoting community-based food systems, which directly connect producers and consumers, can improve the resilience of local communities and reduce dependence on long and complex supply chains. BRICS can support local agricultural markets, producer cooperatives, and distribution systems that favor the consumption of local and seasonal products, while strengthening local economies and reducing the carbon footprint of the food system.

Promoting Integrated Pest Management (IPM)

IPM is an ecological approach to pest management that combines different agronomic, biological, and chemical practices to control pests in a sustainable manner. BRICS can promote the spread of IPM among farmers through training, technical support and incentives, reducing dependence on synthetic pesticides and improving the health of agricultural ecosystems.

Supporting Innovation and Collaboration in Agriculture

Fostering an environment favorable to innovation in agriculture through investments in research and development, collaborations between academic institutions, the private sector and farmers, can accelerate the adoption of sustainable practices. BRICS can facilitate platforms for knowledge sharing, the development of adaptive technologies and the creation of partnerships that promote innovative, environmentally friendly and economically viable agricultural solutions.

Continuous Monitoring and Evaluation

Finally, to ensure that agricultural policies and practices achieve their sustainability and food security objectives, it is essential to implement robust monitoring and evaluation systems. BRICS can adopt sustainability indicators, collect and analyze data on agricultural and environmental performance, and adjust policies based on results, thus ensuring that interventions are effective and that they contribute to the continuous improvement of food and agricultural systems.

Through these continuous and integrated actions, BRICS can play a crucial role in promoting agriculture that is not only productive but also environmentally friendly, contributing significantly to global efforts to create food systems that are resilient, sustainable and capable of supporting a growing world population in harmony with nature.

Deepening strategies for sustainable agriculture and food security in BRICS countries requires a careful examination of new technologies and innovations, together with a commitment to strengthening the climate and environmental resilience of agricultural practices. The continuous evolution of climate conditions and global markets, together with the need to preserve biodiversity and natural resources, underlines the importance of a dynamic and flexible approach that can adapt to rapidly changing scenarios.

Implementing Digitalization in Agriculture

The digitalization of agriculture, through the use of cloud-based platforms, artificial intelligence, and big data, can offer producers advanced tools for crop management, resource optimization and production forecasting. BRICS can stimulate the adoption of these technologies by facilitating access to data and digital infrastructure, and promoting digital training for farmers, especially in rural communities where access to technology may be limited.

Development of Circular Agrifood Systems

Adopting circular economy principles in agri-food systems can minimize waste and improve resource efficiency. This includes the recovery of organic waste for the production of compost or bioenergy, the use of agricultural by-products as resources for new production processes, and integrated aquaculture systems. BRICS can promote policies and incentives that favor the creation of these circular systems, helping to create a more sustainable agriculture with a low environmental impact.

Strengthening Capabilities for Managing Agricultural Risks

Climate change increases uncertainty and risks for agriculture. BRICS can invest in strengthening the capacity of agricultural producers to manage these risks, through training on resilient agricultural techniques, the development of accessible agricultural insurance systems and the promotion of solidarity networks between farmers that can offer mutual support in the event of adverse events.

Integration of Water Conservation Strategies

Given the increasing pressure on water resources, the integration of effective strategies for water conservation in agriculture becomes essential. This may include the adoption of drip and precision irrigation systems, rainwater collection and reuse practices, and the implementation of drought-resistant crops. Promoting the sustainable use of water helps not only to ensure the availability of water resources for future generations but also to protect aquatic ecosystems.

Promoting Agrobiodiversity

The genetic diversity of cultivated plants and animals raised offers a wide spectrum of benefits, from resilience to diseases to the ability to adapt to different environments and climatic conditions. BRICS can take steps to conserve and sustainably use agrobiodiversity, supporting research and development of local varieties and breeds, and promoting agricultural systems that enhance biological diversity.

Collaborations for Research and Sustainable Development

Finally, tackling the complex challenges of sustainable agriculture and food security requires a collaborative approach that combines scientific research, technological innovation and traditional knowledge. BRICS can play a fundamental role in promoting international collaborations for research and development in agriculture, facilitating the exchange of knowledge and good practices, and supporting open innovation platforms that encourage cooperation between research institutes, universities, industry and agricultural communities.

Through these initiatives and their constant implementation, BRICS can not only address their internal challenges in terms of sustainable agriculture and food security but also contribute significantly to global efforts to build food systems that are resilient, productive, sustainable and just, ensuring the well-being of current and future generations in harmony with the planet.

As BRICS become more committed to promoting sustainable agriculture and improving food security, it becomes imperative to further explore and integrate innovative strategies that take into account evolving global dynamics, environmental pressures, and socio-economic needs. The approach must be continuously adapted and enriched to ensure that the proposed solutions are resilient, inclusive and capable of facing emerging challenges.

Enhancing Synergies between Agriculture and Ecosystems

A greater emphasis on creating and strengthening synergies between agricultural practices and ecosystem conservation can lead to more robust and sustainable food systems. BRICS can promote the integration of agriculture with the conservation of natural habitats through practices such as biological corridors and agroforestry, which not only help maintain biodiversity, but also improve soil health and crop resilience.

Supporting the Transition to Sustainable Diets

Addressing consumption and eating habits is essential to achieve sustainable food systems. BRICS can play a key role in promoting diets that are not only nutritionally adequate but also have a low environmental impact, through public awareness campaigns, support for local and sustainable food production and encouragement of responsible consumption practices. This also involves the recognition and enhancement of traditional and local diets, which are often inherently sustainable and nutritious.

Investments in Green Infrastructure and Water Technology

Green infrastructure, such as rainwater collection systems and efficient irrigation technologies, can significantly improve the sustainable management of water resources in agriculture. Investing in these technologies not only helps to reduce pressure on water resources but also contributes to the resilience of agricultural communities to the impacts of climate change. BRICS can foster the development and adoption of these innovative solutions through policies, financial incentives and training programs.

Expanding Research on Adaptation to Climate Change

Research on the adaptation of agriculture to climate change is vital to anticipate and mitigate negative impacts on food production. BRICS can support research initiatives that explore resilient agricultural practices, adaptable crop varieties, and advanced weather forecasting systems. Promoting transnational collaboration in this field can accelerate the development and deployment of adaptive solutions.

Encouraging Financial Inclusion and Market Access

Access to financial services is crucial for farmers, especially for small producers and rural communities. BRICS can work to improve financial inclusion through access to low-cost credit, agricultural insurance, and investments in infrastructure that directly connect farmers to markets. Facilitating access to these services not only improves farmers' economic security but also stimulates the adoption of sustainable agricultural practices.

Promote the Global Sharing of Knowledge and Innovations

In an interconnected world, the sharing of knowledge and innovation between BRICS and beyond can facilitate the rapid deployment of sustainable agricultural practices and food security solutions. Creating knowledge exchange platforms, innovation networks and research partnerships can help overcome technical barriers and accelerate progress towards common agricultural and food sustainability goals.

Through a constant and collective commitment to these advanced strategies, BRICS can not only address the immediate challenges related to sustainable agriculture and food security but also lead the transformation towards global food systems that are resilient, equitable and in harmony with our planet. This proactive and collaborative approach is critical to ensuring the long-term sustainability of food production and the health of the ecosystems on which we all depend.

In the context of BRICS' continued commitment to sustainable agriculture and food security, it is crucial to explore additional areas of innovation and collaboration that can help strengthen the resilience of food and agriculture systems. Adapting to a rapidly changing environment, characterized by complex challenges such as climate change, loss of biodiversity and socio-economic inequalities, requires dynamic and multifunctional solutions.

Valorization of the Blue Economy

The blue economy, which sustainably exploits marine and aquatic resources to contribute to economic growth, food security and environmental health, represents an area of potential interest for the BRICS. Investing in research and development of sustainable fishing practices, aquaculture and marine biotechnology can not only help diversify food sources but also protect vital aquatic ecosystems.

Promotion of Agroecology and Organic Food Systems

Agroecology, which applies ecological and social principles to the design and management of agricultural and food systems, offers a holistic approach to achieving sustainability. BRICS can promote agroecological practices and organic food systems that encourage biological diversity, resource recycling, ecological balance, and support for local economies. Not only do these systems have the potential to improve soil health and crop resilience, they can also contribute to food sovereignty and the well-being of rural communities.

Integrating Animal Health and Sustainable Phytoprotection

Animal health and plant protection play crucial roles in sustainable food production, affecting both productivity and food security. Adopting a "One Health" approach that connects human, animal and environmental health can help BRICS better manage zoonotic disease risks and improve pest and disease management practices in an ecologically sustainable way.

Development of Policies to Support Rural Welfare

Recognizing that agricultural sustainability is intrinsically linked to the well-being of rural communities, BRICS can develop policies that support access to education, health and social services in rural areas. Improving the quality of rural life not only helps to support agricultural economies but can also help prevent the abandonment of agricultural land and the loss of traditional knowledge.

Facilitating Access to Green Finance and Clean Technologies

To accelerate the transition to sustainable agricultural practices, it is essential to facilitate access to green finance and clean technologies. BRICS can work together with international financial institutions and private investors to create dedicated funds that support the adoption of innovative technologies and agricultural practices that reduce environmental impact and improve climate resilience.

Strengthening Transnational Cooperation in Agricultural Research

Finally, transnational cooperation in agricultural research can play a key role in finding solutions to global challenges. BRICS can support collaborative research platforms that bring together scientists, farmers, and other stakeholders to develop new crop varieties, resilient agricultural practices, and innovative technologies. This cooperation can facilitate knowledge exchange and accelerate innovation in sustainable agriculture and food security.

Through these extended initiatives, BRICS can continue to expand their impact and leadership in developing agriculture that not only meets immediate food needs but is also resilient, just and sustainable for future generations. The adoption of a holistic and adaptable approach, which values innovation, collaboration and respect for the environment, is essential to face the complex and interconnected challenges of our time.

In conclusion, the BRICS approach to sustainable agriculture and food security reflects a holistic understanding of the complex interdependencies between food production, environmental health, social equity, and economic resilience. Through the integration of technological innovations, agroecological practices, policies to support rural well-being, and resource conservation strategies, the BRICS are seeking to address the immediate and long-term challenges associated with agriculture and food security in a rapidly changing world.

The adoption of precision agriculture techniques and the digitalization of agriculture offer opportunities to improve efficiency and reduce environmental impacts. At the same time, the enhancement of traditional knowledge and agroecological practices reinforces biodiversity and soil health, contributing to the resilience of rural communities. Policies to support rural well-being and improved access to financial, educational and health services in rural areas are essential to support a transition to sustainable agricultural practices and to ensure that the benefits of this transition are equally distributed.

The promotion of local and regional food systems, together with the reduction of food waste and support for sustainable diets, aims to create a food system that is more resilient and less dependent on long and complex supply chains. In addition, the focus on sustainable water management and the development of resilient crop varieties highlights the need to prepare and adapt to the impacts of climate change.

The integration of water conservation strategies, the enhancement of agrobiodiversity and the development of policies to support rural well-being indicate a commitment to a more inclusive and sustainable approach to agriculture. In addition, the strengthening of transnational cooperation in agricultural research underlines the recognition that global challenges require shared solutions and international collaboration.

Through these integrated strategies and their ongoing commitment to innovation and collaboration, BRICS can not only navigate the challenges of sustainable agriculture and food security but can also provide leadership and inspiration for global efforts to build food systems that are resilient, productive, just and sustainable. The key to success in these initiatives will be the ability to remain adaptable, responsive and proactive in the face of rapidly changing global scenarios, ensuring that policies and practices not only address current needs but are also resilient and sustainable for future generations.

15. Domestic Policy and Challenges: discussion on domestic political challenges and reforms in each country.

The internal political challenges and reforms in each BRICS country (Brazil, Russia, India, China and South Africa) reflect both the unique contexts and the common issues faced by these emerging nations. Each member state is faced with complex internal dynamics, which influence national policies and the ability to respond effectively to the needs of their citizens. Let's review the key challenges and reforms in each country:

Brazil

Brazil's domestic political challenges include corruption, economic and social disparities, and environmental issues. The country has faced several corruption scandals involving high-level politicians and businesses, undermining public trust in institutions. Anti-corruption reforms and the strengthening of democratic institutions have been at the center of the political agenda. In addition, Brazil faces the challenge of balancing economic development with the protection of the Amazon, an issue that has attracted international attention and raised debates about sovereignty and environmental policy.

Russia

Russia is confronted with issues of governance, freedom of expression and strained international relations. Challenges include the centralization of power, restrictions on the press and civil society, and the management of geopolitical tensions, especially in relation to Ukraine and Syria. Internal reforms have often aimed at strengthening economic and political stability, but critiques concern the need for greater transparency and democracy. Energy policy remains a key pillar, given the dependence of many European countries on Russian gas.

India

India faces challenges related to cultural and religious diversity, social tensions, economic growth and environmental sustainability. Economic reforms aimed at stimulating growth, such as the 'Make in India' initiative, coexist with the need to address poverty and inequalities. The tension between the Hindu majority and religious minorities, issues of access to education and health, and the management of natural resources represent additional challenges. Policies aimed at improving digital infrastructure and promoting technological innovation have shown significant progress.

China

China is faced with the challenge of maintaining political and social stability while pursuing economic modernization and international openness. Issues include managing rapid urbanization, environmental sustainability, human rights and civil liberties, and managing autonomist aspirations in areas such as Hong Kong and Tibet. Economic reforms continue to promote growth, but tensions between state control and the free market, and between cultural preservation and innovation, present complex challenges.

South Africa

South Africa faces challenges related to economic inequality, unemployment, corruption and the legacy of apartheid. Despite having one of the most progressive constitutions in the world, the country fights to ensure equality and opportunity for all its citizens. The reforms are focused on improving access to education, healthcare, decent work and land, seeking to address deep social and economic inequalities. Combating corruption and improving governance remain key priorities.

In conclusion, while the BRICS continue to emerge as key players on the global stage, their domestic political challenges and reforms reflect the complexity of navigating modernization, globalization and maintaining the balance between development and sustainability. These challenges are not isolated and require integrated solutions that take into account the specific social, economic and environmental contexts of each country.

Common Priorities and Unique Differences

Despite different challenges, BRICS countries share common priorities, such as the need for reforms to improve governance, combat corruption, stimulate economic growth and address social inequalities. At the same time, their reform strategies reflect the unique differences in their political, economic, and social contexts. For example, while Brazil and South Africa may focus more on issues of social and racial inequality, Russia and China may emphasize political stability and international relations, and India on managing its cultural and religious diversity and on the challenges of urbanization.

Reform and Development Strategies

The reform strategies adopted by the BRICS include strengthening democratic and legal institutions, promoting inclusive economic policies, improving access to basic public services such as education and health, and adopting sustainable environmental policies. In addition, the need for reforms in the energy sector, to balance economic growth needs with environmental protection, is a shared concern, although the specific approach may vary depending on each country's resources and priorities.

Challenges in Implementing Reforms

The implementation of complex reforms is often hampered by political, economic and social obstacles, including resistance from established interest groups, challenges in securing adequate funding, and difficulties in implementing large scale changes in complex and diversified societies. In addition, geopolitical tensions and international relations may influence the BRICS countries' ability to carry out internal reforms, requiring careful navigation of global dynamics.

BRICS Collaboration to Address Common Challenges

Collaboration between BRICS countries, through platforms such as the annual BRICS summit and various sectoral cooperation mechanisms, offers opportunities to share experiences, coordinate responses to common challenges, and support mutual reform efforts. This collaboration can be especially valuable in addressing transnational issues such as climate change, food security, and global economic governance.

Towards a Sustainable and Inclusive Future

In conclusion, internal political challenges and reforms in BRICS countries are intrinsically linked to their development paths and their role in the world system. Effectively tackling these challenges requires an ongoing commitment to reform, international cooperation, and the adoption of approaches that balance growth, equity and sustainability. As the BRICS continue to navigate these complex territories, their experiences offer important lessons on the dynamics of political and economic change in an interconnected and rapidly evolving world.

As the BRICS face their domestic political challenges and pursue crucial reforms, the importance of adapting and responding not only to global changes but also to evolving domestic needs becomes increasingly evident. The internal political dynamics of each country, influenced by economic, social and environmental factors, require careful management and flexible strategies to ensure stability, growth and sustainable progress.

Adapting to Demographic Changes

Demographic changes present both challenges and opportunities for BRICS countries. The aging of the population in some regions, the increase of youth in others, and internal and external migration require flexible policies that can direct education, employment, health and social security in ways that are both reactive and proactive. Adapting policies to meet the needs of a changing population is essential to maintain social cohesion and promote inclusive economic development.

Resource Management and Environmental Sustainability

The sustainable management of natural resources remains a crucial challenge, with increasing pressure on water, energy and mineral resources. The transition to greener and more sustainable economies requires reforms that encourage ecological practices in industry, agriculture and cities. Policies aimed at promoting energy efficiency, renewable energy and the conservation of water and forest resources are essential to ensure a sustainable future.

Strengthening Democratic Institutions and Governance

Effective governance and strong democratic institutions are essential for carrying out reforms and for tackling domestic political challenges. The BRICS are faced with the challenge of strengthening transparency, fighting corruption and ensuring public participation in decision-making processes. Reforms that aim to improve accountability, strengthen the rule of law and protect civil rights are essential to building more just and equitable societies.

Social and Economic Inclusion

Addressing social and economic inequalities is an imperative for BRICS, requiring policies that promote inclusion and equal opportunities. This includes access to quality education, accessible health services, economic opportunities, and the protection of the rights of vulnerable and marginalized groups. Reforms aimed at reducing disparities and promoting greater social equity can contribute significantly to improving social cohesion and political stability.

International Collaboration and Response to Global Crises

BRICS must also navigate the context of complex international relations and global crises, including conflicts, climate change, and pandemics. Collaboration and multilateral diplomacy are crucial to address these challenges. Actively participating in international forums, promoting shared solutions to global problems, and working for more inclusive and equitable global governance can strengthen the role of the BRICS as a leader in world issues.

Continuing on this trajectory, BRICS can not only overcome their domestic political challenges but also contribute significantly to the solution of global issues, promoting peace, sustainability and equitable development. The ability to balance national interests with global responsibilities, adapting domestic policies to reflect both local needs and global changes, will be decisive in shaping the future of these countries and of the international system as a whole.

As the BRICS face complex domestic political challenges and undertake significant reforms, the evolution of the global technological landscape and the urgent need to address issues of digital security and innovation add to an already large list of priorities. The digitalization of the economy and society offers enormous opportunities but also presents unique challenges that require careful and targeted policy responses.

Digital Security and Data Sovereignty

With the increase in digitalization, data security and privacy protection become primary concerns. BRICS must address challenges related to cybersecurity, cybercrime and data sovereignty through reforms that promote the protection of personal data and the security of critical infrastructure. The development of national data protection regulations, together with international cooperation to combat cybercrime, is essential for building a secure digital environment.

Promoting Digital Inclusion

Equitable access to digital technologies is crucial to ensure that all citizens can benefit from digitalization. BRICS must address the digital divide through policies that promote digital inclusion, improve Internet access in rural and disadvantaged areas, and provide training on digital skills. Investing in digital infrastructure and educational technologies can help ensure that the digital transition is inclusive and equitable.

Sustainable Development and Green Technologies

The global climate crisis requires an acceleration in the transition to clean energy and sustainable technologies. BRICS have the opportunity to lead through the adoption and promotion of green technologies in sectors such as energy, transport and agriculture. Reforms that encourage sustainable innovation, through research funding, tax breaks for clean technologies and regulations favorable to renewable energy, can stimulate economic growth while reducing the environmental footprint.

Education and Innovation

To remain competitive in the global knowledge-based economy, BRICS must invest in education and innovation. This includes strengthening education systems to promote scientific research and technological innovation, as well as supporting startups and businesses that work on innovative solutions. Creating an innovation-friendly ecosystem, connecting universities, industry, and government, can accelerate technological development and support long-term economic growth.

Social Equity and Work

Digital and technological transformation brings with it changes in the labor market, with the potential creation of new opportunities and unemployment in traditional sectors. Reforms that address professional reconversion, adult education, and support for workers affected by the digital transition are vital to ensure that no one is left behind. Implementing policies for decent work, social protection and lifelong learning opportunities is critical to building resilient and inclusive societies.

Through a continuous commitment to targeted reforms and strengthened international collaboration, BRICS can successfully navigate the complex challenges of the 21st century, promoting internal stability, stimulating sustainable economic growth and contributing to global governance. The ability to adapt quickly to change, to innovate responsibly and to ensure that the benefits of progress are widely shared will be crucial in defining the future role of the BRICS on the world stage.

As BRICS continue to explore and adapt to changing global dynamics, their domestic policies and the challenges faced require constant attention to issues of social justice, economic equity, and environmental resilience. The reforms undertaken in these countries must not only respond to the immediate needs of their populations but must also foresee the future implications of rapid technological development, demographic changes and environmental pressures.

Improving Quality of Life

A continuous focus on improving the quality of life for all citizens remains at the core of BRICS internal policies. This requires inclusive policies that address income inequalities, guarantee universal access to quality education and health services, and provide adequate housing and social infrastructure. Implementing sustainable urban development programs and affordable housing initiatives can significantly contribute to reducing social disparities.

Responding to Climate Change

The impact of climate change represents a cross-cutting challenge that requires decisive actions at the national level and international cooperation. The BRICS are addressing the need to integrate climate change adaptation and mitigation into their development policies, promoting energy efficiency, the development of renewable energy and the sustainable management of natural resources. The adoption of circular economies, which reduce waste and promote reuse and recycling, can also play a fundamental role in reducing the ecological footprint.

Labor Market Reforms

As the labor landscape evolves due to automation, digitalization, and global economic changes, BRICS must reform labor markets to ensure that they are resilient, flexible, and inclusive. This includes promoting education and vocational training, adjusting social protection policies for self-employed workers and those in non-traditional sectors, and supporting entrepreneurship and innovation as engines of job creation.

Food Security and Sustainable Agriculture

Ensuring food security remains a priority, with BRICS adopting strategies to promote sustainable agriculture capable of meeting the challenges of climate change and growing demand for food. This includes supporting agricultural research to develop resilient crops, investing in sustainable agricultural technologies, and promoting agricultural practices that preserve biodiversity and improve soil health.

Building Resilient and Inclusive Societies

Finally, building resilient and inclusive societies that can face present and future challenges requires a continuous commitment to good governance, civic participation and respect for human rights. BRICS must work to ensure that political and economic reforms are designed and implemented in ways that promote equity, protect vulnerable groups, and encourage broad and meaningful citizen participation in decision-making processes.

As the BRICS navigate these complex challenges, their ability to implement effective reforms, to adapt to new global realities, and to cooperate with each other and with the wider international community will be crucial in determining their success in promoting sustainable development, political stability and economic well-being both nationally and globally. This commitment will require a long-term vision, a holistic approach to public policies, and a willingness to face and adapt to changes with flexibility and resilience.

In concluding this examination of the internal political challenges and reforms in the BRICS countries, it becomes clear that, despite significant differences in their specific contexts, there is a sharing of common challenges and a unique opportunity to collaborate in the search for sustainable solutions. These countries, representing a substantial portion of the world's population and the global economy, have the potential to profoundly influence the course of global development.

The commitment to inclusive and sustainable reforms requires responsible and transparent governance, focused on promoting social justice, economic equity, and environmental conservation. Achieving these objectives involves addressing existing inequalities, ensuring broad participation in political and economic life, and adopting policies that promote innovation and sustainable growth.

The promotion of an open and constructive dialogue between governments, the private sector, civil society and the international community is essential to formulate effective strategies that respond to immediate and future needs. Cooperation between BRICS, through exchanges of knowledge, experience and good practices, can strengthen the collective capacity to navigate the challenges of the 21st century, while promoting peace, prosperity and sustainability at the global level.

Ultimately, domestic political challenges and reforms in BRICS countries are not only issues of national interest but are closely connected to global dynamics and influence the world's ability to achieve sustainable development goals. As the BRICS continue to evolve and adapt to a rapidly changing international environment, their success in overcoming these internal challenges and in contributing positively to global governance will be decisive in shaping an equitable and sustainable future for all.

16. Health and Wellbeing: state of health systems and welfare initiatives in the BRICS.

Health systems and welfare initiatives in BRICS countries (Brazil, Russia, India, China and South Africa) reflect a variety of approaches and challenges due to the different socioeconomic, demographic and political realities of these countries. Although each of these countries strives to improve access to health services and to raise the general level of well-being of the population, they face different challenges in achieving equity, efficiency and quality in their health systems.

Brazil

Brazil stands out for its Unified Health System (SUS), which guarantees universal access to health services to all citizens. This public system finances a wide range of services, from primary care to highly complex procedures. Despite wide access, the system faces challenges related to insufficient funding, regional disparities in the quality and availability of services, and pressure on health services due to factors such as communicable diseases, chronic diseases and recent public health problems, such as the COVID-19 pandemic.

Russia

The Russian healthcare system combines elements of public and private funding, with the government guaranteeing free access to a wide range of health services through the compulsory health insurance program. However, the system is faced with challenges such as the disparity in access to high-quality services between urban and rural areas, the overload of health infrastructure, and the need to improve health outcomes, including the fight against non-communicable diseases and the increase in life expectancy.

India

India faces significant challenges in its healthcare sector, including a marked disparity in access to health services between urban and rural areas, insufficient funding for public health, and reliance on expensive private health services that can lead to financial difficulties for families. In response, India launched Ayushman Bharat, an ambitious initiative to provide universal health coverage and improve primary care services, with the goal of making health services more accessible and equitable for all Indians.

China

China has made significant progress in expanding access to health services and improving public health through reforms such as the Universal Health Insurance System. These reforms have led to a significant increase in insurance coverage and an improvement in basic health services. However, the country continues to face challenges such as inequalities in access to high-quality health services, the aging of the population and the increase in chronic diseases.

South Africa

South Africa is striving to overcome the profound inequalities in its healthcare system inherited from the apartheid era, with significant differences in access to and quality of health services between population groups and geographical areas. The government is working on the creation of a National Health System (NHI) to ensure that all South Africans have access to free and quality healthcare services. Challenges include funding, managing human resources in the healthcare sector, and the burden of diseases such as HIV/AIDS and tuberculosis.

Wellness Initiatives

In addition to health system reforms, BRICS countries are also implementing initiatives to promote healthy lifestyles and prevent diseases. This includes health education programs, vaccination campaigns, public fitness initiatives, and policies to address the social determinants of health. Attention to mental health and psychological well-being is also gaining recognition as an essential component of general well-being.

In conclusion, as the BRICS continue to work to improve their health systems and promote well-being, the sharing of experiences and best practices among these countries can offer valuable lessons on how to address common challenges and take advantage of opportunities to move towards fairer, more effective and sustainable health systems.

As the BRICS advance in addressing challenges related to health and well-being, the emergence of new health technologies and the increasing focus on preventive health offer unique opportunities to innovate and improve the effectiveness of health systems. These emerging nations, with their diverse experiences and resources, can learn from each other and promote transnational collaborations to address some of the most pressing global health issues.

Telemedicine and Digital Health

The adoption of telemedicine and digital health platforms can play a crucial role in overcoming geographical barriers to access health services, especially in the vast rural areas of the BRICS countries. The digitization of medical records, the use of personal health management applications, and remote diagnostic systems can improve healthcare system efficiency, reduce costs, and provide preventive and personalized care.

Artificial Intelligence in Healthcare

Artificial intelligence (AI) offers extraordinary possibilities in the healthcare sector, from the early diagnosis of diseases to the personalization of treatments. BRICS can invest in researching and developing AI-based solutions to address specific health challenges, such as monitoring outbreaks, optimizing health resources, and analyzing data to inform public health policies.

Focus on Mental Health

Mental health is gaining recognition as an essential component of general well-being, requiring an integrated response that goes beyond simple health care. BRICS can implement policies that promote mental health awareness, improve access to psychological support services, and address the stigma associated with mental illness. Promoting supportive work and community environments can contribute to a holistic approach to well-being.

Collaborations for Health Research

Establishing transnational partnerships for health research can accelerate scientific progress and promote innovation in healthcare. Collaborations between academic institutions, biotechnology industries and governments of BRICS countries can facilitate the exchange of knowledge, the sharing of resources, and the joint development of advanced health technologies. These collaborations may focus on priority areas such as infectious diseases, antibiotic resistance, and vaccination technologies.

Sustainability of Health Systems

Addressing the financial sustainability of health systems is a fundamental challenge for BRICS, which requires reforms aimed at optimizing the allocation of resources, improving efficiency and ensuring the quality of care. Policies may include introducing innovative funding models, supporting universal health insurance, and investing in preventive health to reduce the burden of chronic diseases.

Health Education and Promotion of Healthy Lifestyles

Public health education and the promotion of healthy lifestyles
are essential to prevent disease and improve overall well-being.
BRICS can implement national campaigns on nutrition, physical
activity, mental health and disease prevention, aiming at
building a culture of health that supports informed decisions
and healthy behavior among citizens.

Continuing on this trajectory of innovation, collaboration and
focus on prevention and holistic well-being, BRICS can not only
improve the health and well-being of their populations but also
contribute to shaping a healthier and more sustainable future at
a global level. The ability to adapt to new challenges, to exploit
emerging technologies and to promote equity in health will be
decisive in defining the trajectory of health progress in the
BRICS countries and beyond.

As BRICS move toward the goal of improving the health and
well-being of their populations, it becomes crucial to adopt a
proactive approach in addressing emerging challenges in the
global health landscape. Initiatives to promote health are not
limited only to infrastructure improvements or the adoption of
new technologies, but also include the need to address the social
determinants of health, to improve preparedness and response
to health emergencies, and to promote international
cooperation.

Addressing the Social Determinants of Health

To address the deep roots of health disparities, BRICS must
focus on social determinants of health, such as education,
housing conditions, access to safe drinking water and adequate
sanitation, and food security. Implementing policies that
address these issues can lead to lasting improvements in public
health and well-being, while reducing health inequalities
between different sections of the population.

Preparedness and Response to Health Emergencies

Recent pandemics have underscored the importance of rapid and effective preparation and response to health emergencies. BRICS can strengthen their health systems by improving disease surveillance, ensuring the availability of critical medical resources, and developing rapid search capabilities to address new pathogens. Training health personnel on emergency protocols and the promotion of community preparedness plans are essential to reduce the impact of future health crises.

International Cooperation and Health Diplomacy

International cooperation plays a key role in promoting global health and responding effectively to cross-border challenges. BRICS can assume a leadership role in health diplomacy, facilitating the exchange of information, the sharing of best practices, and collaboration in the research and development of health solutions. Actively participating in multilateral health organizations and contributing to the formation of a fairer and more sustainable global health order are fundamental steps towards achieving shared health objectives.

Mental Health Promotion

Recognizing the importance of mental health as an integral part of overall well-being requires a paradigm shift in BRICS health systems. Developing accessible and high-quality mental health services, promoting awareness, and reducing the stigma associated with mental illness are crucial actions. Initiatives such as training health professionals in psychology, creating mental health helplines, and promoting access to therapy and support are essential to address this growing challenge.

Innovation and Health Research

Continuous innovation and research in the healthcare sector are essential to effectively address existing and emerging diseases. BRICS can invest in excellent research centers, promote collaborations between universities, the private sector and governments, and support innovation in biotechnology, drug therapies and medical practices. Research focused on the specific needs of BRICS populations can lead to more targeted and effective health interventions.

Through an ongoing commitment to these key areas, BRICS can not only improve the health and well-being of their populations but also contribute significantly to global efforts aimed at building a healthier future for all. Achieving these objectives will require a forward-looking vision, innovative policies and a commitment to cooperation and partnership at all levels of society and between nations.

The BRICS approach to health and well-being continues to evolve in the face of global challenges and opportunities. To keep pace with the needs of a growing world population and emerging health threats, it is essential to adopt innovative strategies that not only improve access and quality of healthcare but also promote disease prevention and the improvement of overall well-being.

Emphasis on Prevention and Holistic Wellness

A greater emphasis on disease prevention can transform BRICS health systems, shifting the focus from curing diseases to actively promoting health and well-being. Integrating regular screening programs, educational campaigns on healthy lifestyles, and community wellness initiatives can significantly reduce the burden of chronic diseases and improve quality of life. Adopting a holistic approach that considers physical, mental, social and environmental factors will help create healthier and more resilient societies.

Integration of Digital Health Services

The integration of digital health services into national healthcare strategies can offer wider and more flexible access to care, reduce inequalities and improve service efficiency. BRICS can develop digital health infrastructures that support telemedicine, online consultations, remote health monitoring, and electronic prescriptions. This will require investments in digital technologies, training of healthcare personnel, and development of regulatory frameworks to ensure the privacy and security of patient data.

Environmental Sustainability and Health

The link between human health and environmental health requires BRICS to integrate environmental sustainability into their health policies. Tackling air and water pollution, promoting sustainable resource management, and reducing exposure to toxic chemicals are crucial steps to prevent environmental diseases and promote long-term well-being. In addition, adopting sustainable agricultural practices and ensuring food security through resilient and sustainable food systems are essential to public health.

Strengthening Research and Innovation Capacities

Strengthening research and innovation capacities in the BRICS is vital to address unique health challenges and develop solutions tailored to their populations. Investing in biomedical research, public health sciences, and emerging health technologies can accelerate progress toward complex health goals. The promotion of partnerships between academies, industries and governments will facilitate the sharing of knowledge and the commercialization of scientific discoveries and technological innovations.

Promoting Global Collaboration for Health

Finally, the BRICS have a crucial role to play in promoting global collaboration for health. Through shared initiatives, they can help shape a global health agenda that addresses common priorities such as pandemic preparedness, access to essential medicines, the fight against antimicrobial resistance, and support for health systems in low and middle income countries. Actively participating in global dialogue and contributing equally to international health efforts will strengthen collective capacities to respond to health crises and promote equitable and sustainable global health.

By continuing to explore these areas of intervention and implement targeted reforms, BRICS can not only improve the health and well-being of their populations but also make significant contributions to global health, demonstrating the power of cooperation and innovation in overcoming some of the most pressing health challenges of our time.

As the BRICS continue to pursue the improvement of health systems and the general well-being of their populations, attention is increasingly shifting to integrating public health policies with sustainable development strategies. Recognizing that health is a fundamental human right and a crucial pillar of social and economic development, these countries are exploring innovative ways to address complex health challenges that are intertwined with issues of equity, environment and technological progress.

Addressing the Socioeconomic Determinants of Health

A holistic understanding of health requires concerted action to address its socioeconomic determinants. Poverty, education, housing conditions, access to clean water and sanitation, and food security directly affect the health of populations. The

BRICS are trying to integrate interventions in these sectors with health initiatives to create a wider and sustainable impact on the well-being of citizens. The adoption of cross-cutting policies that link the health sector with education, urban planning, agriculture and the economy is essential to reduce health inequalities and promote a healthier society.

Strengthening Public Health Systems for Pandemic Resilience

The recent COVID-19 pandemic has highlighted the crucial importance of resilient and responsive public health systems. The BRICS are working to strengthen their capacities for disease surveillance, for rapid response to health emergencies, and for the production and distribution of vaccines and treatments. The creation of collaborative networks for vaccine research and development, the improvement of logistics and infrastructure for the distribution of vaccines, and the promotion of information campaigns to increase the acceptance of vaccines are key steps towards building safer and more protected communities.

Integration of Technology into Care and Prevention

Health technology, including digital health data, telemedicine, artificial intelligence and robotics, offers revolutionary possibilities to improve access and quality of healthcare. The BRICS are exploring how these technologies can be integrated into their healthcare systems to make services more efficient, accessible and personalized. This requires investments in digital infrastructure, training of healthcare personnel in new technologies, and development of regulatory frameworks to ensure data security and patient privacy.

Promoting Healthy Lifestyles

Preventing non-communicable diseases, such as cardiovascular disease, diabetes and cancer, through the promotion of healthy lifestyles, is another key area of intervention for BRICS. Public campaigns on the importance of a balanced diet, regular physical activity, reduction of tobacco and alcohol consumption, and regular screening can help to significantly reduce the incidence and impact of these diseases. In addition, health education in schools can lay the foundation for healthy habits that last a lifetime.

International Cooperation for Global Health

Finally, the BRICS recognize the importance of international cooperation in promoting global health. By collaborating with multilateral organizations, sharing resources and knowledge, and supporting public health efforts in low- and middle-income countries, BRICS can play a critical role in solving global health challenges. The commitment to promote equitable access to health technologies, to support research and development in the health field, and to promote policies that recognize health as a global common good is essential to create a healthier future for all.

Through these continuous initiatives and the adoption of a collaborative and integrated approach, BRICS can not only address immediate challenges in the health sector but also contribute to building more resilient, equitable and sustainable health systems globally. This collective commitment to health and well-being represents a fundamental step towards achieving sustainable development goals and promoting a healthier and more prosperous global community.

In conclusion, the BRICS face complex challenges but also unique opportunities in the field of health and well-being, due to their growing economic and political influence at the global level, as well as to the diversity and scale of their populations. The evolution of health systems in these countries reflects a commitment to achieving ambitious health objectives, including universal access to care, disease prevention, promotion of healthy lifestyles, and the integration of advanced technologies to improve the effectiveness and efficiency of healthcare.

The promotion of universal access to health services represents a common but challenging goal for BRICS, requiring constant attention to the equity, quality and sustainability of health systems. Addressing the social and economic determinants of health, improving preparedness and response capacity to health emergencies, and integrating innovative technological solutions are essential steps towards building more resilient and adaptive health systems.

At the same time, the promotion of healthy lifestyles and the prevention of non-communicable diseases through public education and targeted legislation can significantly contribute to reducing the burden of diseases and improving the quality of life of BRICS populations. Mental health and holistic well-being emerge as necessary areas of increased attention and investment, reflecting a broader understanding of well-being that goes beyond the mere absence of illness.

In addition, international cooperation plays a crucial role in strengthening BRICS efforts in the field of public health. Through collaboration and partnership, BRICS can not only better address their health challenges but also contribute to global health, promoting equitable access to healthcare, supporting research and development of innovative health solutions, and working together to respond to international health emergencies.

The BRICS path to improving health and well-being requires a long-term vision, policies based on evidence of effectiveness, and a commitment to innovation and multilateral cooperation. With these efforts, BRICS have the potential not only to transform their health systems but also to play a leadership role in promoting a healthier and more equitable global community. The achievement of these goals will contribute significantly to progress towards the sustainable development goals and to the construction of a future in which every individual has the opportunity to live a healthy and productive life.

17. Future of the BRICS: future prospects and potential scenarios for the development of the bloc.

The future of the BRICS (Brazil, Russia, India, China and South Africa) is rich in potential development scenarios, reflecting both internal and external challenges and the unique opportunities offered by their growing economic and political influence at the global level. As these countries continue to navigate the rapidly changing international landscape, their future trajectories will depend on a number of factors, including the ability to adapt to global economic changes, address sustainable development issues, and navigate complex geopolitical dynamics.

Economic Growth and Integration

One of the key future prospects for the BRICS concerns maintaining and accelerating economic growth. This could include deepening economic integration between members through commercial initiatives, joint investments in critical infrastructure, and the promotion of regional value chains that can support industrial and technological development. In addition, the expansion of the BRICS New Development Banks can provide essential financial means to support such development projects.

Global Leadership and Multilateral Cooperation

The BRICS are destined to play an increasingly significant role in global governance, challenging the existing world order and promoting a more multipolar international system. This could involve greater commitment and influence in multilateral institutions, such as the United Nations and the G20, as well as the promotion of new international cooperation forums and platforms that reflect the interests and priorities of emerging and developing countries.

Sustainable Development Challenges

The future of the BRICS will also be profoundly influenced by their ability to face sustainable development challenges, including climate change, sustainable resource management, the reduction of inequalities and the promotion of inclusive societies. Joint efforts to develop and implement green technologies, sustainable urban development policies, and circular economic models could not only benefit BRICS members but also offer replicable models for other countries.

Technological and Digital Innovation

The adoption and development of advanced technologies represent another critical area for the future of the BRICS. Investing in research and development, promoting innovation in the private sector, and supporting education and training in key fields such as artificial intelligence, biotechnology and renewable energy can position BRICS as leaders in the industries of the future, while promoting economic growth and global competitiveness.

Social Dynamics and Internal Policies

The future prospects of the BRICS will also be shaped by the internal social and political dynamics of each country. The ability to manage social diversity, to address inequalities and to ensure effective and inclusive governance will be critical to maintaining social and political stability. Addressing these issues internally and sharing lessons learned could strengthen cohesion within the block and improve its ability to face common challenges.

Development Scenarios and Potential Challenges

Looking to the future, the BRICS could face a range of development scenarios, from rising as a cohesive economic and political bloc that challenges the existing world order, to navigating internal tensions and differences of interest that could limit cooperation. The ability to balance these dynamics, promote common interests and exploit opportunities for cooperation will largely determine the long-term success of the BRICS on the world stage.

In conclusion, as the BRICS face a future full of potentials and challenges, their collective journey will offer unique opportunities to shape global dynamics, promote sustainable development and support a fairer and more multipolar international order. The ability to successfully navigate these changes will depend on a shared commitment to cooperation, innovation, and a long-term strategic vision.

As the BRICS move into the future, they face an ever-changing global landscape, characterized by rapid technological innovations, geopolitical challenges, and a growing need for sustainable solutions. The future trajectory of this block will be influenced by a number of dynamic factors, including the evolution of governance models, economic resilience, strategic partnerships, and the ability to address global environmental issues.

Economic Resilience and Diversification

Economic resilience will emerge as a central theme for BRICS, requiring greater diversification of their economies to reduce dependence on raw material exports and the import of technology. Investing in research and development, promoting high-tech sectors, and encouraging entrepreneurship can help stimulate innovation and support long-term economic growth. The creation of robust domestic markets and the promotion of intra-BRICS trade could also offer a buffer against global market fluctuations.

Global Governance and Leadership

The BRICS could assume a more assertive role in global governance, seeking to reform international institutions to better reflect the evolving balance of power in the world. By promoting norms and practices that promote a more just and equitable world order, BRICS could work to ensure that emerging economies and developing countries have a stronger voice in global issues. This could include advocacy for fair business practices, the fight against climate change, the sustainable management of global resources, and the promotion of international peace and security.

Environmental Challenges and Sustainability

Addressing environmental challenges will become increasingly critical for BRICS as they seek to balance economic growth with sustainability. Actively engaging in global initiatives to combat climate change, promote energy efficiency, invest in renewable energy sources, and adopt sustainable development practices will be vital steps. In addition, cooperation on transnational environmental projects, such as the conservation of biodiversity and the management of water resources, could strengthen intra-BRICS collaboration and contribute to sustainable solutions.

Technological Innovation and Digital Society

The acceleration of technological innovation will provide BRICS with an opportunity to lead in sectors such as artificial intelligence, biotechnology, sustainable energy and smart cities. Promoting a strong digital infrastructure and digitally inclusive societies could improve access to public services, stimulate the digital economy and promote civic participation. However, this will also require addressing challenges related to data privacy, cybersecurity, and fairness in access to technology.

Social Dynamics and Internal Cohesion

Finally, the BRICS' ability to successfully navigate the future will depend on their ability to manage internal social dynamics, including reducing inequalities, promoting social inclusion and maintaining national cohesion. Addressing issues of social equity, ensuring equitable access to economic opportunities, and promoting tolerance and cultural diversity will be critical to ensuring stable and resilient societies.

As the BRICS move towards these potential future development scenarios, their collective trajectory will reflect not only the challenges faced but also the opportunities seized. Their ability to adapt, innovate and collaborate will determine their impact on the world stage and their ability to contribute to a more sustainable, equitable and prosperous global future.

In the context of a rapidly changing world, the future of the BRICS presents a landscape full of complex challenges but also significant opportunities for strengthening cooperation and innovation. The ability of these countries to adapt to geopolitical, technological and ecological changes will profoundly influence not only their development path but also their role in the global architecture.

Revolution in Education and Skills for the Future

To support innovation and economic growth, BRICS will have to face the need to revolutionize educational systems to prepare their populations for the skills required in the 21st century. This includes not only education in STEM (science, technology, engineering and mathematics) but also education in innovation, critical thinking, creativity and flexibility. Educational programs will need to be rethought to incorporate lifelong learning and adaptability, thus preparing people for careers that may not yet exist.

Economic Integration and New Trade Routes

Economic integration between the BRICS could deepen further, with the creation of new trade routes, common standards and digital platforms to facilitate trade and investment. The expansion of the New Development Bank and the creation of alternative payment systems could reduce dependence on Western financial systems and promote greater intra-BRICS economic exchanges. This could also stimulate economic diversification and collaboration in strategic sectors such as renewable energy, digital infrastructure and biotechnology.

Environmental Sustainability as a Global Imperative

Environmental sustainability will emerge as not only an ethical but also an economic imperative for the BRICS, pushing towards a greener global economy. Initiatives could include joint investments in clean technologies, agreements on shared climate goals, and cross-border conservation projects. The adoption of sustainable production and consumption practices not only addresses climate issues but also opens up new markets and job opportunities, positioning the BRICS as a leader in the global ecological transition.

Multilevel Governance and Civic Participation

BRICS could explore new multilevel governance models that better integrate local needs with national policies and global strategies. This could include strengthening local institutions, promoting civic participation through digital platforms, and collaborating with non-governmental organizations and the private sector to address social, economic and environmental issues. More inclusive and participatory governance can contribute to social stability and to the legitimacy of reforms.

Global Health as a Shared Priority

Recent pandemics have highlighted the importance of global health as a shared priority and as a matter of global security. BRICS could take a leadership role in strengthening global health systems, promoting research and development of accessible vaccines and treatments, and working toward the creation of a global health security network. This would include supporting pandemic preparedness, sharing information and resources, and collaborating on international health standards and protocols.

As the future of the BRICS unfolds in these potential development scenarios, their trajectory will undoubtedly be marked by how they respond and adapt to the pressing global challenges of our time. Their ability to promote sustainable development, inclusive innovation and international cooperation will determine not only their individual success but also their collective impact on the future of our interconnected world.

In projecting the future of the BRICS, it becomes essential to consider the impact of demographic trends, energy transitions, and global expectations for greater equity and inclusion. These factors, together with technological changes and geopolitical challenges, will shape future prospects and potential development scenarios for the block in ways that require proactive policies, shared strategic visions, and a commitment to international cooperation.

Demographic Transitions and Social Challenges

Demographic trends, including an ageing population in some BRICS countries and predominant youth in others, present unique challenges and opportunities for economic and social development. An ageing population will require more robust health and social care systems, while a young population will require investment in education and the creation of employment opportunities. Addressing these demographic trends through targeted policies can help BRICS exploit the "demographic dividend" and address potential social challenges.

Energy Transitions and Sustainability

The transition to renewable energy sources and sustainable development practices is critical to tackling climate change and promoting economic resilience. BRICS have the opportunity to lead the global energy transformation through investment in green technologies, the promotion of sustainable energy policies and support for international cooperation in the energy field. This transition will offer not only environmental benefits but also new economic opportunities and the possibility of reducing energy inequalities.

Global Equity and Inclusion

The BRICS, with their different development trajectories and internal challenges, can play a crucial role in promoting greater equity and inclusion at the global level. This includes advocating for a fairer trading system, access to development finance, cooperation to address global inequalities, and supporting human rights and decent work. Promoting equity and inclusion not only strengthens internal social cohesion but also contributes to a more just and balanced world order.

Adaptation and Technological Innovation

Technological acceleration offers BRICS the opportunity to overcome development gaps and to position themselves as leaders in emerging sectors. The adoption and development of advanced technologies in areas such as artificial intelligence, clean energy, biotechnology, and digital infrastructure can drive innovation and economic growth. However, it is essential to address ethical, privacy and security issues related to technological advancement, ensuring that the benefits of innovation are widely shared.

Multilateral Governance and Diplomacy

As the BRICS seek to strengthen their influence on the global stage, the ability to work within and through multilateral institutions will become increasingly important. Contributing to the reformism of international financial institutions, actively participating in global peace and security initiatives, and promoting collaborative solutions to world problems will strengthen the role of the BRICS as key players in global governance. Cultural diplomacy and education can also serve as powerful tools to build bridges and promote mutual understanding between the BRICS and the rest of the world.

As the BRICS move towards these future scenarios, their trajectory will be forged by the ability to manage internal tensions, to navigate the complexities of international relations and to adapt to global changes. By proactively addressing these challenges with a commitment to sustainability, innovation and multilateral cooperation, BRICS can not only secure a prominent place in the future world order but also contribute significantly to a more equitable, stable and prosperous world.

As the BRICS move towards future development scenarios, their ability to positively influence both the global architecture and the well-being of their populations will depend on the strategic navigation of a series of interconnected challenges. Economic resilience, social equity, environmental sustainability and technological innovation will remain fundamental pillars on which to build their future path. In this context, additional strategic considerations and opportunities emerge.

Strengthening Social Capitalism and Entrepreneurship

One of the keys to a sustainable future for the BRICS lies in strengthening social capitalism and entrepreneurship, with a particular focus on startups that seek to solve social and ecological challenges. By encouraging social entrepreneurship through favorable policies, dedicated funding and business incubators, BRICS can stimulate innovation in solving crucial problems such as poverty, access to education and clean energy. This approach would not only contribute to economic growth but also to social and ecological progress.

Integration of Corporate Social Responsibility

The integration of corporate social responsibility (CSR) into the business strategies of companies within BRICS can play a significant role in promoting ethical business practices and contributing to social well-being. By encouraging companies to invest in local communities, protect the environment, and adopt fair working practices, BRICS can create an economic environment that values sustainability and equity as much as profitability.

Development of Green Infrastructure and Smart Cities

The development of green infrastructure and the promotion of smart cities are key areas in which BRICS can innovate to address urban and environmental challenges. Through the adoption of sustainable technologies in construction, the improvement of energy efficiency and the implementation of smart city solutions that optimize transportation, waste management and resource use, BRICS can improve the quality of urban life while reducing environmental impact.

Promoting Education and Global Talent

Education plays a critical role in enabling BRICS to navigate and shape the future. Investing in higher education, vocational training, and lifelong learning can equip their populations with the skills they need to thrive in the global economy. In addition, attracting and retaining global talent through favorable policies can help stimulate innovation and competitiveness.

Strengthening South-South Cooperation

Finally, BRICS can play a crucial role in strengthening South-South cooperation, offering an alternative model of development and international collaboration. Through the exchange of knowledge, experience and resources with other developing countries, BRICS can promote development strategies that are more suited to the realities of the countries of the global South. This could include sharing appropriate technologies, supporting capacity building, and facilitating access to markets.

As the BRICS move forward, their ability to address these issues with vision, leadership, and cooperation will determine their trajectory and their long-term impact. Through a commitment to innovation, sustainability and equity, BRICS have the opportunity not only to shape their destinies but also to contribute to a more prosperous and resilient future for the entire world.

In the context of a constantly evolving world, BRICS face the challenge of remaining relevant and influential as they navigate through the complexities of a global environment characterized by rapid technological change, increasing environmental pressures, and changing geopolitical dynamics. Their ability to anticipate and adapt to these changes, while promoting sustainable growth and social inclusion, will define their role and impact on the world scene in the coming decades.

Promoting a New Global Financial Architecture

Faced with the volatility of global financial markets and the challenges posed by dependence on Western-dominated financial institutions, the BRICS could further explore the creation and expansion of alternative financial mechanisms. Promoting a new global financial architecture, including the potential expansion of the New Development Bank and the creation of currency exchange systems that reduce dependence on the U.S. dollar, could offer greater economic stability to BRICS members and other emerging countries, while strengthening their global economic influence.

Leadership in Climate Change and Biodiversity

As the world faces unprecedented challenges related to climate change and the loss of biodiversity, BRICS have the opportunity to assume global leadership in adopting ambitious policies for the mitigation of climate change and the conservation of biodiversity. This could include significant commitments to reduce greenhouse gas emissions, investments in renewable energy, sustainable agricultural practices, and the protection of critical ecosystems. By taking a leading role, BRICS can not only make a significant contribution to the global fight against climate change but also stimulate innovation and growth in the green technology sector.

Addressing Inequality through Social Innovation

Social and economic inequalities represent a persistent challenge for BRICS, affecting social cohesion and political stability. Social innovation, which includes new business models, work practices and technological solutions aimed at improving social well-being, can offer creative ways to address these inequalities. Through the promotion of social entrepreneurship, investment in education and professional training and the adoption of digital technologies to improve access to services, BRICS can work towards fairer and more inclusive societies.

Building Strategic Partnerships Beyond the Bloc

As the BRICS seek to expand their influence and promote a more balanced world order, building strategic partnerships with other emerging and developing countries becomes crucial. These collaborations may extend beyond economic cooperation, including joint initiatives in research and development, security, education and culture. Such partnerships would not only strengthen the position of the BRICS at the global level but would also contribute to greater South-South solidarity, addressing issues of common interest and promoting sustainable development.

Embracing the Fourth Industrial Revolution

The fourth industrial revolution, characterized by the integration of digital, physical and biological technologies, presents both challenges and opportunities for the BRICS. By actively embracing these innovations and promoting a favorable environment for research, development and adoption of emerging technologies, BRICS can catalyze transformations in the manufacturing, agriculture, energy and healthcare sectors. Investing in the population's digital skills and technological infrastructure will ensure that BRICS are not only active participants in this new era but also leaders in defining its path.

Looking to the future, the BRICS are facing a turning point, with the opportunity to define a new paradigm of international cooperation, sustainable growth and equitable innovation. Their ability to collaborate, both internally and with global partners, to navigate economic and technological transitions and to address pressing environmental and social issues, will determine their trajectory and their impact on the world in the 21st century.

In navigating the future, BRICS have a unique opportunity to reorient global dynamics through sustainable innovation, active diplomacy, and a shared vision for equitable progress. As they seek to consolidate their position in the new world order, they will face and overcome a series of intrinsic and external challenges, adapting to global changes and actively shaping international trends so that they reflect their collective and individual interests.

Strengthening Global Food Security

An emerging priority for BRICS in the long term will be the strengthening of global food security. Faced with population growth, climate change, and geopolitical tensions that threaten global access to sufficient, nutritious and safe food, BRICS could lead international efforts to promote sustainable agricultural practices, improve food supply chains, and facilitate technological cooperation in agriculture. By implementing policies that encourage crop diversification, the efficient use of resources and the adoption of safe biotechnology, BRICS can contribute to a more resilient and just global food system.

Impact on Labor Reform and Employment Dynamics

Technological changes and globalization will continue to transform the global labor market. The BRICS, with their large economies and diversified workforces, will play a crucial role in shaping these transformations. By investing in education and training for future skills, promoting employability and supporting the transition to digital and green economies, BRICS can minimize labor dislocations and maximize opportunities for their citizens. International cooperation to establish fair and sustainable labor standards and to protect workers' rights in a global economy will be critical.

Promotion of International Peace and Security

In the context of growing geopolitical tensions and challenges to international security, from regional conflicts to terrorism and cyber-security, the BRICS could assume a more active role in promoting peace and global stability. Through multilateral diplomacy, participation in peacekeeping operations and conflict mediation, BRICS can contribute to a safer and more peaceful international environment. The ability to mediate between great powers and to offer new perspectives on global problems could position the BRICS as key players in resolving international crises.

Innovation in Governance and International Cooperation

The future will see BRICS potentially innovate in governance mechanisms and international cooperation, challenging existing structures and proposing new models for global dialogue and shared decision. The expansion of BRICS initiatives to a greater number of nations in the Global South and the exploration of new platforms for economic, environmental and technological collaboration may offer alternatives to the dominant Western paradigm, promoting greater inclusiveness and global representation.

Facing the Challenges of Digitalization and Cyber-Security

Finally, the digitalization of the economy and society poses both opportunities and challenges for BRICS, requiring innovative policies to promote digital access, protect online rights and ensure cyber-security. As BRICS explore the potential of emerging technologies for economic and social progress, they will also need to address issues related to data privacy, cybersecurity, and ethics in artificial intelligence. International cooperation to establish global norms and standards in these areas will be vital.

As the BRICS move towards these future scenarios, their trajectory will be characterized by how they balance ambitions for growth and influence with responsibility for global sustainability, social justice and international stability. Their ability to act cohesively, to adapt to global changes and to exert a positive influence in the world will define their role in the future global order.

As the BRICS move into the future, it becomes increasingly evident that their path will be shaped not only by internal policies and development strategies but also by the ability to navigate and influence the global geopolitical and economic environment. The challenges they face, as well as the opportunities they can seize, place them in a unique situation to influence the direction of global progress and international cooperation.

Development and Integration of Emerging Technologies

The integration and development of emerging technologies represent a key opportunity for BRICS to lead in new economic sectors and to set global standards. This includes the frontiers of renewable energy, artificial intelligence, robotics, and biotechnology. By creating innovative ecosystems that favor research and development, BRICS can not only catalyze internal economic transformation but also export technological solutions to the rest of the world, establishing themselves as leaders in sectors crucial for the future.

Adaptation to Climate Change and Environmental Leadership

The BRICS, given their significant ecological footprint and vulnerability to various consequences of climate change, have both the responsibility and the opportunity to adopt environmental leadership. The commitment to sustainable development, through ambitious policies to reduce emissions, protect natural resources and promote climate adaptation, can serve as a model for other developing countries. Cooperation within the bloc to finance green projects, exchange environmental knowledge and technologies, and support global climate action can strengthen their influence in international climate negotiations.

Strengthening South-South Cooperation

As engines of the developing world, the BRICS are well positioned to strengthen South-South cooperation, offering an alternative to aid and cooperation structures dominated by the global North. By expanding economic, technological and development partnerships with other nations of the Global South, BRICS can not only facilitate shared development but also create a counterweight to traditional geopolitical influences, promoting a more balanced and multipolar world order.

Navigating Geopolitical Tensions

The BRICS' ability to navigate growing geopolitical tensions and to maintain internal cohesion in the face of diverging interests will be critical to their future global impact. Diplomatically addressing regional security issues, resource rivalries, and challenges to global governance, while maintaining unity on shared objectives and values, will require a delicate balance. Solidarity with global issues, such as the reform of international financial institutions and Internet governance, can strengthen their collective position.

Demographic and Social Challenges

Finally, BRICS must address internal demographic and social challenges, including inequalities, urbanization, education, and public health, to ensure inclusive and sustainable growth. By implementing policies that promote equal access to opportunities, improve health and education systems, and address regional and social disparities, BRICS can ensure that their development not only contributes to their global influence but also elevates the quality of life of their populations.

Looking to the future, the BRICS are faced with an historic opportunity to shape the course of global development and international cooperation. Their ability to promote innovative solutions to global problems, to support a fairer world order, and to successfully navigate internal and external challenges will define their role in the world of tomorrow. The path they choose and how they respond to these challenges and opportunities will determine not only their destiny but also that of the global community in the 21st century.

In conclusion, the future of the BRICS is imbued with potential transformations that could not only strengthen their global positioning but also offer new paradigms for international cooperation, sustainable development and technological innovation. The direction they will take in the coming years will be determined by their ability to proactively face internal challenges, to navigate the complex network of global geopolitical dynamics and to seize emerging opportunities to promote inclusive and sustainable growth.

Challenges and Opportunities

The challenges that BRICS will face include the need to reform and strengthen their internal economic, political and social systems to address inequalities, improve access to essential public services, and promote economic growth that benefits all sectors of society. In parallel, the management of geopolitical tensions, the promotion of environmental sustainability and the adaptation to rapid technological innovations will require a strategic vision and a collaborative commitment both at regional and global levels.

Global Leadership

BRICS have the opportunity to assume global leadership, promoting a fairer and more multipolar world order that better reflects the current distribution of global economic and political power. Through shared initiatives such as the New Development Bank and the strengthening of South-South cooperation, BRICS can offer alternative models of development and international cooperation, supporting the efforts of emerging and developing countries to address their unique challenges.

Innovation for the Future

Investment in innovation and research will be crucial for the future of BRICS, allowing them to drive progress in critical sectors such as artificial intelligence, biotechnology, clean energy and digital technologies. By promoting an environment that facilitates scientific research, entrepreneurship and the adoption of emerging technologies, BRICS can not only stimulate their economic growth but also help solve some of the most pressing global challenges.

A Future Built on Cooperation

Cohesion and cooperation within the BRICS bloc will be essential to achieve these ambitions. While differences of interest and internal challenges will remain, a shared commitment to dialogue, mutual understanding and the search for common goals will facilitate closer cooperation. In addition, by reaching out to global partners and promoting multilateral diplomacy, BRICS can strengthen their role as bridges between the global North and South, contributing to a more inclusive and equitable global dialogue.

Conclusions

In conclusion, the future of the BRICS is full of challenges but also full of opportunities. Their trajectory in the coming years could offer new ways to address global development issues, rebalance international relations and promote technological innovation. The effectiveness with which the BRICS navigate these dynamics, promote internal and external solidarity and implement policies for sustainable development will determine their impact on the world stage and their contribution to building a more equitable, stable and prosperous global future.

18. Bilateral and Multilateral Relations: examination of key relationships between BRICS members and with other nations.

Bilateral and multilateral relations between BRICS members (Brazil, Russia, India, China and South Africa) and with other nations are complex and multifaceted, influenced by a combination of historical, economic, strategic and geopolitical factors. These relationships are fundamental not only for the internal cohesion of the BRICS bloc but also for their collective impact on the international system. Examining these key relationships provides insights into the current and future dynamics of global power, challenges to world governance, and opportunities for international cooperation.

Internal BRICS Relations

Internal relations between BRICS members vary from close strategic partnerships to complex rivalries.

- **China and Russia** have strengthened their ties through economic, military and technological cooperation, united by a common interest in opposing Western influence and promoting a multipolar world order.

- **India and China**, despite significant bilateral trade, have tensions due to territorial disputes and strategic rivalries. However, both nations have shown interest in working together on global issues within the BRICS forums.

- **Brazil, India and South Africa**, as emerging democracies, share common interests in promoting sustainable development, the reform of global financial institutions and the importance of multilateralism. However, their relations are less structured than the ties they each maintain with Russia and China.

Relations with Other Nations and Blocs

BRICS' relations with other nations and blocs are also decisive for their ability to influence the world order.

- **United States and European Union**: BRICS members maintain complex relationships with the United States and the European Union, oscillating between cooperation in areas such as trade and challenges on issues of security, human rights and geopolitical influences. While trying to promote a fairer global architecture, the BRICS often find themselves at odds with Western policies.

- **Developing Countries**: BRICS seek to strengthen ties with other emerging economies and developing countries through South-South cooperation, promoting economic development, food security, access to energy and environmental sustainability. Initiatives such as the New Development Bank aim to offer alternatives to traditional financial institutions dominated by the West.

- **Regional and Multilateral Organizations**: BRICS actively participate in regional and multilateral organizations, seeking to expand their influence and promote their collective interests. Participation in forums such as the G20, the United Nations, and various regional platforms allows BRICS to contribute to global dialogue on critical issues such as climate change, global financial reform, and international peace and security.

Challenges and Opportunities

BRICS bilateral and multilateral relations face several challenges, including the need to balance national interests with collective objectives, manage regional rivalries, and navigate global geopolitical tensions. However, these relationships also offer significant opportunities to promote positive change, both within the bloc and in the wider international system.

The BRICS' ability to act cohesively, to exploit their growing economies to promote sustainable development, and to exert diplomatic influence to strengthen global governance will determine their success in shaping a global future that reflects the diversity and multipolarity of the contemporary world. As the BRICS explore ways to deepen their internal cooperation and expand their network of external relations, it becomes essential to consider how these dynamics influence not only global geopolitics but also aspirations for sustainable development and global equity.

Collaboration in Non-Traditional Areas

In addition to economic and political spheres, BRICS have the opportunity to intensify collaboration in non-traditional sectors that could have a profound impact on global well-being. This includes public health, education, and digital technology. By sharing resources, knowledge and best practices, BRICS can effectively address global challenges such as pandemics, illiteracy and the digital divide, promoting innovative solutions that benefit not only their citizens but also the wider international community.

Integration of New Members

The potential expansion of the BRICS, through the integration of new members, offers another level of complexity and opportunity. By expanding their scope to include other emerging and developing economies, BRICS can not only increase their economic and political weight but also enrich internal dialogue with new perspectives and experiences. However, this would require effective mechanisms to manage diversity and ensure that expansion reinforces rather than dilutes group cohesion and effectiveness.

Challenges of Internal Rivalry

Internal rivalries, such as those between India and China, present significant challenges to the cohesion of the BRICS bloc. Managing these tensions, through dialogue and diplomacy, will be crucial to maintaining unity within the group and to ensure that rivalries do not hinder cooperation on issues of common interest. The BRICS' ability to address these internal issues constructively can serve as a model for conflict resolution and wider international cooperation.

Dialogue with the Western World

Finally, the future of BRICS' relations with Western nations and existing global institutions will be decisive for their ability to influence the world order. While BRICS may seek to challenge and reform existing global structures to better reflect today's multipolar world, success in these initiatives will require constructive dialogue and a commitment to multilateralism. Cooperation on major global issues, from climate change to international security, could serve as common ground to build bridges between the BRICS and the Western world, promoting a more cooperative and interconnected future.

In conclusion, bilateral and multilateral relations between BRICS members and with other nations will remain a key element in determining their role in the future global order. Their ability to navigate internal challenges, to build strategic partnerships and to contribute to collaborative solutions for global problems will define their legacy and their impact on the international stage. By proactively addressing these issues with vision and diplomacy, BRICS can not only strengthen their position but also contribute to a more equitable, stable and prosperous world.

Navigating the future, the BRICS' ability to intensify their global influence will depend heavily on the balance between internal rivalries and collective aspirations, as well as on their ability to forge constructive relationships with other nations outside the block. This dynamic balance between competition and cooperation, both within the group and in the wider international context, will determine the path that the BRICS will follow in trying to shape a world order that reflects their visions and interests.

Increased Collaboration in Technology and Innovation

A promising area for deeper cooperation between the BRICS is technological innovation and scientific research. By sharing platforms for joint research and the development of emerging technologies, such as artificial intelligence, nanotechnology and personalized medicine, BRICS can not only accelerate their technological progress but also help to define global standards in these fields. Collaboration in these areas could also facilitate the development of innovative solutions to sustainable development problems, improving the resilience and well-being of their populations and those of the world.

Improving Food and Water Security

Another critical domain for expanded cooperation is food and water security. The BRICS, given their vast natural and agricultural resource base, have the opportunity to lead international efforts to improve sustainable agricultural practices, promote efficient water use, and combat desertification and soil degradation. By collaborating on innovative agricultural technologies, efficient irrigation systems and water conservation methods, they can play a key role in ensuring global food security in a changing climate.

Management of Natural Resources and Biodiversity

Cooperation in the management of natural resources and in the conservation of biodiversity represents another crucial area for the BRICS. By working together to protect critical ecosystems, such as rainforests, river basins and marine areas, and to promote the sustainable use of natural resources, BRICS can lead global efforts to preserve biodiversity and combat climate change. This will require a shared commitment to implement effective environmental policies and to collaborate on international platforms dedicated to environmental sustainability.

Expansion of Infrastructure and Connectivity Networks

Expanding infrastructure and connectivity networks is critical to facilitating trade, economic integration and social development among the BRICS and beyond. By jointly investing in infrastructure projects, such as the New Silk Road, interregional transport networks and digital infrastructure, BRICS can improve internal and external connectivity, stimulating economic growth and promoting regional integration. Such initiatives can also serve as catalysts for closer cooperation with other emerging and developing nations, strengthening their collective impact on global development.

Addressing Disparities and Promoting Inclusion

Finally, a cross-cutting theme for BRICS will be the importance of addressing internal disparities and promoting social and economic inclusion. As they seek to expand their global influence, it is crucial that BRICS remain attentive to the needs of their populations, working to reduce inequalities, improve access to education and health services, and promote employment and social mobility. By doing so, they will not only strengthen their legitimacy and internal cohesion but will also help to shape a fairer and more inclusive world order.

In short, as the BRICS advance into the 21st century, their collective trajectory will be marked by how they balance aspirations for global leadership with a commitment to address domestic challenges and promote sustainable development. Their ability to collaborate effectively, both within the block and with the rest of the world, will be critical to realizing their potential as agents of positive change in the global arena.

In the context of a rapidly changing world, the future trajectory of the BRICS will be highly influenced by their ability to adapt and respond to new challenges and opportunities. This includes addressing emerging issues related to cybersecurity, the digitalization of the economy, and the need to ensure a fair and sustainable energy transition. In addition, the BRICS' ability to maintain an open and constructive dialogue not only with each other but also with the rest of the world will be fundamental to navigating the complexities of the global geopolitical landscape.

Cybersecurity and Digital Sovereignty

With the increase of digitalization in all aspects of social and economic life, cybersecurity is becoming an increasingly critical concern for the BRICS. Collaboration to strengthen cybersecurity, protect critical infrastructure, and develop common data privacy regulations can help ensure the digital sovereignty of BRICS countries. This will require a balance between promoting open innovation and protecting against cyberthreats, as well as cooperating with international partners to address challenges that transcend national borders.

Digital Economy and Technological Inclusion

The transition to a digital economy offers immense opportunities for BRICS to promote economic growth and innovation. Investing in digital infrastructure, promoting digital literacy and supporting technological entrepreneurship are essential steps to exploit the potential of the digital economy. However, it is crucial that this transition be inclusive, ensuring that all segments of society have access to the benefits of digitalization and that the risk of new forms of inequality is mitigated.

Energy Transition and Sustainable Development

The transition to renewable energy sources and sustainable development practices is crucial to address the climate crisis and promote long-term economic resilience. The BRICS, many of which are heavily dependent on fossil fuels, must navigate this transition so as not to leave vulnerable communities behind and ensure balanced economic opportunities. Cooperation on clean energy technologies, financing for sustainable development, and climate mitigation policies can strengthen their leadership role in promoting a more sustainable global energy future.

Multilateral Dialogue and Cooperation

Maintaining and expanding dialogue and cooperation with other nations and regional blocs will be essential for BRICS to promote their interests and visions globally. Through active engagement in multilateral forums and through bilateral and multilateral diplomacy initiatives, BRICS can help shape a fairer and more cooperative world order. This includes working toward reforming international financial and political institutions to better reflect the global balance of power and the needs of developing countries.

Addressing Global Challenges through Solidarity

Finally, BRICS have a unique opportunity to demonstrate how international solidarity can address pressing global challenges, such as pandemics, poverty, food insecurity and refugee crises. By working together to promote sustainable and justice-based solutions to these problems, BRICS can not only improve the lives of their populations but also contribute to global peace and stability.

In short, the BRICS' future path in the global context will depend on their ability to act in a cohesive and collaborative manner, to proactively face internal and external challenges, and to exploit their growing economic and political capacities to promote a fairer, more stable and sustainable world. Their trajectory will be a significant indicator of the direction of global progress and of the world's ability to unite to address the most pressing issues of our time.

In further exploring the future of BRICS bilateral and multilateral relations, it emerges that their ability to forge a constructive path in the 21st century will largely depend on their ability to manage internal complexities and international diplomacy, maintaining a balance between national aspirations and global obligations.

Leadership in New Economic Frontiers

As the BRICS continue to evolve, a key to their collective success will lie in their ability to assume leadership in new economic frontiers, such as the blue economy, the circular economy, and digital commerce. By creating markets that value sustainability, innovation, and equity, BRICS can establish new paradigms for global economic development that promote both prosperity and environmental protection. Adopting policies that favor greener and more inclusive trade could not only help reduce global carbon emissions but also generate new economic opportunities for developing countries.

Strengthening Peacebuilding Capabilities

Another crucial dimension for BRICS in strengthening their global impact is the strengthening of peacebuilding and conflict resolution capacities. Through joint initiatives that promote intercultural dialogue and understanding, BRICS can help mitigate tensions in regional and global hotspots, offering alternative models to military conflict resolution. Expanding their participation in United Nations peacekeeping operations and international mediation mechanisms could not only improve global security but also strengthen their legitimacy as responsible actors on the world stage.

Strengthen Integration and Internal Cohesion

Within the BRICS block, integration and internal cohesion will be essential to maximize their collective impact. This will require effective mechanisms for dispute resolution and policy harmonization in key areas such as trade, investment and foreign policy. By strengthening BRICS institutions, such as the New Development Bank, and exploring new areas for economic and technological cooperation, BRICS can improve their economic resilience and collective influence at the global level.

Promoting Global Justice and Equity

BRICS also have the opportunity to position themselves as champions of global justice and equity, challenging existing inequalities in the international system and promoting fairer access to global resources and development opportunities. Through a commitment to reform international financial and political institutions and to support policies that privilege sustainable development and human rights, BRICS can contribute to a more just and equitable world order.

Open and Constructive Dialogue with Other Global Powers

Finally, maintaining an open and constructive dialogue with other global powers, including the United States, the European Union and other emerging nations, will be crucial for BRICS in navigating global challenges. Through collaboration on issues such as climate change, nuclear non-proliferation and the fight against terrorism, BRICS can build bridges and promote international cooperation based on mutual respect and shared interests.

As the BRICS advance, their trajectory will be characterized by the search for a balance between safeguarding national interests and contributing to a global collective good. Their ability to navigate these complex dynamics, promote internal solidarity, and engage in effective multilateral diplomacy will define their role and impact in shaping the future of the world order.

In conclusion, BRICS' bilateral and multilateral relations, both within the block and with other nations and global blocs, represent a fundamental aspect of their rise and influence in the international system. The complexity of these relationships reflects a matrix of challenges and opportunities that BRICS must navigate to promote their collective interests, improve their global position, and contribute significantly to global governance.

Internal relations between BRICS members, characterized by a combination of cooperation and competition, require a continuous effort to strengthen the cohesion and effectiveness of the block. The ability to manage differences, deepen economic and political collaboration, and promote a shared vision will be crucial to their collective success. At the same time, strengthening BRICS institutions, such as the New Development Bank, and exploring new areas for sectoral cooperation can provide solid foundations for wider global impact.

In the context of their external relations, the BRICS are faced with the challenge of balancing the search for autonomy and the aspiration to reform the world order with the need to collaborate with existing powers and global institutions. Their commitment to renewed and more inclusive multilateralism, combined with efforts to promote sustainable development, global security and economic justice, could not only amplify their voice in global issues but also contribute to a more equitable and stable world.

Looking to the future, the BRICS' potential to act as catalysts for global change and cooperation will depend on their ability to:

- Successfully navigate evolving geopolitical dynamics, maintaining balanced and productive bilateral and multilateral relations both inside and outside the block.

- Proactively address domestic challenges, including social and economic inequalities, and promote policies that support inclusive development and shared prosperity.

- Take a leadership role in critical global issues, from the climate crisis to the reform of international financial institutions, demonstrating a commitment to sustainable and justice-based solutions.

- Promote innovation and cooperation in emerging fields, such as digital technology, clean energy and cybersecurity, establishing new standards and models of international cooperation.

- Strengthen dialogue and collaboration with other emerging economies and developing nations, expanding the concept of South-South cooperation and offering alternatives to the Western-dominated development model.

In short, as the BRICS continue to navigate the complex global landscape, their collective future will be forged by their ability to act together in a cohesive manner, to address global challenges with determination and to promote a development agenda that reflects the principles of equity, sustainability and multilateral cooperation. Their trajectory will not only define their role in the world but will also help shape the architecture of global governance in the 21st century.

19. Criticism and Controversies: analysis of the main criticisms and controversies concerning the BRICS.

The BRICS, a block of emerging economies comprised of Brazil, Russia, India, China and South Africa, have attracted significant attention on the global stage, both for their potential to influence the world economic and political order, and for the various critiques and controversies that surround them. These critiques emerge from a variety of issues ranging from the internal policies of individual member states to the dynamics of the block as a whole.

Disparity and Internal Cohesion

One of the main criticisms concerns the economic and political disparity within the bloc. The BRICS are extremely diverse in terms of economic size, population, levels of development and political regimes. This diversity raises questions about the cohesion and effectiveness of the block in achieving shared objectives. China, for example, has a significantly larger economy than other members, which can lead to an imbalance of power within the group.

Human Rights and Governance Issues

Several criticisms of the BRICS come from issues related to human rights and governance in member countries. Some member states have been accused of suppressing press freedom, limiting civil and political rights, and maintaining authoritarian governance practices. These issues raise concerns about the credibility and integrity of the bloc in promoting a fairer, rules-based world order.

Environmental Policies and Climate Change

The environmental policies of the BRICS countries have also been criticized, especially in relation to climate change. Given their rapid industrialization, BRICS countries contribute significantly to global greenhouse gas emissions. While there is a growing commitment to clean energy and sustainable development, some critics argue that much more must be done to address their environmental footprints and to lead the global fight against climate change.

International Relations and Geopolitics

The geopolitical ambitions of the BRICS, especially those of Russia and China, have generated concerns in some areas of the world, in particular among Western nations. Moves to challenge the Western-dominated international order are seen by some as attempts to erode international norms and promote an authoritarian agenda. In addition, territorial tensions and regional rivalries, such as that between India and China, add another level of complexity to the global dynamics of the BRICS.

Economic Development and Inequality

Despite economic growth, BRICS countries face criticism for not having adequately addressed internal inequalities and for not improving the quality of life of all their citizens. Challenges include poverty, unemployment, limited access to basic services, and income inequalities. These issues raise questions about the effectiveness of BRICS development models and their ability to provide equitable and sustainable benefits.

Response to Criticism

In response to these criticisms, some BRICS members have taken steps to address specific environmental issues, improve governance, and promote sustainable development. In addition, the bloc continues to seek ways to strengthen internal and external cooperation, promote a multipolar world order, and contribute positively to global governance. However, overcoming disputes and achieving shared objectives will require commitment, transparency and continuous reforms on the part of the BRICS.

In summary, while the BRICS represent an important economic and political force with the potential to significantly influence the world order, the critiques and controversies surrounding them underscore the need to address domestic issues and to navigate complex international dynamics with caution and responsibility. Their ability to respond constructively to these critiques will be crucial to their long-term success and legitimacy on the world stage.

The BRICS' ability to effectively deal with criticism and controversy is not limited only to the internal resolution of issues, but also extends to their interaction with the international community and the way in which they shape global governance in response to emerging challenges. As the BRICS strive to strengthen their role as a leader in the global south and as a balancing force in the world order, responses to these critiques become essential for building trust and legitimacy.

Global Economic Cooperation and Reforms

In the midst of growing global economic challenges, BRICS are often seen as catalysts for the reform of international financial institutions. The criticism that the bloc faces is how it can actually contribute to making the global financial system more inclusive and equitable. The commitment to greater representation in global economic forums such as the International Monetary Fund and the World Bank, and the strengthening of alternatives such as the New Development Bank, are fundamental steps. However, the challenge remains to ensure that these initiatives are accompanied by policies that promote transparency, debt sustainability, and equity.

Environmental Leadership and Sustainable Development

Environmental issues represent another area of intense criticism for the BRICS, many of which are among the world's largest emitters of greenhouse gases. While the bloc has taken a stand on issues such as the Paris agreement and has promised investments in renewable energy, concrete actions and the pace of change are often seen as insufficient. Addressing this criticism requires not only a renewed commitment to ambitious environmental policies but also cooperation to overcome technological and financial barriers to sustainable development, highlighting the BRICS leadership in the transition to low-carbon economies.

Human Rights and Governance

Issues of human rights and democratic governance remain critical points for some BRICS members, with impacts on the perception of the bloc as a whole. The balance between national sovereignty and international human rights standards is a delicate challenge. The BRICS, while respecting internal political and cultural diversity, could seek ways to promote dialogue on human rights and governance, supporting initiatives that strengthen legality, transparency and civic participation, in order to improve their image and strengthen internal and external cooperation.

Multilateralism and International Relations

The critique of the role of BRICS in promoting alternative multilateralism and challenging the existing world order raises questions about how they can build productive international relations while pursuing the reform of global governance structures. A commitment to open dialogue with Western powers and other emerging economies, the search for common ground on global issues such as security, trade and public health, and the promotion of multilateralism that reflects the diversity of the modern world are essential to navigating this critique.

In conclusion, while the BRICS face a range of critiques and controversies, their response to these challenges is critical to defining their future role in the world. Through reformed domestic policies, a renewed commitment to multilateral cooperation and sustainable development, and a constructive dialogue with the international community, BRICS can overcome these criticisms, strengthen their cohesion and legitimacy, and play a key role in shaping a more equitable and inclusive global order.

As the BRICS seek to navigate and respond to the criticisms and controversies surrounding them, it becomes imperative to consider the future of their cooperation strategies and how they might adapt or reform to effectively address emerging global challenges. Long-term commitment to political, social and economic innovation, combined with active and inclusive diplomacy, could offer ways to overcome negative perceptions and reaffirm their role as a positive force on the international scene.

Social and Economic Innovation

To address critiques related to internal inequalities and unsustainable development practices, BRICS could intensify efforts towards social and economic innovation aimed at inclusive progress. This includes the adoption of economic models that not only promote growth but also distribute benefits more equally within society. The promotion of social enterprise, investment in green technologies and the encouragement of responsible business practices are examples of how the BRICS can drive a new paradigm of economic growth that values sustainability and equity.

Strengthening Inclusive Multilateralism

In the international sphere, BRICS can respond to criticism of their geopolitical ambitions and the challenge to the existing world order by strengthening their commitment to inclusive multilateralism. By creating dialogue platforms that welcome a wider range of voices, including small states and civil societies, BRICS can demonstrate their commitment to a global architecture that reflects the diversity and needs of today's world. This approach could also facilitate more meaningful cooperation on transnational issues such as climate change, international security, and global health.

Commitment to Environmental Sustainability

Faced with criticism for their environmental policies, the BRICS have the opportunity to take a leading role in promoting environmental sustainability. By expanding investments in renewable energy, adopting circular economy practices and collaborating on conservation initiatives, BRICS can challenge existing perceptions and become pioneers of a sustainable future. Collective commitment to ambitious climate goals and the implementation of international climate agreements could further strengthen their position as a leader in the fight against climate change.

Open Dialogue on Human Rights and Governance

Issues related to human rights and governance require an open and constructive dialogue within the BRICS bloc and with the international community. Through discussion forums and review mechanisms that promote the exchange of best practices and cooperation on strengthening democratic institutions and human rights, BRICS can address these criticisms while maintaining respect for national sovereignty and cultural diversity. Such a commitment would demonstrate the BRICS will to promote progress that is not only economic but also social and political.

Enhanced Cooperation on Global Security

Finally, dealing with disputes related to global security will require strengthened cooperation from the BRICS, both internally and with other nations. Working together to address threats to peace and security, from international terrorism to nuclear proliferation and regional conflicts, BRICS can play a crucial role in promoting global stability. Collaboration with international organizations and active participation in peacekeeping missions can further consolidate their commitment to a safer world.

In conclusion, overcoming the criticisms and controversies surrounding the BRICS will require an ongoing commitment to innovation, cooperation, and dialogue. By proactively addressing these challenges, BRICS can not only strengthen their cohesion and legitimacy but also promote a positive global impact, leading the way to a fairer, more sustainable and inclusive world order.

As BRICS strive to face and overcome criticism and controversy, it is critical that they explore innovative ways to improve their internal cooperation and extend their positive influence globally. This involves not only responding proactively to existing concerns but also anticipating and adapting to future challenges, promoting a model of growth and development that is sustainable, inclusive and respectful of human rights and national sovereignty.

Promoting Diversity and Inclusion within the Block

To further strengthen their internal cohesion, BRICS will need to value and exploit the cultural, economic and political diversity that characterizes their member countries. Promoting the inclusion and equal participation of all members in collective decisions and initiatives is crucial to ensure that policies and strategies reflect a full range of perspectives and interests. This could include the establishment of dedicated platforms to facilitate cultural exchange and interaction between civil societies, academics and private sectors of the BRICS countries, thus enriching dialogue and cooperation.

Innovation in Financing Sustainable Development

Faced with criticism for their environmental impact and pressure to contribute more actively to the fight against climate change, BRICS can explore innovative models of financing sustainable development. This could include expanding the role of the New Development Bank in financing green projects, the introduction of climate bonds, and the promotion of responsible investments that take into account environmental, social and governance (ESG) criteria. Strengthening cooperation on climate finance would not only help BRICS to manage their energy transitions but also to position themselves as a leader in global sustainable development.

Expanding Dialogue and Cooperation with Other Countries and Regions

To address criticism related to their geopolitical aspirations and strengthen their legitimacy as an influential voice in the international system, BRICS will need to seek to expand dialogue and cooperation with a wide range of countries and regions. This includes strengthening relations with G7 nations, engaging with least developed countries, and exploring synergies with other regional coalitions such as the African Union, ASEAN and CELAC. This expanded multilateral approach could facilitate consensus building on critical global issues and promote collaborative solutions to transnational problems.

Commitment to Transparency and Accountability

Responding effectively to critiques of human rights, governance and transparency will require a renewed commitment to public accountability from the BRICS. Taking steps to improve the transparency of internal and external policies, strengthen accountability mechanisms, and encourage civil society participation can help build trust and improve the BRICS image globally. Such a commitment to open and responsible governance would not only strengthen the block's legitimacy but also promote democratic and human rights principles at the international level.

Ultimately, the BRICS journey through criticism and controversy will be defined by their ability to adapt, innovate and collaborate both internally and on the world stage. By constructively addressing issues of development, governance and international cooperation, BRICS can not only overcome immediate challenges but also shape a future in which they contribute significantly to solving global problems, promoting a more just, sustainable and peaceful world order.

In conclusion, the critiques and controversies surrounding the BRICS are significant challenges that require careful attention and targeted action. These challenges range from internal concerns regarding governance, human rights and social inequalities, to external issues related to the environment, geopolitics and the impact on existing global structures. The BRICS response to these criticisms will be crucial not only for their internal cohesion and prosperity but also for their role and influence in the global context.

BRICS, through a joint commitment to transparency, responsible governance and inclusion, have the opportunity to address and potentially overcome critiques related to human rights and internal governance. Promoting an open dialogue on political and economic reform, supporting social innovation, and raising living standards can help mitigate concerns about domestic practices.

In the environmental context, by taking a leading role in sustainable development initiatives and in the fight against climate change, BRICS can respond effectively to criticism of their ecological footprint. Investing in clean technologies, promoting renewable energy and collaborating internationally on environmental projects will demonstrate their commitment to a sustainable future.

On the geopolitical scene, mitigating tensions through diplomacy and multilateral cooperation, strengthening relations with other nations and blocs, and promoting a more balanced and just world order, are essential steps. The BRICS' ability to act as a united block that respects internal differences, while maintaining a constructive dialogue with other global powers, will strengthen their position in the international system.

In addition, by expanding engagement with civil society, the private sector and academic communities, BRICS can enrich their perspectives on global issues and promote more inclusive and representative policies. This holistic approach to governance and development can help build a wider consensus both within the BRICS countries and in the wider international community.

In short, by addressing these criticisms with concrete actions and a commitment to continuous improvement, the BRICS have the opportunity to overcome controversy and emerge as a more cohesive, responsible and influential block. Their ability to implement internal reforms, to promote principles of sustainability and equity, and to collaborate effectively on the world stage will define their contribution to global progress and international governance. Through these actions, BRICS can not only strengthen their legitimacy and cohesion but also play a crucial role in shaping a world order that reflects the dynamic changes of the 21st century, promoting peace, prosperity and sustainable development at the global level.

20. Conclusions and Final Reflections: summary of key points and reflections on the future role of the BRICS in the world.

The BRICS discussion reveals a complex fabric of opportunities, challenges, critiques and potentials surrounding this influential block of emerging economies. As the world approaches the third decade of the 21st century, the BRICS are in a unique position to influence the global order, promote sustainable development and contribute to the solution of pressing international challenges. The summary of the key points and the reflections on their future role in the world offer a holistic vision of their journey and of the possibilities that open up before them.

Key Points

- **Diversity and Cohesion**: The BRICS are characterized by significant diversity in terms of economy, politics, culture and society. Their ability to maintain internal cohesion, despite these differences, underlines the potential for cooperation based on common interests and shared objectives, such as sustainable development and the reform of global financial institutions.

- **Economic and Political Influence**: With their rapid economic development, the BRICS have acquired significant economic and political influence. This positions them as key players in promoting a more balanced global architecture, able to represent emerging and developing economies more effectively.

- **International Challenges and Cooperation**: BRICS face internal and external challenges that require innovative and cooperative solutions. Their response to issues such as climate change, economic inequalities, human rights, and governance will define their impact and legitimacy on the global stage.

- **Leadership Potential**: There is growing recognition of the potential of BRICS to lead on global issues, offering alternatives to the Western model and promoting practices of sustainable development, multilateralism, and South-South cooperation.

Reflections on the Future

Looking to the future, the BRICS have an opportunity to consolidate their position as a driving force for positive change at the global level. Their ability to act cohesively, to deal with criticism constructively, and to reform themselves internally will be critical to their success and influence. The future role of the BRICS in the world will depend on several factors:

- **Adaptability and Innovation**: The BRICS' ability to adapt to changing global dynamics and to promote innovation in the fields of economy, technology and sustainable development will be crucial to maintaining their relevance and driving global progress.

- **Diplomacy and Multilateral Cooperation**: A renewed commitment to active diplomacy and multilateral cooperation, especially in response to transnational challenges, could strengthen the position of the BRICS as peace brokers and leaders in sustainable development.

- **Internal Reform and Global Responsibility**: The BRICS' ability to promote internal reforms that address inequalities, improve governance and strengthen human rights, parallel to their commitment to global responsibility, will define their credibility and long-term impact.

In conclusion, as the BRICS continue to navigate a complex and interconnected world, their collective success will depend on their ability to join forces for a common good, while maintaining respect for diversity and individual sovereignty. Looking to the future, the role of the BRICS in shaping a more just, balanced and sustainable world order appears not only possible but essential to face the global challenges of our time. Their trajectory in the coming years will offer crucial indications on the direction of global progress and on the nature of international cooperation in the 21st century.

Concluding this in-depth review of the BRICS, we navigated a wide range of themes that illustrate the complex and evolving role of this block of emerging economies in the global context. From the analysis of their economic formation and growth, to their development policies, geopolitical influences, environmental challenges, and beyond, the book sought to provide a holistic view of the aspirations, challenges, and potential of the BRICS in shaping the future world order.

Summary of Key Points

- **Training and Objectives**: BRICS represent a coalition of emerging economies that aim to promote economic cooperation and reform global financial institutions to reflect a more balanced world order.

- **Economic Growth and Development**: Despite their different economic trajectories, the BRICS have shown significant growth, placing them as key players in the global economy.

- **Geopolitical Influence**: Through multilateral initiatives and the promotion of a more inclusive multilateralism, the BRICS seek to rebalance international power dynamics.

- **Environmental Challenges and Sustainability**: The management of natural resources and the commitment to sustainable development remain at the center of BRICS policies, despite criticism for their environmental policies.

- **Criticism and Controversies**: BRICS face challenges regarding internal cohesion, human rights, governance practices, and environmental responsibility, which require attention and action.

Useful Resources

For those seeking to further deepen their understanding of the BRICS and their global impact, here are some useful resources:

- **Official BRICS Site**: http://www.brics.utoronto.ca/ - A research portal that offers analysis, documents and updates on BRICS leaders and related policy issues.

- **New Development Bank (NDB)**: https://www.ndb.int/ - The official website of the BRICS-founded development bank, which provides information on funded projects, sustainable development initiatives and investment opportunities.

- **The Diplomat**: https://thediplomat.com/ - An international online magazine that often offers insights and analysis on BRICS foreign policy and their interactions in the global system.

- **World Bank Data**: https://data.worldbank.org/ - For economic data and development indicators of the BRICS countries, useful for comparative analysis and research.

- **International Monetary Fund (IMF)**: https://www.imf.org/ - Offers economic reports and analyses, including those specific to BRICS countries, that can illuminate their economic policies and growth prospects.

Final Reflections

As the BRICS continue to navigate the complex waters of global geopolitics and sustainable development, their journey offers valuable lessons on the power of transnational economic cooperation and the search for a fairer and more inclusive world order. By successfully confronting internal criticism and strengthening their unity and cooperation, BRICS can not only overcome immediate challenges but also drive positive change globally. Their evolution will remain a topic of critical relevance for anyone interested in the future of global governance and the dynamics of the world economy in the 21st century.